T0248066

COMPTON IN MY SOUL

STANFORD STUDIES IN COMPARATIVE RACE AND ETHNICITY

Compton
IN MY SOUL

A Life in
Pursuit of
Racial Equality

Albert M. Camarillo

STANFORD UNIVERSITY PRESS
Stanford, California

Stanford University Press
Stanford, California

Printed in the United States of America on acid-free, archival-quality paper.

Library of Congress Cataloging-in-Publication Data
Names: Camarillo, Albert, author.
Title: Compton in my soul : a life in pursuit of racial equality / Albert M. Camarillo.
Other titles: Life in pursuit of racial equality | Stanford studies in comparative race and ethnicity.
Description: Stanford, California : Stanford University Press, [2024] | Series: Stanford studies in comparative race and ethnicity
Identifiers: LCCN 2023040286 (print) | LCCN 2023040287 (ebook) | ISBN 9781503638198 (cloth) | ISBN 9781503639317 (ebook)
Subjects: LCSH: Camarillo, Albert. | Stanford University—Faculty—Biography. | Historians—United States—Biography. | Mexican American college teachers—Biography. | Mexican Americans—California—Compton—Biography. | Race discrimination—United States. | Compton (Calif.)—Biography. | United States—Race relations. | LCGFT: Autobiographies.
Classification: LCC E175.5.C255 A3 2024 (print) | LCC E175.5.C255 (ebook) | DDC 979.4/092 [B]—dc23/eng/20231024
LC record available at https://lccn.loc.gov/2023040286
LC ebook record available at https://lccn.loc.gov/2023040287

Cover design: Derek Thornton / Notch Design
Cover art: Childhood photo, courtesy of the author; Downtown Compton, 1962, courtesy of the Gerth Archives and Special Collections, California State University, Dominguez Hills; map, Wikimedia Commons.

For our grandchildren
Avery, Jaxson, Cameron, Sloane, Jayce, Maya, and Diego

CONTENTS

PART III
Circling Back to My Origins

COMPTON IN MY SOUL

Prologue

As the plane approached to land at Los Angeles International Airport, I peered through the small window that offered a bird's-eye view of most of South LA. I could easily spot Compton, a small suburb sandwiched between four freeways. I was born and raised in this city, and Compton, in so many ways, is in my soul.

That warm September morning in 2001 was a special one for me. I was flying to visit my eldest son, Jeff, whose undergraduate school outreach experiences had inspired him to begin his teaching career at a Compton middle school. He'd invited me to speak to his eighth-grade history class. Excited as I was about the chance to see him in action on my old turf, my thoughts mostly centered on the city's recent troubles. From the airport, I drove a rental car to Vanguard Learning Center, a public school located on Compton's westside. I couldn't help but wonder if Jeff's experiences working with students and families in Compton might be shaping him in ways that resembled what I'd experienced growing up there.

While exiting the I-110 Harbor Freeway to enter Compton's city limits, my thoughts quickly shifted to how different our experiences were from his grandfather's, given how much the city had changed. Nearly a century

1

earlier, my father, as a ten-year-old, had trekked with his uncle 1,800 miles from Michoacán, Mexico, to Compton in search of an absent father said to be working on local farms.

I'd visited Compton on occasion after moving from the area in 1975 to begin a long career on the faculty at Stanford University, yet much of what I'd heard about my hometown came from the media's headline-grabbing stories. They were typically tragic, blood-and-guts TV news reports, with graphic images. Violence gripped the city. Gang warfare was rife, and it was not only Black-on-Black—the infamous Crips versus Bloods—it was also Latinos against Blacks.

In the late 1980s, Compton had gained the dubious distinction of being the "murder capital" of the nation, and it was still routinely listed in the top ten most dangerous cities in America. The crack cocaine epidemic, which spurred much of the gang violence, had wreaked havoc on so many neighborhoods, families, and individuals. Police brutality and violence against African Americans, though a longstanding issue, had become widely known due to the fame of local rap groups, such as N.W.A., and that violence headlined many films and documentaries. Latino immigrants and their children, on the way to becoming the majority in the city by the 1990s, sometimes found themselves at odds with their Black neighbors. To make matters worse, oversight of Compton's public schools had descended into a state of disarray by 1990, which had led to bankruptcy and to the district's schools being taken over by the state, a first in California history. It made me sad—and mad—to learn about the troubles plaguing the city of my youth.

But if you dug deeper, amidst the mayhem of the 1980s and 1990s, stories of the resilience I had seen there as a child emerged from within the growing cultural lore about the city. Compton's narrative included Venus and Serena Williams learning to play tennis on the city's courts and the roots of now-famous rap and hip-hop artists, as well as other cultural icons from the city. I knew instinctively, however, that there was much more to Compton than these success and failure narratives. Jeff, among the newest teachers at the middle school, had become my lifeline to reconnecting with the city and its people.

I was excited to meet his students, who called him "Mr. C." After checking in at the school's front desk, I made my way to his classroom. The thirty-two students, all African American and Latino/a, immediately checked me out as I opened the door. One quickly jumped up from his desk, pointed a finger my way, and shouted, "Hey, it's the *original* Mr. C!" I barely contained my laughter.

Jeff asked me to talk about Compton's past, about the years when I was the age of his students. They listened attentively to what the city was like long ago—which probably seemed like ancient history because I was about their grandparents' age. Meanwhile, my memories flashed back to the early 1960s when, not far from Vanguard Learning Center (VLC), I'd sat in another middle school classroom at a time when the westside of Compton had rapidly become mostly African American.

I snapped back to the present when a young man raised his hand, waving it excitedly back and forth. I expected it to be something history related, as were the questions that followed. Instead, he asked: "Did you whup Mr. C's booty when he was our age?" I couldn't contain my laughter this time.

Visiting Jeff's class that September unleashed an avalanche of memories in the days that followed about my long, winding journey from this little city to places I couldn't have imagined as a young person. Born in Compton's segregated Mexican American *barrio*, I had attended grammar schools and middle school on Compton's westside during a fleeting moment of racial integration that quickly gave way to Black majority neighborhoods. My final years living there had returned me to a segregated setting once again after my family moved from West Compton when I was a fifteen. After the misguided urgings of my eldest sister, my family had moved to a home located on the eastern border of Compton city's limits, and I'd enrolled at Dominguez High. This was the segregated "White" high school, where I became a student leader during a tumultuous time of tensions over racial integration.

When I left Compton in 1966, it was as a naïve, impressionable eighteen-year-old seeking to navigate an uncharted path as a "minority" student at a major public university. I had no way of understanding at the time how my experiences growing up in this multiracial city had deeply shaped me as a person, and later, as an educator. The values I hold dear about family and community, interracial relations, fairness, and equity were forged in Compton. I also had no way of knowing when I entered UCLA, at a time when Black and Mexican American students made up less than 1 percent of the student body, that being born and raised in Compton would launch me on an educational trajectory in search of racial justice during an era of anti-war and racial identity movements and the dawning of ethnic studies.

This unlikely journey of a "Chicano kid" from Compton took me along an unmarked road through higher education and beyond. The stories I tell are my own personal memories but often reflect experiences of others in the baby boom generation, who also came of age in the second half of the twentieth century. More specifically, my story is part of a narrative about how educational opportunities for "historically underrepresented minorities" reshaped the hopes and dreams of millions of Americans.

I also share personal reflections in the broader context of what I learned during a lifetime of teaching and writing about the history of race and ethnic relations in America. Decades of community-based work in support of marginalized people and serving as an expert witness in many voting rights and affirmative action–related legal cases also broadened my views about problems of inequality. My stories unmask many contradictions in American life in the twentieth century: racial injustice and interracial cooperation, inequality and equal opportunity, racial strife and racial harmony. I write about experiences of family, community, and relationships that cross racial boundaries, set during decades of sweeping demographic changes that transformed Compton and the nation. I write with messages of hope for the future and for a better, more tolerant, inclusive America. I also tell stories of stubborn resistance to social change and devastating legacies of inequality that still haunt our society.

My story is a quintessential American chronicle about the worst and best of who we are as a people and as a nation. It is only one individual's account, among tens of millions of stories from my generation; but I have learned that understanding history through the eyes of one person can be powerful. My hope is that when my grandchildren and their generation are old enough to read my stories, although they are growing up in a different America, they will have a better sense from my history of how to find their own guiding light.

PART I

Rooted in Compton

ONE

My Barrio Playground

With the extra time I had before I headed back to LAX, I decided to drive through West Compton neighborhoods on the way to the city's Mexican American neighborhood where I was born. Compton is a small city in size, only about eight square miles, so within ten minutes I was back in my old hood.

The neighborhood, cleaved in half by the tracks of the LA Metro Blue Line, looked different, yet strangely the same. I parked my car in front of the drab 1920s-era Catholic parish where my mother had dragged me to church on Sundays. This bare-bones chapel, no bigger than most elementary school classrooms, once held worshipers crammed into about fifteen rows of pews on each side of a single aisle. The building was converted into the parish activities hall after a larger church was built at the end of the block in the late 1950s. The home my family had lived in for over a quarter century laid in the path of the new church's construction, prompting our move out of the barrio to another Compton neighborhood when I was in third grade. When I walked to where our *casita* once stood, an asphalt parking lot greeted me. Across the street the homes looked pretty much the same as before. As I walked around the block toward the railroad tracks in the hopes of finding remnants of family history, a train sped by on the same tracks that streetcars had traveled when I was a kid.

Fronting the railroad tracks were several small stores, the Alatorre Market being the most visible. Though the store's original sandstone block walls had been plastered over and repainted, it was still basically the same building my father and grandfather had built around 1930. It became the Gonzáles Market, the *mercadito* I knew while growing up in the barrio. I peeped into the storefront, and only a few people were shopping, all Mexican folks.

Heading back to the car to drive to the airport, I passed the narrow alley at the back of the market. I stopped momentarily to eye where I had regularly played with my barrio homies. The weeds still flourished nearly fifty years later, and litter still dotted the dirt path between the church property on one side of the alley and homes and small businesses on the other.

I spotted a young boy at the end of the alley messing around with a stick in his hand, poking something on the ground. Long ago that little guy was me. My stories of Compton begin here, in this alley, in the Mexican neighborhood we simply called "*el barrio.*"

"Hey, Beakie, let's go, man," my best friends would call to me from the trash-strewn alley behind our beat-up casita. Even at the age of five, in 1953, we little *vatitos* (homies) were free-range kids in the hood. Though I am thankful my nickname didn't stick long—we all had nicknames there—the bonds I shared with my best buddies shaped many of my early experiences outside of home and family. Popito, Luli, Beegie, and I were like little rats scurrying around, always having fun and getting into mischief, while finding ways to make a few cents to spend on candy and soda pop.

We were the first generation born in the United States of Mexican immigrant parents who had settled in this area nestled in about eight square blocks. Several hundred Mexicans resided in the barrio, which was located in the heart of metropolitan Los Angeles, and on the north and central boundaries of the city of Compton that border Willowbrook (an unincorporated area of Los Angeles County) and Watts, an area of South Central Los Angeles.

Regardless of what I learned later about how the barrio had developed on Compton's westside, for us little guys it was our social universe. It was our playground. Our parents, grandparents, *padrinos/as* (godfathers and god-mothers), and nearly all our relatives planted roots here in the years before and immediately following World War II. Only much later, as a student of history at UCLA in the late 1960s, did I learn that this area of Compton was the only part where Mexicans were allowed to rent and buy property. Some Japanese American tenant farmers (a total of sixty-nine in 1940) were scat-tered across the town, the only other people of color before the 1940s. There were no Blacks among the 16,000 residents in the city in 1940.

The Pacific Electric Railway tracks (for the streetcars popularly known as Red Cars) once bisected the small neighborhood, with a few mom-and-pop businesses nearby. Gonzáles Market and Gutíerrez Market—another family-run market on Willowbrook Avenue—provided a focal point for barrio residents, as did a barbershop and two *tortillerias*. One of these tor-tilla shops also sold delicious *pan dulce*, the Mexican sweet bread I could never get enough of. The single non-Mexican-owned business locally, To-celli's Liquor Store, was run by the only Italian American family in the neighborhood.

Religious offerings abounded. On the corner, across the street from Gonzáles Market, was a house, the size of a two-car garage, turned into a church where White evangelical Protestants—we called them "*las aleluyas*" and "holy rollers"—held meetings and tried to lure unsuspecting Catholics to their faith. Beegie and I once ventured into their shack of worship when one of the proselytizers offered us candy to join in, as members sang loudly, prayed, stomped their feet, and wildly waved their hands. We thought they were *locos* but liked their candy. After a few minutes of chomping on it, we eyed each other as a signal to leave. Good thing we never told our parents, much less the Catholic priest in our barrio parish located down the street, because we would have received a good *nalga* (butt) whippin'.

It was the local parish built in the 1920s or the 30s that brought nearly everyone together in the neighborhood for Sunday Mass and for all the re-ligious rites of passage honored by Catholics (baptisms, First Commun-ions, confirmations, and weddings). My favorite event at Sacred Heart (La Sagrada Corazón) Church was definitely not Sunday Mass. I had trouble sitting still for very long, and, for some strange reason, I always had a stomachache on the sabbath. But when it came to the *Jamaica*, a carnival sponsored by parishioners, my buddies and I were first in line for this annual church event. Games, food booths, decorations, and music made our little poorly constructed Mexican parish come alive every year.

We were lucky this parish met all the religious needs of barrio residents back then. I learned as an adult that Mexicans could not attend services at the White Catholic Church on the city's eastside before about 1950, reflecting a longstanding national policy of the Catholic Church to build parishes that separated the "ethnics" from predominantly White parishioners.

In a similar vein, I didn't know as a kid that our neighborhood was the poorest in Compton, or that it was among the last settled areas to have its dusty, potholed dirt roads paved by the city. Most families settled in the barrio between the world wars, before the city finally paved the streets and extended sewer lines into the neighborhood. Former agricultural land that had once defined Compton gave way back then to the construction of modest working-class homes throughout the city. By the time I was born in 1948, one of the few remaining sections of Compton still under the plow was the appropriately named Richland Farms, a neighborhood on the city's south-central boundary.

Most homes in the barrio were built from the 1920s to the late 1940s. They ranged from tiny hand-built houses of wooden slats to stucco homes. Some looked more like shacks than actual homes, and a few still had outhouses, such as the Mata house (where Beegie and his many siblings lived a few doors down from us). Meanwhile, some larger, nicer homes owned by Whites occupied the edge of the barrio.

Our dad did his best to improve the little wooden house he had bought in the 1920s when he and mom settled on N. Culver Street to raise a family. My older brothers and sisters still recall what a wonderful gift the indoor bathroom was, because they had shared a four-foot-square outhouse for years with my grandmother, who lived next door, and all six of her children. Luckily, before I was born, our father, a cement worker and a good handyman, had built that indoor bathroom for the family. I can't imagine what it would've been like to share a stinky old outhouse with fifteen other family members.

That didn't mean toilet use wasn't a sibling issue—or actually, a gender issue. "Put the damn seat down, you little *cabrones*," I would hear Rita, our eldest sister and the sibling boss of the family, yelling at my brothers as she shut the bathroom door with one of her cuss words.

We lived in the middle of the barrio, where almost everyone had elders and parents who had settled in El Norte (the United States, the north) before, during, or after the chaotic years of the Mexican Revolution. The revolution lasted from 1910 into the early 1920s, resulting in the loss of about 2 million lives. Several blocks to the south were mixed neighborhoods interspersed with poor White folks. Further south, below Rosecrans Avenue, which was one of the city's main east-west streets, were exclusively White neighborhoods of working-class and lower-middle-class families. Rosecrans Avenue, according to my Uncle John, formed an informal racial boundary for the barrio in the 1930s, a borderline that no one from there was supposed to cross.

Uncle John was the López family (maternal) storyteller, who shared a funny, revealing account about Rosecrans Avenue of years ago. In his own words, he'd been "a real hell-raiser" as a teenager growing up in the barrio during the 1930s. "A group of us crossed Rosecrans Ave and we came across a group of *gabacho* (a derogatory term for White) kids hanging out next to their car," he recounted with a sly smile on his face. Uncle John didn't say what provoked the encounter, but as the bad boy he was, I'm sure it involved lots of cussing and middle fingers and probably a lot more. "We ran back to the barrio, and the White boys jumped in their car chasing us," John said. He and his buddies stopped near the church and hid in the alley as the car with White teenagers cruised by on the street. To lay a trap for the gabachos, one of the boys went out into the street as a decoy. The White kids saw him and jumped out of their car and chased him into the alley. "As the White kids searched for us, we tipped their damn car over on its side and took off again." The barrio boys ran and hid behind a house down the street, but within sight of the overturned car. When a police squad car pulled up, Uncle John shared with me, the cops obviously told the White teenagers to flip the car over and go home, which they did. "We taught them a lesson," John said with a devilish look and a laugh, "because they never came back again."

Just a few blocks to the east, and bordering our neighborhood, were many light manufacturing companies along Alameda Avenue (which runs north and south). This area is now known as the Alameda Corridor, a twenty-mile expressway connecting the Port of Los Angeles in Long Beach with rail and truck transportation hubs in central Los Angeles.

Beegie, Popito, Luli, and I frequented the small industrial plants on Alameda, jumping the fences after hours or on weekends to play among the huge containers of products made there. Our favorite building housed Fry Roofing Company, a business that caught fire at least once every few years, creating a spectacle for our young eyes. We forced our skinny little bodies between an opening in the padlocked gates and played log rolling atop large round packages of roofing tar. One day Luli came up with the brilliant idea that the tar was like chewing gum or tobacco, so we all started to chew on bits of tar chipped off the rounds. "You're a real *pendejo*, Luli," shouted Popito, as the first to spit out the nasty tasting stuff. "Yeah, you dumb ass," Beegie quickly added, "this stuff is caca." Remarkably, none of us became ill.

If that wasn't toxic enough, we were exposed, in our "playground," to lead contamination—not from lead-based paint but from handling lead shavings. Gabriel's Plumbing Company was located on Willowbrook Avenue between Gonzáles Market and the home of Laurie, the local "lady of the night."

The back of Gabriel's business, directly across the alley from my home, was where his workers routinely dumped a heap of metal pieces along the fence in the alley. Luli, whose brother worked in the neighborhood chrome plating shop, somehow knew this stuff was valuable. "Look for the softer pieces," Luli instructed us, as he bit a small piece of lead to show us it was not as hard as the other bits of scrap metal. We sorted through the mound of shavings by hand to locate the lead pieces, putting them in a paper bag to take to a small welding shop on Rosecrans Avenue. At the shop across from our elementary school, the welder weighed the contents and gave us little recyclers a quarter or so each, with which we'd head off to Gonzáles Market to buy candy and "real" chewing gum.

Always in need of our sugary junk food fix, we also wandered the barrio in search of empty pop bottles. They could each be redeemed for one penny. Sometimes when our recycling business went bust, at night we'd jump the fences to the Gonzáles and Gutíerrez Markets and steal a few empty bottles to redeem the following day. We were smart enough not to take too many bottles at one time for fear of being found out. In fact, I was such a good customer and reliable redeemer of bottles at Gonzáles Market (owned by Padrino Ramón, the godfather to my mother and all my siblings) that Pinky, the friendly, pretty sister of the co-owner of the market who lived down the street from us, allowed me to establish a fifty-cent line of credit for my growing addiction to sweets of any kind. No wonder my mouth was filled with cavities as a kid.

Though we patrolled the barrio on foot and on old junky bikes, we somehow understood not to venture too far beyond its boundaries. It was okay to cross the tracks into the barrio that extended several blocks south and north into unincorporated Willowbrook, an area locals referred to as "El City" in reference to Mexico City, but not much farther.

On the other side of Willowbrook lay Watts, an area that was mostly Black when I first ventured there as a little kid with my father for haircuts at a Mexican-owned barbershop. And I occasionally went there with my mother who shopped at Sewaya's Clothing Store on 103rd Avenue, the small business district of the area. Through the first half of the 1900s, Watts had been a multiracial community, but by the mid-1950s, African Americans predominated as Whites and some Mexican Americans moved out.

The barrio in Compton resembled many immigrant neighborhoods scattered across urban and suburban America: they were places where a first generation born in the United States came of age in a time of language and other cultural changes. Spanish-speaking, *serape*-clad grandmothers were a common sight in the barrio, while English-speaking teenagers ran around dressed in jeans. While our parents spoke only Spanish to each other, use of that language diminished with age, or became combined into Spanglish. I never used my halting Spanish with my siblings, except Spanish cuss words with my brothers. And, in my family at least, by the time I came along as the youngest of six, the kids only spoke English to one another.

Spanish-speaking elders always kept an eye on kids as we wandered the barrio, so we were safe, despite our mischief. Our mothers never seemed worried about where we were for much of the day, other than at mealtime. After roaming free all day, at dinnertime, my mother would ask one of my brothers to go out into the neighborhood to fetch me. I learned to be fairly close to home at that time of day, because if I was out of earshot of my brother's call or whistle, I'd get my ass beat. Home in the tumbledown house that my father mostly built may have been crowded, but it was a happy place. As a child, I didn't know what poverty was about because most Mexican families in the barrio were poor like ours.

Our father was a real homebody, so we rarely went much beyond Compton and the immediate area. Dad expected us to eat every meal at home. Good thing our mother was a great cook, producing deliciously fresh tortillas hot off the *placa* with *frijoles* and *arroz* on the side for every low-cost meal. Dad also expected us to sleep in our own beds every night, not even allowing me to stay over at my cousin's house, the son of his closest brother, and only three houses down from us.

My mom occasionally allowed me to go on outings with my friend Luli because the Gonzáles family patriarch was her godfather. Luli's dad Charlie (Rosalio) was an avid fisherman and went to the beach often with his kids. Charlie was a carefree guy, and the butcher at Gonzáles Market, the store owned by his brother, Ramón.

"Do you want to go with us to Tin Can Beach?" Luli asked me one Saturday morning when I was around six years old. "Sure, but let me ask my mom first," I replied. "But why do you call it Tin Can Beach?" I asked Luli. He laughed as he said, "You'll see."

Four of us kids sat in the back seat of Charlie's cool 1951 Buick convertible for a long ride on surface streets—there were no freeways in South LA then. This beach, later developed as Bolsa Chica State Beach, was located in adjacent Orange County. As soon as we parked and set foot on the sand, I looked up and immediately understood why the name Tin Can Beach was spot-on—tin cans, broken bottles, and other junk was strewn everywhere. "Watch where you walk and stay on the path," Charlie shouted to us kids, "because I don't want to take any of you *chavalitos* home with cuts on your feet."

Tin Can Beach may have been hazardous, but it was safe in different ways. It was a so-called open beach, an "anything goes" type of recreation spot, where poor White folks pitched tents, itinerants and teenagers got drunk, and dark-skinned Mexican people could gather without harassment. That was needed because racial segregation reigned in Southern California from the 1910s to the 1940s, and African Americans, Mexican Americans, and Asian Americans were banned from many recreational places, including public swimming pools and parks. Certain beaches in the Southland were also off limits to people of color—not by law, but by custom. Along with the option we had of Tin Can Beach, I learned many years later about a "Negro Beach" in Santa Monica on the westside of Los Angeles. And, as I grew older and wanted to have fun in the sand and surf, my sister Rita, who could easily pass as White, would take me to a clean public beach in downtown Long Beach.

Tin Can Beach was a leftover that we were dealt as part of what I call "Jaime Crow." Jim Crow in the South was already well entrenched as a system of White supremacy, codified into law and maintained by social custom and vigilantism, by the time Jaime Crow flourished in the Southwest in the early 1900s. Sometimes I imagine Jim Crow as a virus, a kind of plague, that spread its racial virulence over various communities of color. This virus mutated; and depending on the location and the color of the host, it deployed many and various ways to keep certain groups down. "Jim" spread west from Texas to California, becoming "Jaime" as it mutated.

Jaime Crow targeted Mexican people with racially restrictive practices enforced by social custom rather than by law. These practices and customs were common before World War II, but many of them had begun to break down by the time I was growing up in Compton in the 1950s. Gone were the signs in storefront windows and overtly segregated public places that my parents remembered in Compton and elsewhere in the 1920s and the 30s. The barrio itself, a product of racially restrictive real estate covenants and government programs that redlined people of color into certain neighborhoods, was a scar on Compton's landscape left by the disease of Jaime Crow.

Our separated-out lives weren't unusual. Like my siblings and me, most Mexican American children—and their Black and Asian counterparts—lived apart from Whites during the first half of the twentieth century. We grew up in segregated barrios and *colonias* in rural, agricultural areas from the small towns in Texas's Rio Grande Valley to California's Central Valley to the growing cities across the Southwest.

In the Los Angeles area, dozens of smaller barrios, much like our neighborhood in Compton, had sprouted up in former agricultural areas that gave way to suburbanization during the 1940s and 50s. And then there were the large barrios of East Los Angeles—Boyle Heights, Lincoln Heights, Belvedere, and others—that morphed from multiethnic places to predominantly Mexican American barrios by the 1950s. By the time I was growing up in Compton's small barrio of 1,000 people, East Los Angeles's Spanish-speaking population had the largest concentration of Mexican-origin people in the nation. Over half of the 600,000 Mexican Americans in the greater LA area in 1960 lived on the eastside (at the time, only Mexico City had more Spanish-speaking people in North America).

When my buddies and I turned six in 1954, our carefree days of outdoor play ended as we entered kindergarten at Rosecrans Elementary School. Most of the hundreds of thousands of Mexican American kids who grew up in the 1940s and 50s in the United States attended public schools that segregated children of color into separate classrooms or separate schools. But some of us grew up in smaller barrios where we attended school with White kids.

Located about a quarter mile from the heart of the barrio, Rosecrans—built in 1923 and named after Civil War Union Army General William Rosecrans—introduced us to life outside the barrio cocoon. At Rosecrans Elementary, and later at other schools I attended in Compton over the next twelve years, I was exposed for the first time to White, Black, and Asian classmates.

I had certainly seen Whites at times in our neighborhood, and Black folks when I tagged along with my mother to pay our utility bills in downtown Compton and to shop with her in Watts, but I had rarely interacted with them before kindergarten. My brother Art, who is nine years older than me, had befriended the first African American kid to enter Rosecrans in 1949. Joe's family was one of the early Black families to move into northwest Compton, not too far from the barrio. He and Art were close buddies for years. Joe was even nice to his friend's little brother, while visiting our home many times and sometimes staying for dinner. And Harpo (Art's nickname because of his light skin color and long curly hair that resembled Harpo Marx) often went on weekend outings with Joe's family. Such outings led to another of Uncle John's tales.

"I was driving west on Rosecrans Ave," my mom's younger brother recalled, "and I see this little white hand waving and waving at me from the bed of a truck ahead of my car, which was filled with about five or six Black kids." Laughing at recalling the whole thing, John continued, "As I pulled up closer to the truck, I see this little white face attached to the hand . . . it was Harpo."

A few years later, in 1956, I met Willie—one of three African American kids in my kindergarten class at Rosecrans—and we were cool together, reconnecting several years later as football teammates in junior high school. There were two Black girls in our elementary school class, and about half the remaining students were Mexican American or White. The truth is, I just didn't think much about racial differences back then, as I hadn't experienced the kind of discriminatory treatment my parents once faced in Compton and elsewhere. I don't remember White children in our kindergarten class ever saying or doing anything to make Willie or me self-conscious about being a "minority."

Through the mid-1950s, Compton did not segregate students in schools by race. But this changed in the late 50s, when the number of African American students increased sharply. Compton neighborhoods, which were still largely racially separated at the start of the decade (including the northwest section where we lived, and the westside in general), were in the throes of a huge demographic shift as I attended grade school and entered junior high school.

I preferred being home watching TV or messing around in the barrio with Luli, Popito, and Beegie over school at first. I tried to stay home as often as Mama would allow, knowing that a phony cough here, or "I'm feeling kind of sick today" there, would get me an occasional reprieve from Rosecrans. Also, I didn't like my kindergarten teacher. Miss Griswald was a short, skinny White woman, and I don't remember her ever smiling much. One day she reinforced why I didn't like school, or her.

Kindergarteners all had to take a short, mid-morning nap, or at least rest on the mats the school provided. We were asked to bring our own blankets to the classroom for naps and leave them in cubbies. Early in the school year, my dad had returned from San Diego, where he worked for a while paving sidewalks, and he brought some gifts back from nearby Tijuana, the border town of Baja California. My prize was a beautiful Native American–style blanket, rich with colors and geometric designs. It is now obvious that it was a cheap, knockoff blanket, but I didn't know that. I thought it was really cool, so it became my kindergarten nap blanket.

One day, a classmate—a little White boy who always dressed in cowboy shirts, straight out of a TV western, with horseshoe symbols and frilly shit on the pockets—had my blanket in his hands and was ready to lay down for a nap. What the hell! Having three older, bigger brothers, I was well versed in claiming and protecting my possessions. "That's my blanket!" I yelled at him as I rushed over and yanked it out of his hands. He shyly backed away without a word.

"Mission accomplished," I thought to myself, as I walked over to my nap mat with my precious, colorful blanket in hand. A moment later, it was tugged from me by little Miss Griswald. "Why did you steal Billy's (or whatever that little bastard's name was) blanket?" she shouted at me. "It belongs to me," I said, watching her hand this treasure to "cowboy Billy." I tried to pull it way again until she stepped in between us.

Miss Griswald pointed to the corner of the classroom. "Go stand there and face the wall," she demanded. I did so for the entire nap period and never told my family about this incident. But on the last day of the school year, I took that damn blanket, hid it in my jacket, and went home. I finally got back at that *cabrona* (bitch) and that little cowboy fool for doing me wrong!

Growing up in the barrio had partly taught me to protect personal belongings, because I didn't have many. My mother and sister Annie often laughingly reminded me in later years about how I once lined up my barrio buddies outside the kitchen window to frisk them for my valuables they might've concealed. They understood, as I patted them down to make sure none headed home with any of my stuff.

My teachers from first through third grade at Rosecrans School turned out to be nice women, but none motivated me to learn. We had daily newspapers at home, but no books. Even if we'd had them, our mother simply had no time to read to any of us, and our father's English skills were poor.

Not having much experience with reading, I especially hated when asked to read out loud in class. I didn't do well, and likely talked too much or was otherwise a pest in class, judging from the many U (unsatisfactory) marks for citizenship I received on every grade card sent home. I was not a good student, but I sure liked recess and playing games on the playground, and hanging out with the barrio boys whenever I could.

TWO

El Norte, a New Beginning

Like most people in the United States, my life is the product of a migration story. The experiences of those who came before me shaped who I was as a boy growing up in Compton and the man I became. Understanding the stories of what my parents and elders went through while settling into their adopted country inspired my success in life and career as a historian. The lives of Benjamín and Rose, my parents, though unique in many ways, are also part of a much larger story about millions from Mexico and other nations who sought better lives for themselves and their families in a new land.

Most Mexican American households in Compton's barrio were like ours—lower-working-class families with four to seven children trying to eke out a living as best they could. Prescription birth control wasn't an option in general until the 1960s, and with my parents, the Catholic Church would have excommunicated them for that. Large families were the norm in Mexican immigrant families, especially those from traditional agricultural backgrounds where children were expected to contribute to the family's welfare.

My family couldn't pay a physician for prenatal care and delivery of babies at a hospital. Our mother called a doctor to the house at 1716 N. Culver Street each time she was ready to give birth. Mama lost her first child, who was stillborn, and her third child at age four due to an accident, as well as my little brother David, who died at age two. Six of us survived to live in the increasingly cramped quarters of the expanding Camarillo family.

The search for opportunity and stability that lured the first White residents to incorporate the farming town of Compton in the late nineteenth century drew others as well. Like multitudes of immigrants who came to the United States over the centuries, the families of my father and mother planted roots in Compton's barrio with hopes of earning a slice of the American pie. Though they endured much pain while becoming good citizens here, they were grateful for opportunities that came their way.

I didn't listen closely to the immigrant experiences of my father Benjamín, and the journey that first led him to Compton in 1911, until I entered UCLA. "Sí hijo" (Yes son), my father explained, "I came to Los Angeles when I was ten looking for my father who had left the family the year before in Quiringicharo [a small *pueblo* in Michoacán, Mexico] to work in California."

Always with a sad look, Benjamín retold the story about facing starvation on a meager diet of beans, tortillas, and sometimes the corn his family picked for the local landowner whose hacienda encompassed the pueblo. Seeking to better his family's situation meant spending his early adolescent years working in the United States while saving every penny to reunite his family in Compton. After returning twice to Quiringicharo, Benjamín became one of hundreds of thousands of Mexicans who settled permanently in El Norte following the Mexican Revolution.

When this revolution of 1910 spread across Mexico, warfare between revolutionaries and federal troops cut a swath of chaos, bloodletting, and economic despair everywhere. My paternal grandfather sought relief by going to California. "Él fue a buscar trabajo en el norte" (He went to look for work in the north, the United States), my father told me, his head turned down sorrowfully with the furrows of his dark, weather-worn brow showing his advanced age, "pero él no regresó" (but he did not return).

As the eldest male in the family and now sole wage earner, Benjamín had been trying unsuccessfully to feed his younger siblings. He headed north in search of his father and to earn some money to send to his mother. His favorite Tío Trino (Uncle Trinidad), who had traveled with my grandfather to the United States in 1910, returned temporarily to Quiringuicharo before heading back to California. Benjamín, at ten years old, pleaded to join him so he could see his father who'd settled in the Los Angeles area. Trinidad agreed.

While walking to the railhead miles from Quiringuicharo, they saw bodies of men hanging from the telegraph poles next to the tracks—the violence of the revolution had come to Michoacán. My great-uncle and his tall, man-child nephew hopped the first freight train heading north and eventually reached Ciudad Juárez, the border town on the Rio Grande River connected by a bridge to El Paso, Texas.

The dry desert heat in July made walking across the bridge intense. On the U.S. side was one of the few immigration stations then established along the almost 2,000-mile-long border. Mexicans easily crossed over in 1911. Sometimes immigration service agents didn't even bother to ask migrants to fill out an entry card.

Trino was retracing the steps he and Donaciano, Benjamín's father, had taken the year before, which involved locating El Paso's Union Depot, a major regional railroad hub. Trino again figured out which freight trains were headed west toward California instead of north or east; he and my father waited patiently to jump into an open freight car as it began slowly rolling out of the railyard.

After about two days of riding the rails, the duo jumped off near Santa Ana in Orange County, about thirty miles from Los Angeles. A cousin, Octaviano Camarillo, had settled in the small town a few years earlier to work on a ranch as a *vaquero* (cowboy). Weary from their long journey, they stayed briefly with him before pushing on to Los Angeles.

The Camarillos in Santa Ana continued a family tradition from Mexico as *charros* (horsemen), a skill that certainly didn't reach the Camarillos in Compton. I am afraid of horses, unlike Leo Camarillo, my third cousin, who became a five-time national team roping rodeo champion and ProRodeo Hall of Fame inductee.

However, the final leg of my father's journey, which he recounted with a mischievous little smile, included riding time. He and his uncle came across a corral of horses after walking for many miles and decided to "borrow" two, despite not being good riders. After running the sweating horses for hours, they stopped to let them drink from a stream. They didn't know that horses have to cool down first, so the horses' muscles seized up, and they refused to move. Luckily, my uncle and his nephew weren't caught, which could've led to a hanging back then, and they reached the Los Angeles area.

Compton in 1911 was a village of a thousand people surrounded by family farms. The only people of color in town were a crew of about a hundred Mexican immigrant railroad workers and farmworkers, the majority of whom were clustered on two streets. My grandfather was among them.

Benjamín soon learned what Tío Trino had hidden: my grandfather had taken up with another woman and started a new family. My dad, quiet by nature, never openly condemned this family betrayal. When he spoke about this, though, his eyes were downcast and voice lowered, suggesting the emotional wounding of this abandonment.

After several months in Compton, and earning wages working on local farms, Benjamín and his uncle returned to Quiringuicharo to help support family members. They eventually persuaded my grandfather to return south too. Donaciano returned home occasionally over the next few years, leaving my grandmother pregnant two more times before disappearing entirely.

Worsening conditions in Michoacán caused by the revolution prompted Benjamín to return to Compton again. Cristín, the husband of his older sister Maria, asked Trino to take him along on the return journey north so he, too, could support his struggling family. So all three jumped on a Central Mexican Railroad train headed north. But by 1912 the revolution had seriously disrupted railroad travel. Trino knew something was wrong when about halfway to the U.S. border the train headed east toward Monterey. Two days later, the threesome found themselves in Piedras Negras, the Mexican border town across the Rio Grande River from Eagle Pass, Texas. Instead of the 800-mile train ride envisioned to LA, the trio now faced 500 extra miles to reach El Paso first.

Trino, Benjamín, and Cristín decided to bypass the Texas border entry area and walk along the riverbank to find a place to wade across the Rio Grande. The river was running too fast though, so they walked further from town until they found a man in a boat willing to ferry them to the U.S. side for a few pesos. When they finally landed and walked back to Eagle Pass, there were no U.S. trains traveling west toward California.

Out of money, the three walked much of the 150 miles north to San Antonio, sometimes stopping at farmhouses to work for food. Trino knew they had to reach "the Alamo City" to jump a train going west to California. Along the way, though, Cristín became ill. My father said Trino wanted to leave Cristín behind, but Benjamín pleaded with Trino, and the strong family ties held. My father's brother-in-law recovered, and after many exhausting days of marching, they reached San Antonio. A few days were spent working for a little cash, and then they located a train heading west to El Paso and then another one headed to California.

Trino and Cristín fully settled into Compton in 1912, earning enough money to send for their wives back home to join them. My father had other plans. After a short stay in Compton, he set out with a friend to ride the rails, jumping on and off freight trains for about a year, doing the only work he knew—harvesting onions in California's coastal towns and picking sugar beets in Colorado and Wyoming. He stashed away daily wages while working alongside some of the many thousands of Mexican immigrants who harvested the expanding agricultural bounty of the western states in those days. Then he gathered his savings and returned to Texas on the way back to Quiringuicharo.

Benjamín had one goal in mind: bring enough money to family in Michoacán to keep them from starving and then immediately head back to California to work, taking his next youngest brother, my Tío Rosendo, with him. In 1914, Benjamín and Rosendo were thirteen and twelve, yet they immediately found jobs as day laborers in the booming Los Angeles construction industry. With enough money saved after two years, Benjamín sent my grandmother train fare. The family, without my grandfather, soon reunited in Compton. It would be fifty-six years before my father visited the pueblo of his birth again.

Benjamín's immigrant saga is a familiar one for Mexicans back then. He was part of the first massive immigration to the United States—the first great wave—of people fleeing their revolution-torn homeland between about 1910 and the late 1920s. An estimated 1 million Mexicans—about a tenth of the entire population of Mexico—ventured north and settled mostly in border states from Texas to California. They worked on rural farms, labored as railroad repairmen, and helped build infrastructure projects of booming western cities while searching for some modest measure of greater stability for themselves and their families. Many returned to Mexico after the civil war violence eased, but hundreds of thousands relocated permanently in the United States, as did my relatives in Compton.

It didn't take long for Mexican immigrants like my dad to know they'd entered a country where their labor was wanted and needed, but where opportunities were doled out unevenly—and they were socially despised. Early twentieth-century America was an extremely race-conscious society, and if you were Mexican, African American, or Asian, you learned which boundaries not to cross. The signs in storefront windows in many public places provided constant reminders: "No Mexicans, Negroes, or Dogs Allowed," "White Trade Only," "Este Baño es Solamente para Americanos" (This Bathroom is for Whites Only). When Mexicans saw the word "Americanos," they knew what it meant.

Benjamín encountered these signs before 1940 everywhere in Texas during his cross-border journeys, and not infrequently in California. Shared prejudices and informal practices among White realtors and property owners, for example, meant most Mexicans, Blacks, and Asians knew which neighborhoods in rural towns and cities were off limits. By the 1920s, informal practices to steer Mexicans and other people of color to certain neighborhoods often had become reinforced by racially restrictive real estate covenants. A deed of sale for property typically included a paragraph with a blank line for a seller to write in the names of any racial minorities (the excluded group varied by location) who were to be kept out of White neighborhoods.

Compton was hardly an exception. The president of the local realtor association openly stated in a response to a survey about race relations that "All subdivisions in Compton since 1921 have restrictions against any but the White race . . . we have only a few Mexicans and Japanese in the old part of the city." The barrio was one place where Mexicans were allowed to buy property and build homes. And they did. In the mid-1920s, my father and a small but growing number of other Mexican immigrants helped this Compton neighborhood take shape. My mother's father, who befriended Benjamín, was another one of those immigrants.

Francisco López, like my paternal grandfather, first ventured to Califor-

nia in 1910. Together with his father Gerónimo, he left Puruándiro, Michoacán, to seek work in Los Angeles. My mother didn't know how her father
and grandfather ended up on Santa Catalina Island, located about thirty
miles off the coast of Long Beach, but there they were living in a boarding
house in April 1910, when a U.S. Census enumerator listed them among the
island's Mexican laborers.

Francisco saved enough money to return to his small pueblo to fetch
his wife Josefa and his son and brought them to Catalina Island. Josefa was
pregnant with my mother. Francisco was part of a crew of Mexican workers
hired by a labor contractor to work on this privately owned island, later purchased in 1919 by William Wrigley, the chewing gum manufacturer. Avalon,
the small tourist village built on the island in the early twentieth century,
was a rather exotic resort destination for wealthy Los Angelenos. My mother
Isabel López, the second child and first daughter of the López family, was
born in Avalon, not long after the family settled there in 1911. My children like to joke that their grandma was the first Pacific Islander/Mexican
American in California. Either way, not many who were born early in the
twentieth century could claim this tiny, rocky island as their birthplace!

When my mother, called Isabel then, was seven, the family moved to
Compton. Her father had found plenty of work on area farms and in construction. The family rented a small building that was nothing more than
a barn on the edge of the small downtown section of Compton. The area
was near the Southern Pacific Railroad housing for laborers—a row of little
shacks next to the tracks where mostly Mexican railroad workers lived. "I
hated that awful little barn," my mom recalled, "because it had no running
water, and you had to hold your nose to use the outdoor toilet, which was
really just a hole in the ground."

There was an upside for Isabel to reside in this part of the city: attending the one grammar school in town, where she learned to speak and read
English fluently. She also acquired a new name. One day while entering the
first-grade classroom after playing at lunch time, her teacher commented on
the light-skinned girl's rosy-colored cheeks. From then on, she was known
as Rosie or Rose.

Despite enjoying school and being a good student, her education stopped
in the seventh grade when her father quickly gathered the family to move

out of the area. According to my mother and older siblings, my grandfather, though friendly and well-liked, was an alcoholic and not very responsible. In the early 1920s he cultivated some land near Compton as a tenant farmer and occasionally hired other Mexicans to help with harvests. At some point, he failed to pay their wages, and some threatened revenge. The López family quickly fled to California's Central Valley and joined the migrant farm-workers picking crops up and down the valley for nearly two years. That itinerant time, my mother claimed, was by far the worst of her life.

Her formal schooling ended as they spent weeks picking one crop and then another. They moved often from farm to farm, while calling shacks or horse stables "home," with no running water. And Rosie first experienced the pain of how Jaime Crow operated while living temporarily in valley towns notorious for raw discrimination against Mexicans, Japanese, and Filipinos. Restaurants, movie theaters, barbershops, you name it, were off limits to people of color.

The meager wages she and her two brothers earned went to their father to help keep food on the table, and there was not enough for much else. When Rosie was about fourteen in 1925, they returned to Los Angeles to live for a time in the *El Jardín* (garden) section of Watts, a majority Mexican neighborhood in this multiethnic area just north of Compton.

Racial prejudice against Japanese and Mexicans in Compton existed, but it wasn't the virulent, sometimes violent racism that existed in rural areas. Instead, when the López family returned to Compton in the mid-1920s, lines of residential segregation were hardening as new housing subdivisions were built in the growing town of about 12,000 people.

Other forms of discrimination also surfaced to prevent race comingling. The Compton Theater, the first movie house to open on Main Street (later named Compton Boulevard), had seating that separated Whites from non-Whites. When Mexican and Japanese moviegoers entered the theater, an usher directed them to designated areas downstairs or to the balcony. It was simply understood that minority folk could not sit in the White-only sections. At least once, though, light-skinned Rosie López ignored that. On a movie outing with darker-skinned Mexican American friends, she split off from her friends while approaching the usher with ticket in hand and said, "Thank you very much, sir," in perfect English. Looking back at her friends in line before she passed through the doorways to the White section of the small theater, Rosie smiled and winked about her momentary immunity from the Jaime Crow virus in Compton.

My parents met in Compton while my dad was working construction there. My mother's father, Francisco López, became friends with the fellow Michoácano, Benjamín Camarillo. And while attending gatherings at the López home, Benjamín met Rosie. They secretly courted for over a year, needing to stay under the radar of Francisco's closely guarded watch of his daughter, who, at seventeen, was forbidden to even go out with men. They eloped to Santa Ana and got married there in 1929. Rosie was not quite eighteen, and Benjamín was twenty-eight.

Marrying freed Rosie from the hard reality that her stern, overly demanding mother had forced on her as the eldest daughter. Though her mother didn't speak to Rosie for a year afterward, marriage meant avoiding doing the laundry—by hand—and cooking for the López family of ten. Rosie's mother had not allowed her to attend school again after returning to Compton a few years earlier, so that she could focus primarily on feeding and cleaning up after four younger brothers and a sister. Our grandmother, whom we called Mama Pepa, was a bitter woman who suffered at the hands of her alcoholic husband, who died of cirrhosis of the liver at age fifty-three. She resented Rosie for leaving the household to start her new life with Benjamín.

My parents rented a cottage in the center of the emerging Compton barrio, and with money Benjamín had saved during bachelorhood, they bought two tiny homes on lots adjacent to the recently built Catholic parish. Not long after they moved into one of the homes, while renting out the other to my grandfather, the Great Depression took hold. My father had steady work paving streets in the Los Angeles area during the worst years of the economic crisis from 1929 to 1939, but my grandfather was mostly unemployed then. In a kind gesture to familia, my father graciously transferred title of his rental property to Francisco and helped feed his in-laws and mother's siblings during these hard times.

A woman of great fortitude but with a playful side, Rose shouldered all the household responsibilities for the family while navigating the English-speaking world that surrounded Compton's barrio. She made sure we were washed, fed, clothed—always perfectly ironed—and on time for school and church. A kiss on the cheek or a big hug didn't come every day, but we understood her unconditional love for us. We complied with respect to whatever request she made for this or that, and she rarely needed to raise her voice to us. No wonder that, despite being short in stature, *La Jefita* (the little boss) was what my older brothers called her, as she provided the glue that bonded our family together during good times and bad.

This is not faint praise, given the dedication Rose had to her children, despite the crises and profound losses she experienced, some of which she shared with me and my siblings as adults. The sorrow over the deaths of three of her small children was etched in her face every time she mentioned them. Her first pregnancy ended in the stillbirth of a baby girl. Rosie was only eighteen years old then; she had no access to prenatal care and couldn't ask advice from her own mother about how to a handle pregnancy. Yet Rose always regretted not being more conscientious about eating healthy foods during gestation. She took better care of herself when pregnant with my eldest sister Rita, born a year later. Adela and Anita (Annie) followed, each two years apart. Our dad probably began to worry if Rose could bear him a son, but over the next dozen years, four boys joined the crew.

The death of Adela, her second child, at age four was far more traumatic than the stillbirth of her first daughter—and might've been avoided. Adela, sporting a full cotton dress, was playing in our kitchen with a López uncle who lived next door. Mom was cooking on the stovetop and stepped away briefly until screams from Adela made her run back into the room. Adela's dress and long hair had caught fire; Mom snuffed out the flames with her bare hands, badly charring them. Realizing that Adela had suffered serious burns all over her back and neck, she got the uncle to quickly fetch Benjamín, who was outside visiting with our grandfather.

Dad rushed inside to see his little girl screaming in pain while wrapped in a blanket in her mother's arms, the smell of burning hair and flesh filling the kitchen. Benjamín took her and his injured wife by car to the nearest hospital. Luckily, La Campanas Hospital was close by in Compton.

With Dad holding Adela in his arms, Rose told a nurse what had happened and asked for a doctor right away. "Do you have cash to pay for the hospital visit?" was the only thing the admitting nurse at the private hospital asked. They didn't. "Then you will have to go to a different hospital," she said matter-of-factly. Our mother always claimed they didn't accept Adela because, back in 1938, it was a segregated hospital for Whites only.

Benjamín drove nearly fifteen miles north to Los Angeles County General Hospital where they knew Adela would be admitted. The hospital took her in, but she died that night from shock and pneumonia. Whenever Adela's name surfaced in family discussions while I was growing up, tears quickly welled up in Mom's eyes. I can only imagine the toll on my parents from losing one of their little girls.

Like many family stories kept from children's ears, it wasn't until I was a student at UCLA that my mother first shared the Las Campanas Hospital part of the story and her belief that Adela's life could have been saved with immediate medical attention. That old hospital ironically had Spanish mission–style architecture. Its adjacent sanitarium attended to people seeking asylum from drug and alcohol abuse, including some famous Hollywood stars such as Judy Garland. Good thing that goddamn place was closed by the time I learned they'd denied emergency care for my sister's traumatic injury. In my more radical college days, I would've considered burning that racist place down.

Jaime Crow could be brutal, and he was alive and well in Compton before my time. When I think about our family horror story of racial injustice, I am also reminded of how so many poorer Americans and people of color are still facing legacies of inequality in medical care on a daily basis.

As my interest in U.S. history grew during early college days, I began asking family members about other hush-hush stories that I vaguely remembered bits of as a child. Many new tales surfaced almost every time I returned home to visit. These stories from my mother and sisters Rita and Annie (seventeen and thirteen years older than me, respectively) included a few about my uncles and began to help me connect my family's experiences with discrimination in Compton to broader historical events.

"I know that Uncle Frank spent time in jail when he was a teenager, but what happened to him?" I asked Mom and Rita directly. "He was only sixteen years old [in 1940] when he was sent to a juvenile camp before he was transferred to San Quentin State Prison when he turned eighteen," Rose said, about the fate of her little brother. "*Pobrecito*, he was only sixteen," she repeated, sadness in her voice as she covered her mouth and held back tears. As the story goes, Frank and two close friends from the barrio, Luis and Freddie, were out one night when they encountered a prostitute, who propositioned them for sex. A dispute over payment followed, and though no one knows exactly what transpired, something went afoul. The White woman called the police and claimed she'd been raped and robbed by three young Mexicans. The three teens were arrested without bail and arraigned for rape, assault, and robbery. With no funds to hire legal counsel for their defense, the three kids were at the mercy of the court, until Gladys Root, a well-known attorney who sometimes handled high-profile cases for the poor, took on their case.

"Frank told us that he and the other two boys had sex with the prostitute, but she wanted more money," my mother recounted. "But after they refused, she called the cops and said she was raped and robbed." "People in the barrio," Rita added, "said they were framed."

Frank was convicted on charges of second-degree robbery and assault with intent to commit rape. He was seventeen years old. Though Root helped to have the rape charges dropped, Frank spent a year in a juvenile correctional facility, and after he turned eighteen, he was transferred to San Quentin State Prison, where he remained for several years.

I'd always wondered, as a kid, why Uncle Frank seemed so aloof and was always drunk. "He was such a polite, nice, good-looking kid," my mother recalled, "but he was never the same after he was released from prison." Rita agreed.

This story began to make sense as I learned more about the era when Mexican American youth were targeted by police and the LA criminal justice system: they were characterized as deviant, violent *pachuco* gang members and thieves. By the late 1930s, a new generation of Mexican American youth had come of age, and law enforcement officials and the press marked some of them as part of the "Mexican problem." With their hair fashioned in distinctive styles, and attire that brought attention to these Brown teenagers, they were viewed as un-American. They also often spoke *caló*, a street genre of Spanglish.

Stereotypes and other characterizations associated with the so-called Mexican American youth problem were rampant during the infamous

"Sleepy Lagoon" murder trial in 1942. Police were called to investigate the death of a young Mexican man who had attended a party the night before at a home near a reservoir just south of downtown Los Angeles. The swimming hole frequented by Mexican American kids was called Sleepy Lagoon (after a popular song of the day). Residents reported to police that a group of Mexican American youth had crashed the party, and fights had broken out. Without direct evidence or witnesses, the police blamed the murder on a group of young men labeled the "38th Street Gang."

Seventeen teenagers and young men were summarily arrested by the LA Police Department and charged with second-degree murder, the largest mass arrest for murder in American history at the time. The murder case made the front pages of the *Los Angeles Times* and other newspapers. Twelve of the defendants were found guilty and sentenced to San Quentin. In an unbridled display of racism, the judge held the twelve without bail during the entire judicial proceedings and didn't allow them to change clothes or cut their hair because, he argued, the jury needed to see them for the uncouth criminals they were. With the help of members of the Mexican American community and White liberals and attorneys, the state court of appeals overturned the convictions in October 1944, citing insufficient evidence and failure to provide due process under the law. All twelve young men were released from prison.

Although they were freed two years later, the police and the media during the early years of World War II continued to stoke racist fears about the evils of zoot suit–clad "Mexican pachucos." The zoot suit, a popular style worn by tens of thousands of young men across the nation, became a touchstone for racial hatred toward Mexican Americans in Los Angeles. Only six months after the three-ring circus of the Sleepy Lagoon trial, the largest race riot in the history of western America up to that time broke out in downtown LA and raged on for five days.

It started in early June 1943, when hundreds of U.S. sailors and other military personnel took taxis from military bases in and around Los Angeles and began to patrol downtown streets looking for Mexican men, whether in zoot suits or not. What became a field day for brutalizing young Mexican Americans attracted support from some White civilians, who offered sailors and soldiers free rides to find the "brown bastards" and wipe them out. Mexican American kids were pulled from movie theaters, yanked from streetcars, and pummeled while innocently strolling down sidewalks. Some sailors even entered East Los Angeles neighborhoods to assail Mexican kids in their homes.

Meanwhile, the police idly watched the mayhem as young men were beaten by the sailors, stripped of their clothes, and left bleeding in the streets. Only then did the cops move in—to arrest them, often hauling off their girl-friends to jail as well. They were booked for—preposterously—disturbing the peace. The LA newspapers proudly pronounced that the military would rid the city of the pachuco problem even if the local police did not.

The hysteria stoked by the media and police in the late 1930s and 40s about the supposedly deviant, criminal behavior of Mexican youth gave me context for what happened to Uncle Frank in 1941, and to another López uncle afterward. While Frank served time in San Quentin during the war years, his brother Mike, at fifteen years old, liked to sport his cool zoot suit. What Mike didn't know was that wearing his suit in early June 1943 placed a target on his back. As news of the riots in downtown LA spread, other cities and towns in California, including Compton, experienced copycat-style vi-olence against Mexican American kids.

Mike and his family lived next door in our grandmother's place and, according to my older siblings, spent more time in our home than in his own. Rose was more like a mother to him. "I'll never forget that day," my sister Annie said emphatically, "we were all so scared when Mike burst into the kitchen all bloodied and beat up with his zoot suit torn." "Give me one of your butcher knives, Rosie, so I can kill those *pinches*" (fuckers), Mike pleaded with his sister, as Rita and Annie looked on in horror. (Benjamín was away that evening.)

Some White servicemen had been spurred on by the Los Angeles riots and had attacked Mike nearby. "When Mom wouldn't give Mike a knife," Annie recalled, "he quickly rummaged through a kitchen drawer and ran out the door with a potato masher." It was hardly lethal, but our mother was terrified his retaliation would land him in prison like Frank. They heard yelling and commotion in the alley outside our home. "Don't go near the windows," La Jefita shouted to the girls, while running to lock the back door.

Though the fight that day between Mike and the servicemen ended without any further violence, it was just one more trauma my mom suffered in the late 1930s and early 40s. The ordeal of losing children—and seeing a brother be sent to prison and another beat up by soldiers—was compounded by worry about whether her brother John would return from the war in Europe. He and tens of thousands of other Mexican American young men proudly volunteered or were drafted into the armed forces to serve their nation. Rose's worries were amplified by recent news that two of her Camarillo nephews had been killed in action overseas in 1944. To make matters worse, her father, Papa Gordo as my siblings called him, died in her arms in 1944. Too poor to afford a hospital room, he succumbed to liver cancer at home. Despite all this, Rose endured and gave birth to me and my younger brother over the next decade.

THREE

Growing Up, Chicano Style

Stories by Camarillo and López elders of their life in Compton helped educate me about my family's past. Growing up in Compton in the 1950s and 60s was a huge part of continuing my education. By the time I came along in 1948 as the sixth Camarillo child, my family had lived in our old wood-framed home for nearly two decades. The house was unusual on the block for being backward: that is, the front entry faced the dirt alley and the back side of other houses and small businesses on the next street. The rear entry was set way back on the lot facing N. Culver Street; you entered through a screened-in laundry room—as much an outdoor as an indoor space—before entering the kitchen.

Despite working all week on construction sites, our father always tried to improve the casita with his handyman skills. By the time Art came along as the fifth child in the 1930s, our father had added on rooms for the growing brood. But it wasn't until my brother Max was born at the start of World War II that Dad built an indoor bathroom, which was the only room with a door. He also added on a big bedroom for all the boys—we called it "the dormitory."

Benjamín slept in the dormitory with us as a means of birth control, yet my birth was followed seven years later with another "mistake" in our little brother David. Seniority mattered, with older brothers having their own single beds instead of sharing bunkbeds. Rita and Annie slept on an old sofa that folded down into a bed in the tiny room that led to the equally tiny bedroom of our parents. That bedroom opened to the dormitory, which had an entrance from the back of the house. With no closets anywhere in the house, we hung clothes on nails pounded into the walls.

We gathered for meals in our little add-on kitchen that Dad continuously worked on expanding, as part of keeping our casita as livable as possible on his meager wages. The living room had a couch to seat a few of us and a single chair next to a portable, non-vented heater we occasionally used in winter months. The heater had a makeshift connection to a gas line that ran across the floor.

One of my earliest memories was sitting around a huge radio console in the living room with my siblings listening to *Inner Sanctum Mystery,* a program that scared the shit out of me as a four-year-old! But our entertainment source was repossessed when my mother defaulted on the installment plan during a lengthy illness of our father.

Besides home projects, Benjamín once tried his hand at being an entrepreneur when my grandfather Francisco convinced him to become a partner (likely without providing any funding of his own) in building a small performance theater in the barrio. This was just one of many examples of barrio members pooling resources to help each other out. They completed the theater and hoped to bring in musicians and Spanish-language vaudeville acts from downtown Los Angeles, but the Great Depression quickly snuffed out their business venture. My father lost much of his investment and sold the property to Ramón Gonzáles, the padrino to my mother and all my siblings, who developed his family-run grocery store. Benjamín continued his day job paving streets and sidewalks while Francisco stayed mostly unemployed and spent the little money he did earn on alcohol.

At almost six feet tall with broad shoulders, skinny legs, and medium-brown skin color, Benjamín was quiet in demeanor and pensive by nature. An intelligent man who had never spent one day in school in Quiringuicharo, he taught himself to read in both Spanish and English as an adult, with help from my bilingual mother. He knew the virtue of hard work in support of his family. Starting as a day laborer at age twelve and then as a street-paving construction worker, he developed skills over time as a cement finisher and eventually joined the Cement Masons Union around 1940.

From doing low-wage hard labor as the family's sole breadwinner, Dad also understood the value of education. "Stay in school, hijos," our father would say. He didn't want any of us, especially his sons, to follow in his footsteps. Our mother, who had been forced to withdraw from school in the seventh grade, reinforced the need to do our homework and get a formal education. For my older siblings, that education included the humiliation of abruptly having to learn to use English regularly, as Rosie only spoke Spanish to my father and to the kids, until I came along.

Rita, who started school in 1937, didn't know the words to ask her kindergarten teacher permission to use the bathroom, for instance, so she peed in her pants. "I vowed never to speak Spanish at school again," she said decades later. Punishment could come quickly for speaking Spanish in the classroom or on the playground, in the form of a ruler slap across the wrist or a pinch on the ear from the teacher.

The classroom sometimes provided a much-needed escape from home, however. Our father's inner demons awakened when he drank liquor. He was a binge drinker who, at least twice a year, would skip work and get drunk non-stop. This could last for a week or even two before he came to his senses as money ran out for the family's food and bills. Besides the toll this took on his family, particularly Rosie who handled the childrearing and all other household matters, he paid a price in suffering withdrawal symptoms after bingeing. His employers always welcomed him back to job sites, though, because he was such an excellent cement finisher.

Taking care of us kids and Benjamín, who never lifted a finger for our daily needs, was La Jefita's task. She took on even more when I was three years old, and times became even harder for the Camarillos than they had been during the Great Depression.

Dad became very ill with tuberculosis in 1951, requiring a lengthy hospitalization. My mother and I would take a long bus ride, with several transfers, to Long Beach to visit him at a sanitorium for TB patients. I had to speak to him through a screened window because no one was allowed to go inside the World War II–style bungalow that served as the ward. "When will they let you come home, Daddy?" I would ask each time, and he would reply in his heavy accent, "Pues hijo" (Well son), "the doctors won't let me go home yet." My response over the eighteen months of ward visits, according to Mama, was, "Damn doctors!" The silver lining was that he didn't drink for nearly five years after his release.

I did not realize then that my mother had almost no financial safety net to rely on, other than her older children. When my father fell ill, Rita, the eldest sibling, had just graduated from Compton High School, which was quite an achievement for a Mexican American girl at the time. She spoke English well by then and had recently found a bank job, being careful not to reveal her Mexican status. Only later, after she had proven her typing and shorthand skills at their downtown location in Los Angeles, did Farmers and Merchants Bank learn they had a Mexican American employee (some thought her surname was Italian rather than Spanish).

My next eldest sister Annie, a junior at Compton High, worked cleaning homes for some of her teachers to help earn a few dollars in the family's time of great need. And, despite caring for six children, my mother did the same part-time work for a schoolteacher. She took me along to Mrs. Belben's house each week, where a big ass cookie jar sat on the kitchen counter filled with sweet goodies. I had never seen one, except on TV, and, when Mama wasn't looking, I reached into that beautiful clear glass jar and devoured a few.

Household money still remained scarce. Desperate for help, Rosie applied for aid for the poor, but the LA County caseworker suggested that my eldest sister's full-time employment should suffice. My mother ignored the suggestion that Annie, seventeen, could quit school and go to work. To make matters worse, Max developed a severe pulmonary problem that required a three-month stay in Children's Hospital in Los Angeles at the same time our father was recovering from TB.

What saved the family until my father could work again was Ramón Gonzáles of Gonzáles Market. Ramón, our mother's padrino, gave us a credit line at the store to put food on the table. He knew that Benjamín would eventually pay him back, which he did.

Compadrazgo, or godparent relationships, were important for Catholics in general, and especially for poor Mexican folks tied together through these quasi–family-religious connections. In the case of Padrino Ramón, he had taken his charge seriously a few years earlier as well. As the story goes, my great Tío Trino, my father's closest uncle who lived a few doors down from us, came over with some nice women's dresses he thought my mother would like. Rosie was a good seamstress, so she graciously accepted the gift from Trino and immediately used the beautifully patterned material for dresses for Rita and Annie.

Trino was known for buying goods from winos in the barrio, who likely had stolen the merchandise to fence so they could buy some cheap liquor. Well, a day or two later my sisters proudly sported their new dresses in downtown Compton. A few minutes after they returned home, Rose replied to a loud knock at the door to find an irate White woman, her husband, and standing behind them, an LA County Sheriff's deputy. When my sisters appeared at my mom's side, the woman yelled, "These are the girls who stole my clothes," pointing a finger at the two, as my mom tried to explain their dresses.

The entire Camarillo family—including my two-month-old self in Mom's arms—were locked up together in a single cell at the sheriff's substation located in nearby Willowbrook, where Annie and Ben Jr. (nicknamed Sonny) cried inconsolably. Allowed to make one phone call, my mother contacted her Padrino Ramón. The outraged godfather posted bail and demanded the deputies release the family. Fortunately, the charges of receiving stolen property were later dropped, though I can now say I was once an incarcerated infant.

We were fortunate to have this connection with Ramón, who was a no-nonsense man with dignity and grace and the leader of Compton's Mexican American community for twenty-plus years. Born in 1905, he was fluently bilingual and had graduated from high school. An advocate for education and sports recreation, he served as a spokesperson to Compton's White majority until his death in 1963. He was largely responsible for helping to build the first public baseball field in Cressey Park on the westside (renamed Gonzáles Park in his honor) and for bringing semi-pro baseball teams to the city. And Gonzáles was the first Mexican American and person of color elected as a trustee to the Compton School Board in the late 1950s.

We lived a few doors away from Ramón and his kind wife Sarita. In the back of their house, at the rear of the market, lived his brother Charlie, the market's butcher and the father of my friend Luli. In fact, in almost every direction you looked from our home, relatives were close by. My great Tío Trino's house was just two properties over from the Gonzáles home, and across the alley was our father's closest sibling, Tío Rosendo, and all of our cousins. Next to us lived our cranky Mama Pepa, and within a few blocks in any direction we had aunts, uncles, cousins, and other grandparents. Such extended, supportive family networks were the norm for many barrio residents and a common reality of immigrant America, past and present.

These relationships provided kinship and cultural ties, even though they partly resulted from having no other options to live elsewhere in the city at the time. The barrio also had its share of dysfunctional people that Beegie, Luli, Popito, and I knew—the winos, drug addicts, and grumpy old men.

Yet even as we kept the traditional respect for our elders, we were different for being born in the U.S.A. We were the first mass crop of "Chicanos/as" a term often used in some barrios like ours throughout the Southwest. In my family, it was used interchangeably with "Mexican" to refer to another Mexican American person or family in our community. It took on a new significance with many of my generation as we became more politically and culturally aware in the late 1960s. But before then, our in-between-ness was noticed by our elders. They always saw us, endearingly, as *los pochos* (Americanized Mexicans). And we were.

I used to tag along with my dad to visit his Tío Trino's house on Sundays for card games. After hanging out while they played, I asked my father, in English, for a few pennies to go buy bubblegum or some other store treat. Trino playfully interjected, almost always with a cuss word, "Habla español, cabrón!" (Speak Spanish, you little bastard!). My testy response, which always drew his laughter, was, "Why don't you speak English?"

Although all six Camarillo children graduated from high school, the educational system was a difficult rite of passage for most Chicanos/as. The norm in California throughout the first half of the twentieth century was de facto racial segregation of Mexican Americans and other children of color in public schools and widespread school failure. Mexican Americans had become the largest ethnic minority group in the state during the 1920s, and the children of immigrants were tagged by many educational leaders and race-baiting politicians as "educational problems" in local public schools. This aspect of the "Mexican problem" centered on three insidious characterizations of Mexican American students. They were deemed to be naturally un-intelligent (i.e., low IQs when tested) and unable to speak English well, and, as a result, expected to slow down the pace of learning for White classmates. Mexican American students also lacked proper hygiene, some administrators argued, and thus jeopardized the public health of White children (the stereotype of the "dirty" Mexican). On top of these two assumptions, and sealing their educational fate, some school personnel believed Mexican kids lacked the personal motivation and parental guidance to succeed in school. Over time these characterizations found their way into local educational policies.

Never mind that, in the 1910s and 20s, Progressive Era public education leaders across urban America believed that education was key to forging good citizens out of the children of foreigners. In California this educational mission took a back seat to the racial imperative of separating, when possible, children of color from White students. The result was that, by 1940, about 80 percent of all Mexican-origin students, whether or not they spoke English or were legally classified as being White, attended separate "Mexican schools" or were segregated into separate classrooms. In part, because Mexican Americans provided the backbone of agricultural labor in the state's rural areas and important labor in the growing cities, there seemed no need for this group to continue beyond grade school. Combine these low expectations with informal policies of racial segregation of Mexican Americans, reinforced by residential segregation, and you can understand the stifling impact these policy-driven views had on educational outcomes for the state's largest ethnic group.

The practice of many school districts in California to establish so-called remedial Mexican schools to justify segregation of Mexican American students did not go down without a fight. It was contested by some parents in Orange County in a federal district court case in Los Angeles in 1947. The judge in the now-famous case, *Mendez v. Westminster School District of Orange County*, ruled that forced segregation of Spanish-speaking students violated their rights under the Fourteenth Amendment. An appeal by the school district lost. But the *Mendez* case was limited to rejecting school segregation in the form of remedial Mexican schools, and only in California. Mexican Americans endured other discriminatory social and cultural educational practices long after.

By the time I entered middle school in 1960, the median number of
school years attained by Mexican Americans in the Southwest was only
eight, and ten years for non-Whites, versus the full twelve years for Whites;
in other words, Whites more often achieved high school graduation. In California, these figures for Mexican Americans were only slightly better. The
legacy of high dropout rates, school failure, and a big gap in total school
years attained affected college attendance rates as well. In 1960, 22 percent
of Whites had some college education, while for Mexican Americans it was
less than 6 percent (with most attending community college). It was rare for
a Mexican American to earn a university degree.

It took until the early 1970s for this pattern of "denial of equal opportunity by exclusionary practices" at the regional and state level to be called out
in a series of reports from the U.S. Commission on Civil Rights. The final
report of the commission, released in 1972, concluded:

> The dominance of Anglo values is apparent in the curricula on all educa-
> tional levels, in the cultural climate which ignores or denigrates Mexican
> American mores and the use of the Spanish language; in the exclusion of
> the Mexican American community from full participation in matters per-
> taining to school policies and practices.

In effect, the commission's report captured the disenfranchising effects of
decades of educational segregation and inequality on Mexican American
children.

You didn't have to look very far in the barrio for signs of this educational
failure and neglect. Very few of my aunts, uncles, and older cousins had
high school diplomas. And my older sisters and brothers can recall how at
each step along the educational ladder, from grammar school through high
school, fewer and fewer Mexican American students matriculated alongside
them. For far too many, schooling seemed a dead end instead of stairsteps
to opportunity.

But not for all. Fortunately for me and my siblings, education became a
ladder to climb. Beyond graduating from high school, four of us attended
college, three earned undergraduate degrees, and two went to graduate
school, though it could have worked out very differently for me.

FOUR

Chasing California Dreams

Your humanity is not only shaped by the family you come from, but by those with whom you rub elbows growing up. My path was changed in part by new friendships made when we moved from the barrio to the westside in 1956, just when the Black population was changing Compton's predominantly White landscape.

The altering demographics in my home city mirrored a larger chase for the American dream, fed by a World War II economic boom for which Los Angeles was ground zero. Like a siren call, developing Southern California suburbs beckoned millions of Americans from all quarters of the country to uproot, turning their backs on places of origin for a chance to live the good life out West.

Los Angeles and Southern California epitomized the suburban idyll through most of the twentieth century. The region had the historic pull of a temperate Mediterranean climate and rich soil. Native peoples, the Tongva or Gabrieleño, as Spaniards had called them, inhabited the region for thousands of years before that country established the colonial settlements of Alta California in the late 1700s. Missions, military garrisons, sprawling cattle ranches, and civilian towns dotted the sparsely settled region through the Spanish period (1769–1820) and Mexican era (1821–1848). After California's annexation by the United States in 1848, following the war with Mexico, a family farming economy took hold in the second half of the nineteenth century and well into the 1900s.

What had been a steady migration westward before 1940 accelerated to a dizzying volume during and after World War II, drawing Americans of all colors, religions, and cultural backgrounds to Southern California (Los Angeles County's population of under 600,000 in 1920 soared to above 4 million by 1950). As the staging ground for the war in the Pacific, the Los Angeles metropolitan area had in fact mushroomed into the fastest-growing region in the nation. The same applied to the city of Los Angeles, which grew from about 570,000 residents in 1920 to nearly 2 million by 1950. The booming metropolis had a vibrant industrial economy and sprouted bedroom communities in all directions. These suburbs offered multitudes of newcomers open space, abundant affordable housing, beautiful beaches close by, and a mild sunshine-filled climate nearly year-round.

Compton was one of the earliest incorporated towns (1888) in the Los Angeles area. A small number of farmers lived there, including the Reverend Griffith D. Compton. He purchased land that was originally part of Rancho San Pedro, a huge Spanish/Mexican land grant ceded to Juan José Domínguez, a prominent leader in Mexican California.

When my father first came to Compton in 1911 and when my mother and her family arrived in 1918, it was still more like a farming hamlet, with just 1,000 people. But thousands of new arrivals in the 1920s and 30s helped turn the sleepy little town into an emerging suburb. By the time I entered kindergarten in 1953, Compton was home to about 50,000 people. The city, like its counterparts throughout the region, was growing as if on steroids. By 1960, almost 72,000 people lived in what became known as the "Hub City" for being located at the center of the metro region.

Much like the adjoining suburbs of Lynwood, Southgate, Downey, and Huntington Park to the north, and neighborhoods in Long Beach and Lakewood to the south, Compton in the first half of the twentieth century was predominantly open only to White folks (up until the late 1940s). Most Caucasian newcomers originated from east of the Rocky Mountains, especially from the Midwest. In 1940, for example, well over half of all male heads-of-households in Compton were born in midwestern states. Only about 7 percent were native-born Californians, and 10 percent originated in other western states.

The Hogelen family, whose daughter Pam was a high school friend, was among the many eastside residents who had come from midwestern farming communities. Pam's father Don had grown up in the small town of Laurel in far eastern Nebraska. As a young man, Don got his first taste of California when he was hired to drive cars from Nebraska to Southern California before the war. In 1942, while preparing to enter the army, he married his sweetheart Ione, who was from the nearby town of Belden. The couple headed to East Compton in 1948, where Don started a decades-long job at a nearby car dealership. Pam remembered her neighborhood, which was close to Long Beach Boulevard, as one "Where you walked everywhere, left the front doors of your home unlocked, and returned home only when you heard Dad's loud whistle."

Compton, in fact, earned the title of All-American City in the early 1950s. Though unremarkable in most ways, it offered residents in the 1940s and 50s a simple, safe, and comfortable place to raise a family. The city's two-block-long downtown district was a typical mid-century Main Street, U.S.A. A variety of small businesses lined both sides of Compton Boulevard, and, by the time I first remember walking through downtown in the early 1950s, a few national brand companies had opened stores.

The majority of White folks who purchased property on the city's eastside were also working-class families. But there was a middling and professional class in older neighborhoods that had tree-lined streets and larger homes. One was known as the "Hollywood of Compton," with some beautiful Spanish-style stucco homes, front lawns with white picket fences, and colorful flowering plants. Some white-collar professionals owned these homes, but these few square blocks were bordered by less affluent, skilled blue-collar and working-class families—also all White.

To be sure, some poor White folks on the eastside lived in apartments and duplexes, but most of the east part of Compton was home to hard-working blue-collar and white-collar people who valued good suburban schools for their children, an excellent community college (Compton Junior College was regionally recognized), reliable public services, and safe neighborhoods.

Perhaps most importantly were the abundant employment opportunities nearby. Eight miles to the south in Long Beach, thousands of jobs could be had in the aircraft and aerospace industries (such as with McDonnell Douglas) and in shipping and ship maintenance facilities (such as the Port of Los Angeles). These and other war-related industries had converted to a peacetime economy and expanded production during the Cold War years.

Just to the north of Compton was also one of the largest auto manufacturing plants in the nation: the General Motors assembly factory in South Gate; and just a few miles beyond that were the large warehouse and railroad freight shipping facilities of Los Angeles. Jobs in light industry were also available along the entire twenty-four-mile Alameda Corridor, from Long Beach to Los Angeles.

Another big South LA employer was the oil industry, whose presence dated from the Southern California oil boom in the early 1900s. It, too, had roots near Compton. Los Angeles and its suburbs were among the largest oil-producing places in the nation through much of the twentieth century. All told, the industry employed thousands and thousands of workers in places such as nearby Dominguez Hills, Long Beach, and Compton. That included the future president, George Herbert Walker Bush, who brought his family to live in Compton's eastside for a time in the late 1940s, as he followed his budding oil business career to California. George W., the forty-third U.S. president, was a little boy at the time. (Was George W. the little White boy who stole my favorite blanket in kindergarten?)

The Hub City was also known as the place for new and used car dealerships that lined Long Beach Boulevard, the main north-south artery that connected Compton to Long Beach. Interspersed between the boulevard's dealerships were small businesses of many types, including Jerry's BBQ, a 1950s style drive-up restaurant that could have served as a set for George Lucas's classic film *American Graffiti*. The eastside was bordered by the Long Beach Freeway (one of the first in California), which ran along the Los Angeles River. By the time I was growing up in Compton, the river was a massive, ugly, concrete flood control channel that rarely carried much water to the ocean via Long Beach.

A favorite draw for me and other kids was the two-story JC Penney's in downtown, which had the first and only elevator in town. When I accompanied my mother and sisters to the store, I liked playing elevator operator to pass the time, up until one harrowing incident at age five. My mom and Annie had split up to shop elsewhere, both assuming that the other one had "Baby Albert" in tow (I was the youngest in the family for seven years). When I exited the elevator, my sister and mother were nowhere in sight. Petrified, I started yelling, "Mama, Mama, where are you?" Tears welled up in my eyes and an employee quickly came to comfort me. Just then I looked up to see my mother and Annie burst through the front entrance with panic-stricken faces that quickly turned to relief when they saw me.

In the era before shopping malls, Compton's downtown had everything families needed. The Compton Theater, two banks, two "variety" or "five and dime" stores, as we called them—including a Woolworth's with its old-school lunch counter—were mixed in among a few clothing and jewelry shops, a hardware store, and other small businesses. Many downtown buildings along Compton Boulevard were about twenty years old by then, having been rebuilt or newly constructed after the devastating Long Beach earthquake of 1933. City Hall, the LA County Library, and the Compton Police Department buildings also had been rebuilt on the western edge of the city's downtown area, fronting the Pacific Electric Railway tracks that ran next to the Great Depression–era post office.

Bordering the train tracks on the eastside was the Red Car (streetcar) passenger waiting station, a personal favorite because of its best lunch counter–served milkshakes in town. Mama often rewarded me with this delicious treat for going on errands with her.

Across from the streetcar waiting station was a shoe repair shop that I hated, because my brother Max (seven years my senior) liked to torture me there. Prominently displayed in the shop window was a weird mechanical puppet-like shoe repairman figurine who raised its arm with a hammer in hand as he pounded a nail into a make-believe shoe. It looked like something from the *Twilight Zone*, and Max knew I was deathly afraid of this goddamn little mechanical guy. When he was charged to watch after me while Mom shopped, he would press my face up against the window saying, "The little man is going to get you." Even as I grew older, I avoided walking by the shoe repair shop like it was the plague. I still don't like puppets. Thanks Max.

In front of the shoe repair shop was a Yellow Cab bench for taxi customers, and a few steps further away was a grocery store and the Compton Bakery. (When we bought pastries or bread, one of our López cousins who worked there always offered me a few broken cookie pieces for free.) Near the grocery store was Marshall's Bike Shop, another favorite stop downtown where you could survey the coolest and newest Schwinn bicycles. Until the third grade, I rode around the hood on an old, hand-me-down bike from my brothers that was kept alive with salvaged parts from even older bikes. Few in the barrio dared own a new bike because it might not hang around long.

Among the other White folks who settled in Compton were the Smiths, the family of my best high school buddy Danny. His parents opened their mom-and-pop grocery store in West Compton in the early 1950s, near General Rosecrans School. These White transplants from Arkansas earned enough from that store to afford a modest home on the westside, but after a few years they relocated to East Compton.

A small population of European immigrants also ventured west with their families in tow, before restrictive immigration policies were put in place by Congress in the 1920s that shut the door to further trans-Atlantic migrations. In 1940, about 10 percent of Compton residents were born in various central and northern European countries. A small number of Jewish families were among them, including the Markensons, whose granddaughter became a high school friend.

Wolf (William) Markenson, with his wife Sarah and baby son Albert, had fled the Pale of Settlement that is now eastern Poland and includes parts of western Russia, Belarus, Ukraine, and Lithuania. A wave of anti-Jewish pogroms into the early twentieth century pushed tens of thousands to flee regional violence and poverty and immigrate, primarily to the United States.

The Markensons arrived in the United States in 1911 and made their way to St. Louis, Missouri, where three more sons and a daughter were born. After serving in the navy during the war, eldest son Albert returned to St. Louis and convinced his brothers to follow him to California. They settled in Compton in 1947, and the Markenson brothers and a brother-in-law went into business together. Albert and Audrey had a home built for their young family on the eastside of Compton after their newly established westside grocery store, Bargain Town, became profitable. This was the market my family and I frequented after we moved out of the barrio when I was eight.

Sharon Markenson, my high school friend, remembered that "Not too far from our home there were some larger, much nicer homes, and we were all close to the neighborhood schools, stores, and the Compton Jewish Community Center." Sharon's parents helped found the center, which played a key role in supporting the city's small Jewish community.

Some families who lived on the westside headed to the eastside as Blacks moved in, preferring the eastside to joining the "flighters" who moved to more distant White suburbs. For instance, James Webb and his wife moved from Virginia to Hagoton, Kansas, a farming community, to plant roots and rear five daughters. One of those daughters, Corena, married her sweetheart, Herbert Dwyer, in Hagoton. The Webbs and the Dwyers were part of the migration of thousands of Dust Bowlers who headed west when family farms became destitute during the Great Depression. After a stint as migrant farmworkers, James brought his family to Richland Farms on the southwest side of Compton in 1933 and built a home there. His daughter and son-in-law followed a few years later, and James helped them build another home on his large lot so the extended family could be reunited. One of Mr. Dwyer's children, Doug, briefly attended Walton Junior High with me, and we later reconnected as high school football teammates.

The Smiths, Markensons, Dwyers, and other families were proud to live in the All-American City, a designation bestowed on Compton in 1952 by the National Civic League. Roughly a dozen cities every year garnered this coveted recognition. To receive this award, a city had to claim more than just availability of jobs; it had to be a good place to live. Having good public schools, public services, affordable suburban lifestyle, single-family homes, a good climate, and "good people" were all part of earning the reputation as "All American."

But "good people" to the National Civic League was code for "White people." Compton, which in 1952 had been overwhelmingly White, would not stay that way for long. Good people come in all colors, and the lure of Compton drew African Americans as well. But not at first, because until the late 1940s, Blacks had been systematically excluded from buying or renting in the city, and there were no recorded Black residents there in 1940. By 1950 African Americans made up about 5 percent of the total population of Compton, but a whopping 40 percent were already residents on the westside.

Had the National Civic League officials in 1952 looked more closely, especially at Compton's far northwest neighborhoods within city limits, they would have noticed a change underway as the first African American families broke the color line. Thousands of working- and middle-class Blacks had been hemmed into deteriorating neighborhoods in South Central Los Angeles and in Watts during the 1930s and 1940s. For them, buying a home in Compton represented a big down payment toward reaching that elusive American dream.

African Americans, like their midwestern White counterparts, ventured to the southern half of the Golden State in search of golden dreams. But in this case, Black people planted roots in the hope of distancing themselves from the cruelty and humiliation of the apartheid-like Jim Crow system in the South. About 5 million southern Blacks were part of the Great Migration in the first half of the twentieth century; the majority settled in large industrial northern cities. The onset of World War II redirected hundreds of thousands of others to the war-related opportunities out West.

The trickle of African American southern migrants before the war suddenly became a tsunami during the 1940s. But they soon realized that a version of Jim Crow had hitched a ride and followed them to California. "James" Crow, as some Black Angelenos called it, was not codified by law as in the South and was less oppressive in terms of daily life, but it nonetheless stifled opportunity and freedom for African Americans who moved to California.

Nothing reflected James Crow's handiwork more than the growing concentration of Blacks into racially designated, residentially bound neighborhoods of South Los Angeles after the Second World War. Black settlement in LA did not start this way, though. A growing population of African Americans were residents there early in the twentieth century, about 10,000 people in 1910 and 30,000 by 1920; and they mostly lived in multiracial, multiethnic neighborhoods south and east of downtown Los Angeles. As more African Americans from the South arrived, they tended to cluster in affordable homes south of downtown areas along the Central Avenue corridor, which they bought at a rate that far exceeded that in other American cities. A thriving "Negro Central Avenue" cultural and commercial district developed south of downtown LA until the 1940s, and it, too, was still multiethnic.

As their numbers increased, however, real estate covenants became more widespread, forbidding Blacks from buying in certain neighborhoods and suburbs. In 1920 about 20 percent of cities in LA County were covered by such racial covenants; this reached about 80 percent by the 1940s. Not only did many realtors and White homeowners try to hold the line—sometimes violently—against Black entry into certain neighborhoods, but the federal government made it even more difficult for them to buy through its mortgage loan policies.

In the wake of massive mortgage foreclosures during the Great Depression and as part of New Deal reforms beginning in the mid-1930s, the federal government got into the home loan business. First through the Home Owners Loan Corporation (HOLC), which offered amortized loans with low down payments for citizens who had defaulted on previous home loans, and soon after, through the new Federal Housing Authority (FHA), the feds provided guaranteed home loans with low down payments to millions of Americans. These loans through private lenders spurred home buying, particularly in California's rapidly expanding housing markets of the 1940s and 50s.

There was a catch, however. Race and ethnic background were allowed to be deciding factors in determining *where* individuals could secure a loan with the government's backing. "Redlining," as it came to be known, was invented by the federal government and its bureaucrats at HOLC, FHA, and the Federal Home Loan Bank Board. They devised a color-coded system of guidelines with which they mapped the cities and neighborhoods across the nation. "Green" areas (first grade) and "blue" areas (second grade) were considered good, desirable, safe locations for federally financed home loans. Those areas marked "yellow" were viewed as risky and third grade. The loan arbiters wrote off those marked "red" (fourth grade) as being too hazardous, way too risky. As a result, potential homeowners who looked in mostly multiethnic neighborhoods and in areas with Black and Brown folks found it nearly impossible to get government-backed loans to buy or renovate homes.

Which communities in the LA metro area do you think were mostly out-lined in yellow and red?

The HOLC and FHA officials' perspective in surveying Compton as part of South LA is particularly instructive. They gave "blue" or "grade 2" rat-ings to most of the central and eastern areas of the city; elsewhere, a different story unfolded after their visits. "The industrial section adjacent to the area on the east," along Alameda Street next to the barrio, they noted, "contains many nondescript structures largely inhabited by Mexicans and other sub-versive racial elements." The investigators also noted that "subversive racial elements from the north" threatened Compton's future for FHA loans.

These so-called racial subversives were African Americans in Watts and in the unincorporated neighborhoods adjacent to Compton's northwestern boundaries, where some Blacks resided. Is it any wonder the HOLC survey and map "redlined" the Mexican American barrio in which I grew up, and the northwest quadrant of Compton?

More than any other group, African Americans bore the brunt of the double whammy of racism in the housing market—restrictive neighbor-hood housing covenants and federal mortgage policies—especially because their migration numbers were skyrocketing. By 1950, the Black population reached 171,000 within the LA city limits and represented 78 percent of all Blacks in the metro area. The number of Black residents in LA soared to 340,000 by 1960. The residential areas of Black South LA expanded at the same time they became more concentrated and overcrowded. Impressive oc-cupational gains occurred for Blacks regionally in terms of blue-collar and industrial jobs during the war and post-war years (only after enormous pres-sure was placed on President Roosevelt by civil rights leaders). Yet African Americans were bottled up in an expanding section of South LA that was surrounded by race-restricted White suburbs in every direction. Regardless of status—poor, working class, middle class, or professional—if you were Black, you struggled to move beyond the confines of South LA neighbor-hoods. But the cap on the bottle of race-restricted housing was beginning to pop off in the late 1940s as blue-collar and middle-class Blacks focused their eyes on the prize of Compton.

In 1948 the U.S. Supreme Court handed down a decision in *Shelley v. Kraemer* that made racially restrictive real estate covenants illegal, and five years later the Court held that such covenants specifically could not be enforced because they violated the equal protection rights of African American homebuyers under the Fourteenth Amendment. The armor that James Crow had used to help shield White-only neighborhoods had been pierced.

Emboldened by the high court's decisions and with the support of a growing legion of White liberals in California, communities of color pressed harder to access historically restricted suburbs that had been guarded, especially from entry of African Americans. Among the brave early African American families to purchase a home in the All-American City of Compton was Bernice "Mama" Woods. From Port Arthur, Texas, this granddaughter of a minister dreamed of moving beyond the laundry work she did as a teen. After marrying Melvin, who was very light-skinned, in 1941, they settled in Watts. But when opportunity rang, they bought a home in Compton. To do so, Melvin insisted he alone meet with a realtor for viewings. After they became the first Black family on their block, darker-skinned Bernice recalled neighbors staring at her, making her feel uneasy. When a White postman nearly hit one of her kids on the street with his mail truck—which she remembered as a purposeful act of intimidation—she feared for the children's safety when playing outside.

"Mama" Woods—a label of endearment and respect Bernice earned over decades of public service in Compton—became a pioneering Black leader. She was elected to the school board and city council, and she advocated for youth and community program development. "My husband Melvin," Bernice said to me with a wide smile in 2011, a few years before she died, "always used to say, 'Whatever Bernice wants, Bernice gets.'"

Meanwhile, Black families predominated in the Woods's neighborhood within a year or two, causing a mad rush of property sales and the beginning of "White exodus," a much more rapid type of White flight. White and African American realtors swept in to make a financial killing in such neighborhoods in transition.

The profile of the north-westside rapidly changed block by block as hundreds of African American homeowners claimed a piece of coveted Compton property. Joe, my brother Art's friend, and his family were part of this early movement of Blacks into the city. But the change from White to Black homeownership on the westside in the early 1950s did not go uncontested.

In 1948, for example, after the first Blacks purchased homes on the outskirts of the city's northern boundaries, Compton realtors and others pledged to "Keep the Negroes North of 130th Street." This quickly failed, and by 1953, the boundary of White versus Black housing had moved south to Rosecrans Avenue, the same street that years earlier had separated barrio families like mine from adjoining all-White neighborhoods.

Some desperate White homeowners banded together to threaten White neighbors and realtors if they sold to African Americans. And some residents resurrected an obscure city statute that prevented the "peddling" of real estate in Compton, using this municipal ordinance to ask police to arrest certain realtors who had sold homes to Blacks. When all else failed, some directly harassed and intimidated the first African American families to penetrate south of Rosecrans Avenue.

Similar scenarios happened in nearby neighborhoods. In June 1953, Herman White and his wife and little daughter were the first Blacks on S. Dwight Street, on the westside, one block from an elementary school. A month before they moved in, another Black family in a neighborhood close by had experienced attacks by an angry White mob. The first week for the White family went by without trouble. That changed one night in late June 1953.

As was reported in the *California Eagle*, the newspaper of Black Los Angeles, "The uneasy truce in Compton cracked wide this week, when the forces of intimidation once more leaped into the open." Someone burned a cross on the White's front lawn and hurled a rock through a bedroom window, narrowly missing the head of their two-year-old daughter Francie. This racist incident occurred just a block from Longfellow Elementary, which I attended with Francie after we moved to westside Compton three years later.

To continue to claim the property to which they had legal right, Maxcy Filer, who moved to Compton in 1952, recalled how he and other members of the newly formed Compton chapter of the NAACP in 1957 used the "double escrow" ploy—a White buyer purchased a home and immediately resold to an African American—as a way to gain entrance to White neighborhoods. Called block busting, it was intentionally used to sell a home in a formerly all-White area to a Black family to "bust" up the neighborhood (while boosting realtors' sales). Filer marveled how quickly a neighborhood could transition. "Once a Black would move into one block in Compton," he recalled, "then you'd see 'for sale' signs in that whole block" as "Black and White realtors . . . would go and tell the Whites, look, the Blacks are moving in, the Negroes are moving in, and I can get you a good price on your property and you better sell now or the value is going down." But at the start, armed with bats or sometimes shotguns, Maxcy Filer and male friends took turns holding all-night vigils to protect Mr. and Mrs. Pickens, the first Black family to jump the racial divide across Rosecrans Avenue in the early 1950s.

Maxcy Filer first heard of Compton from a fellow soldier while stationed on Okinawa in the South Pacific in the years following Japan's surrender to the United States and Allied Forces. A young man from Watts had talked up features such as Compton Community College, the Compton Invitational Track and Field Meet held each year, and the good suburban life. "I'm going to move to California and the suburbs," Maxcy decided. After attending a business college in Indiana and meeting his future wife Blondell, they ignored family ties in other cities and bought in West Compton.

But Maxcy soon realized that Blacks lacked certain job opportunities in Compton—in civil service and police and fire departments—as well as elsewhere in the city. Over time, he and other Black friends used their NAACP local chapter to gain a foothold on the westside during the 1950s and to increase employment opportunities for their people into the 1960s.

Hundreds of other Black families rushed in once the door of homeownership was pried open. For instance, David Newman grew up in the mostly Black westside into the early 1960s. "[African Americans] families in Compton back in those days were . . . one big happy neighborhood family," he recalled. "There were no worries as to where you walked or what you did because everybody looked out for you," he fondly reminisced. "Compton back in the day . . . it was like a step up."

Not all of the city's changes were happenstance. Helen Phillip-Caver, an Alabaman, moved with her husband into a newly built tract home on Compton's northwest side in 1951. The land had previously been tilled by Japanese and Mexican tenant farmers, and she had visited on weekends to ride horses at the stables amid the farms. After the war, Compton annexed these lands, and a developer constructed hundreds of modest single-family homes, the first to sell property to prospective buyers regardless of race.

"Out here, at first it wasn't anything but gardening," Helen remembered, while pointing in all directions from her forever home: "The Mexicans used this lot to grow greens and flowers. Down the street where Centennial [High School] is, that was a horse ranch. Out here was way out . . . before they developed it," she said, referring to the city that some initially had called "[the Black] Beverly Hills." "When we moved in here . . . we had doctors, lawyers, schoolteachers, nurses, everybody was working. We would go to downtown Compton shopping," Helen recalled fondly. "And it was beautiful."

The same factors that influenced African Americans like the Phillip-Cavers, Newmans, Filers, and Woods to move to Compton played a part in my childhood memories. In that time period, for good and for bad, my family moved to Compton's westside.

FIVE

Barrio Boy's New Neighborhood

My time in the barrio came to an end when I was just eight years old. In January 1956 the priest of our tiny parish, La Sagrada Corazón Church, asked five property owners on the church's side of Culver Street—including my parents and grandmother—to sell their land to them. A new, larger church was to replace the cramped, ugly, decades-old structure in which all of us barrio kids had been baptized. For the Catholic Church, my parents agreed, of course. They sold our home for the huge price back then of $7,000.

I didn't understand when La Jefita told us Dad was looking for property to build a replacement for the only casita I'd ever known. The only friends I'd ever had lived nearby. I was happy in my barrio. How dare the church force me to move from the house where my siblings and I were all born and the community where all our relatives resided! But thoughts of persuading my parents to reject the church's offer quickly gave way to excitement about moving into a newly built home before year's end.

Little did I know about my mother's joy in leaving Culver Street behind. Mainly, Mama's happiness stemmed from leaving the proximity of Mama Pepa, as we called Grandmother Josefa. An unhappy woman through most of her married life with our heavy-drinking grandfather, Mama Pepa became increasingly angry and vindictive after our Papa Gordo's death in 1944 from cirrhosis of the liver. She not only treated her five daughters-in-law horribly (two aunts have recounted to me how venomous she was toward them), but she began to turn against my mother around the time I was born.

From my earliest memories of her when I was a small child, old, grumpy, and mean-spirited are what come to mind. This was especially unfortunate because she was the only grandparent I had a chance to know. My mother once told me, and my sisters confirmed, that Mama Pepa resented her for being our grandfather's favorite daughter. Francisco constantly visited our home back then from next door, partly because of his friendship with our father of nearly twenty years, whom he felt grateful to for granting ownership of the home where he raised our uncles and aunt. Mama Pepa's resentment of our mother and her family intensified, especially as her mental health deteriorated over time.

Several incidents helped my mother see that moving away from our grandmother was a dream come true. After our grandfather passed away, Mama Pepa had ordered her to select one of my older siblings to sleep over at her house every night from fear of being alone (all five of her children were gone and married by this time). My brothers and sisters had to obey—except introverted, easily frightened Ben, who got on his knees and pleaded to avoid this as the eldest brother. The rest shared that they dreaded the nights when they had to sleep in the same bed with our grandmother, especially as she routinely talked in her sleep.

La Jefita was pushed to the brink by mistreatment of my brother Harpo (Art), who stayed over at grandmother's house one evening when our Aunt Mabel (my mother's younger and only sister) and some others gathered there for some talk and drinking. Not wanting Art to hear the adult conversation in the living room, Aunt Mabel ordered him out of the house; when he hesitated, she physically threw him out the door. With bruised feelings and a bruised arm, Art came home and reported to Mama what had happened. When our big (literally) sister Rita with her maternal tendencies and big temper learned the details, she stormed into our grandmother's house and confronted her aunt. They squabbled and pushed each other, but Mabel was no match for her niece physically—and landed nalgas first on the floor. After that, Mama Pepa never again spoke to her daughter Rose, or to any of us, and ordered all my mother's siblings to do the same. Most shunned our mother for many years.

Mama Pepa also had a six-foot-high cyclone fence, with wire barbs on the top, constructed between our two properties, which looked as menacing to me as the Berlin Wall. Our mother endured the insult, which may have been the result of mental illness or meanness, without complaining, but she realized her mother was beyond salvation.

Not long after that fence was built, when I was about seven, my mom became scared of what Mama Pepa might do to us children physically. I was outside playing one day in the yard alone when Mama Pepa called to me as she stood next to the fence holding something in her hand. "Ven aquí, Albertito" (Come here, little Albert). Even though she had never paid attention to me before, much less offered me anything, I hesitantly responded to her repeated command. As I walked closer, I saw through the wire fence that she held what looked like a Hershey's bar. I loved Hershey's chocolate—or any chocolate. I took the candy bar from my grandmother's outstretched fingers. And, as I began unwrapping it to take a bite, my mom burst through the back door/front door of our home. Running full speed toward me, she swiped a hand and knocked that delicious-looking candy bar to the ground. In the next second she'd grabbed me by the arm and pulled me into the house.

I stood there stunned, having never received anything from Mama Pepa but cold stares and harsh warnings not to play on her rare sliver of front lawn with my cousins. The only thing Mom said was, "Never take anything again if Mama Pepa offers it to you. Entiendes!?" (Do you understand!?).

After we moved from the neighborhood a year later, I never saw my grandmother again until her funeral nearly a decade later. By then, my mother had explained her fright that day and the possibility that "Mama Pepa was trying to poison you." All I know is that I didn't lose my love for Hershey bars!

The nail in the coffin came from my mother's general fear about the safety of her boys in the barrio. On the street corner nearest to our home, across from Sacred Heart Church, you could often find a few local young vatos shooting craps. This dice game probably involved only small amounts of money and was considered no big deal to residents, until some guys in a

Chicano gang from Watts made their way into our barrio and wanted to play. One day my older brothers, Art and Ben, were standing near the street, maybe 100 feet from the craps game. They ducked after a car drove by, and they heard what sounded like exploding firecrackers. But as Art swiveled to run away, he saw stray bullets ricochet off the block wall in front of our home that Dad had built. Mama was also worried that Art might be influenced by such barrio gangsters, even though he'd started to get into playing football more than hanging out with vatos.

After the home sale had been decided on, Benjamín chose to purchase a lot and build a home, reducing overall costs by doing the foundation and concrete-related work with some family help. I got to tag along with my dad and mother, and baby brother David, in the search of vacant lots.

The first lot Dad showed interest in buying was in Lynwood, the city just north of Compton. After seeing the lot, we drove to a real estate office, and Dad went in to speak with a realtor. He quickly returned to the car but said nothing as we drove home. Another lot Dad found, this time in southwest Compton, turned out to be the winner, and our new home, in a neighborhood called Richland Farms.

Not until many years later did my mother tell me that my father, who spoke broken English with a heavy Spanish accent, hadn't expected the visit with that Lynwood realtor to end abruptly. Benjamín's interest in buying a lot there had been met with a courteous reply of, "I'm sorry sir, but we don't sell property in Lynwood to Mexicans." Though racially restrictive covenants could no longer legally keep Blacks and Mexicans out of Lynwood during the 1950s, and had stopped effectively doing so in Compton, that cabrón realtor was applying informal pressure to produce the same effect.

Luckily, another realtor welcomed Dad's offer to purchase a lot in Richland Farms. Benjamín found a contractor to build the structure who would let him serve as the concrete sub-contractor. And partly to thank our mother for keeping the family together during his hospitalization with TB, he gave Rosie what she wanted most in her new home: a kitchen with a built-in stovetop and plenty of cupboard space, and a separate bathroom for the four boys with a large shower. It must have been torture for her and my sisters to have shared one small bathroom in our barrio home with four dirty boys who never put the toilet seat down after they peed.

Though Luli, Beegie, and Popito knew I was leaving the barrio, I didn't manage to say a formal goodbye to them. I assumed we would meet again, but we never did. After my brother Art became a cop on the Compton PD, he shared that Luli was found stabbed to death on a Compton street in the late 1970s. One of my cousins told me that Popito was shot to death in a drug deal gone bad. I don't know if Beegie survived.

The vacant lot our father purchased in 1956 sat on the edge of Compton's southern-most city boundaries, facing what was then one of the largest undeveloped parcels of land in southern Los Angeles County. Not until fifty years later—when Art and I, together with my two grown sons, visited Michoacán—did I realize the visceral draw for him of this unique area of Compton. The many farms that dotted the landscape across the street from our new home, with Dominguez Hills in the background, resembled our father's birthplace village of Quiringuicharo.

On Thanksgiving weekend in 1956, we made the move. Dad borrowed a huge flatbed truck from the construction company he worked for to move all our belongings, including scrap building materials he had accumulated from many job sites over the years, which had been piled high on our side yard (Benjamín was a pack rat). As a result, we must have looked to our new neighbors like a version of the old TV show *The Beverly Hillbillies* while unloading all that junk. For us, the move was more like the family sitcom of the 1970s and 80s, *The Jeffersons*, but with an upwardly mobile Mexican American family instead of a Black one. The Camarillos of Compton were also "movin' on up" in the mid-1950s. But unlike the Jeffersons, who moved to the eastside, we moved to Compton's westside.

This huge step up was helped by the fact that our dad was now staying sober and working regularly as a unionized cement finisher in 1956 (his weekly paycheck was about $100 per week, or about $959 in 2020 dollars). Pulling off all the finances to build our new home became a family affair, though. My older brothers worked every summer for Zavala Paving Company, where my dad had worked for years, and they handed over their weekly earnings to La Jefita. Rita, who still lived with us at age twenty-five, bought most of the new furniture for the home on credit. And there was sweat equity. My older brothers and father did all the concrete work on the driveways and walkways. I worked on many weekends helping my father load up our pickup truck with beautiful natural stone pieces excavated from a new home construction site where he worked, which was about fifteen miles from Compton. Dad used this "Palos Verdes" rock to build planters, light posts, and walls. My brother Ben took it upon himself to plant a big lawn from seed, which was something we'd lacked before, and it served as the football field for my older brothers.

Our home was at the southern edge of Richland Farms on a large lot that had been subdivided into three smaller ones. When the neighborhood—about two-thirds of a mile long and a half-mile wide, bordered by Wilmington Avenue on the west, Alondra Boulevard on the north, Greenleaf Street on the south, and Oleander Street on the east—was developed, the landowners made much larger lots than elsewhere in the city, ranging from about a quarter acre to one acre. And, unlike all other Compton neighborhoods, some streets there lacked sidewalks or storm drain gutters, lending a rural flavor to the area, which filled in quickly in the post-war years.

Richland Farms had mostly modest two-bedroom, one-bath homes on large lots, with an occasional larger home owned by some middle- and upper-income White families. As I roamed the area on bike soon after moving, I found homes that had backyard horse corrals, barns, and chicken coops. As an extension of a nearby farming community, these rural features came thanks to Reverend Griffith Compton, who had designated that a certain section of the town be zoned for raising livestock and other farm animals (which still applies).

Our home fronted the huge agricultural area nearly two miles long by one-and-a-half miles wide that encompassed the southern boundary of Compton and the adjacent unincorporated area of Rancho Dominguez. Its nearly 2,000 acres of land were cultivated by several tenant farmers (mostly Mexican and Japanese) to produce everything from beets, carrots, turnips, string beans, and onions to alfalfa and hay. Standing on the side of our home looking southward, the hills of Rancho Dominguez lay half a mile away; less than a hundred feet away was the start of an enormous hay field, separated from our home by a slim piece of property hosting tall electrical transmission lines that buzzed constantly.

This Richland Farms borderland now hosts one of largest planned industrial parks in Los Angeles County when developed in the late 1970s.

Having this beautiful "side yard" in Richland Farms two decades earlier helped turn this barrio boy into a quasi-country boy. With no friends in the neighborhood at first, my best buddy was my dog Butch, a young collie and chow mix. We wandered through the fields of hay that grew way over my head by late spring. In early summer when the hay fields were cut, Butch and I would roam about to spot a jackrabbit, quail, or pheasant. Butch ran after them, always in vain, and I sometimes had my bow and arrow on hand but always came up short as well. Richland Farms also had a real creek to wander along about a quarter mile away from home. Compton Creek was a concrete channel where it ran north-south through the city, but it turned into a natural creek as it meandered to the Los Angeles River. I tried to catch crayfish in the litter-strewn creek.

Sometimes Butch and I also took long walks along the Red Car tracks that crossed the creek and led to Dominguez Hills, where you could find a nineteenth-century adobe rancho nestled on a lush hill that had been turned into a Catholic seminary (not far from scattered oil drilling rigs). I knew to stay away from the vegetable fields planted by the tenant farmers who lived nearby in old run-down wooden houses. But we benefited from access to loads of fresh-picked veggies, as Dad became friends with a Mexican tenant, whom I called Tío Chuy.

No Blacks or Mexicans lived in Richland Farms when we moved into its eastern-most boundary. But across Oleander Street from us was a neighborhood with small homes on small lots where several Mexican American families—and at least one Filipino family—mixed in with working-class and some poor White families. The families included that of my father's closest sibling, Tío Rosendo, who followed his older brother out of the barrio. The two Camarillo households, located across the street from each other, numbered eighteen people—so we took over the neighborhood in this part of Richland Farms.

The summer fun of playing in open fields in 1956 trailed by my faithful dog—fishing for crayfish in the Compton Creek and watching horseback riders on nearby trails—gave way to the uneasy reality of transferring to a new elementary school. Mom had enrolled me in Longfellow Elementary about one mile away in the heart of West Compton.

SIX

Changing Westside Colors

I entered Ms. Vocila's third-grade classroom in mid-fall semester as one of seven Mexican American kids out of thirty-seven students. In lots of ways, this new classroom was like General Rosecrans School, except there was not one African American student in my class and, as best as I can remember, only a few in the entire school. Ms. Vocila was a kind and gentle teacher, but even so, I still didn't have much interest in education.

Transferring to Longfellow School meant having no friends at first, as none of the kids in the class lived near me, except for two girls with whom I walked home sometimes. It did open me up to the fact that other families had different realities. On one walk home with Melody (who lived two blocks from me) and her friend Eileen, Melody asked if I wanted to come into her home to play. I had no interest in girls at that time, and I had only ever been inside Mexican Americans' homes but said "sure." After a few minutes, Melody asked if I wanted to hear her play the piano, which I'd never seen except on TV. She sat down at the keyboard and impressed me with her skills. "Do all the homes of White folks have pianos?" I wondered.

Sometimes, my brother Max (who was seven years older) and I would wander the open fields in Richland Farms together. On one occasion, during what was the last week of the school year, a ride with Max on the front handlebars of his bike added to my childhood isolation at the time. Max was going really fast on a dirt road in a nearby hayfield when one tire hit a rut, sending us flying about five feet in the air. Max, a big fifteen-year-old, landed on the road and skidded along; the problem was my head had become the cushion between him and the dirt. I was knocked unconscious and felt foggy headed when I came to.

Max stood me up with a gasp that I couldn't register since I was still in a daze. "Get back on the bike so I can ride you home!" Though barely conscious, I was savvy enough to stumble home instead. In shock, I didn't feel any pain. But when my mother and sister Annie (who was living with us at the time while her husband was stationed in Korea) saw me, they cringed and immediately took me into the bathroom for cleaning up. I cried at seeing the half of my face that had hit the road was nothing but a mixture of dirt and blood, with tears now adding to the bloody mess embedded on my cheeks.

For nearly two months into my first full summer in Richland Farms, the left half of my face, from the chin to forehead, was one massive, nasty-looking scab. During the first week, with bandages nearly covering my entire head, I looked like a fricking mummy as the slow healing process began (being from a working-class family, there was no visit with a doctor). When the bandages were removed, I took on a split-faced zombie look, fresh out of a horror movie.

I had been a skinny kid until we moved to Richland Farms. No child in his right mind, though, would want to play with me that summer in 1957. So, I spent my time doing what made me happiest—watching television and gorging on sandwiches and chocolate milk. The nickname "Bones" I'd earned from my brothers as a skinny five-year-old roaming the streets of the barrio with my friends was used to taunt me now instead. From not playing outside as I used to, I got pudgy.

"Hey, where is Bones?" one of my brothers would yell while playing basketball or football in the yard; another would reply, "He's watching TV again." Then Art would usually say, "Get his fat ass out here to play!" I'm so grateful they dragged me out of the house for some exercise. And thanks to my big brothers, this started my love for sports. It took almost a year for me to slim down.

It helped that I made friends with a couple of boys in Mrs. Bailey's fourth-grade class, which is where I had one of the most racially mixed experiences of my education. In a class of thirty-six students, there were twenty-three White kids (including one Jewish girl), five Mexican Americans, and seven African Americans. The rise of the Black population was already happening in westside Compton.

Though shaded by race, the memories of the fourth grade etched into my brain were not about Black classmates. Early in the school year in 1957, Mrs. Bailey—a heavyset, fiftyish White woman, and a no-nonsense type of teacher—gave us a compulsory, boring assignment: to learn about the Spanish missions.

We were tasked with building a cardboard mission complete with drawings of saintly priests or "padres," who, we were taught, had traveled north to rescue the "mission Indians" from their hedonistic ways. (Only recently has this assignment faded from the curriculum in the state's public schools.) Mrs. Bailey placed us in small groups to work on painting our cardboard mission. For some reason that I don't remember, the six White kids in my group started discussing ethnic backgrounds. "What are you?" one of the classmates asked another, and she said, "I'm Irish," while another kid shared, "I'm German." Another girl, Holly, said "I'm Jewish," which I didn't understand. When my turn came, I looked around and opted to say, "I'm Spanish." I knew damn well I'd lied but to say "I'm Mexican" in a group with all White kids? I knew instinctively that it would make me seem inferior to these classmates.

What I didn't know then was that historians of race and ethnicity often describe the 1950s as a period of Anglo conformity and forced assimilation. For at least a few seconds, I took on the racial/ethnic identity of being Spanish, just like the preferred characters in our lesson about California missions. It was an era when a nine-year-old Chicano transplant from the barrio would be more likely to opt to Whiten himself up so that he could be accepted by his peers.

My choice is a sad commentary on a society that had made anything Mexican seem tainted, and dirty, as a cultural identity. It was also the only time in my life I concealed my identity, though pressures from society made this coverup all too common for young Mexican Americans by mid-century.

As early as the 1920s, some educators had identified Mexican American students as a drain on public schools, and some public health officials blamed Mexicans for spreading communicable diseases (such as a smallpox epidemic that occurred in LA in the 1920s). It was not a huge leap for authorities to label Mexicans as "welfare" problems during the Great Depression, especially in the southwestern states where Mexicans became concentrated. Federal authorities added fuel to the fire of a growing anti-Mexican immigrant sentiment.

As the economic depression unfolded in the early 1930s, President Herbert Hoover was among the first to sound the alarm about Mexicans taking scarce jobs away from Americans in his home state of California and for depleting local welfare coffers. Over the course of several years beginning in 1931, federal officials, in conjunction with local agencies in LA and other cities, developed a two-part plan. The first part involved "scaring" Mexicans into returning to Mexico voluntarily through newspaper reports that immigrants would no longer be allowed to accept local charity. Thousands accepted the initial government offer of free transportation to emigrate. When this failed to produce the repatriation numbers desired, the government began to physically round up Mexicans and deport them involuntarily.

Hundreds of thousands of Mexican immigrants and their American-born children were deported or repatriated during the next few years of the Great Depression. Estimates of such forced removals that ruined lives range from a low of 400,000 to a high of almost 1 million. As a result, this was one of the largest federally orchestrated involuntary movements of people in U.S. history.

My mother recalled wondering "what happened to families that seemed to disappear overnight from the barrio" with a shrug of her shoulders. For myself, I didn't know about this dark chapter in American history until I was a student at UCLA. It's still hard to even imagine what it would have been like, growing up in Compton in the early 1930s, to have been forced to move to a country where I had few personal connections.

The net result of these deportations was that the Los Angeles area lost an estimated 20 to 33 percent of all Mexican-origin people by the late 1930s. Those who stayed were disproportionately Mexican American citizens, especially the children of immigrants like my siblings and me.

Coupled with the rise of the Mexican American "gang problem" associated with the Sleepy Lagoon case and the Zoot Suit Riots in the early 1940s, it is little wonder that so many in my post-war generation of Mexican Americans internalized negative associations with the term "Mexican." In the wake of powerful social forces—schools, television, print media, Cold War politics—anything less than assimilation to a White, All-American norm had become suspect. The impact was widespread, as by 1960 about 80 percent of California's approximately 1.5 million Spanish-origin people (primarily Mexican) were like me: a U.S.-born citizen of immigrant parents (34 percent) or of U.S.-born parents (46 percent).

Another activity related to our lessons about California missions added to my feelings of alienation. Mrs. Bailey allowed some of us to work with obsidian stone, the black volcanic glass Indigenous people in the region used to make arrowheads. A lover of bows and arrows, I began using rocks as a chisel to fashion an arrowhead.

Man, my final product was a cool-looking, beautiful black arrowhead with a very sharp point. Proud of my skillfully made arrowhead, I went up to Melissa—a nice, freckled-face White girl—who was standing at a nearby table working on her own project. "Hey, Melissa," I said excitedly, while pushing the prize closer to her, "look at my arrowhead!" As Melissa turned quickly to look, her left arm swung out, and the arrowhead struck her arm. She immediately recoiled, grabbed her arm, and walked away.

She hadn't said anything to me, but some thirty seconds later while I was showing off my arrowhead to other kids, I felt a sharp pain in my back. As I screamed, "Ouch!" and quickly turned to see who had done this, there stood Mrs. Bailey with a horribly mean look on her face and a sharp pencil in her hand that she'd used to stab me. "You mean little . . . !" She didn't say the next word, but it wasn't going to be "Spaniard." Pointing a finger toward Melissa, she added, "Look what you did to her," as I noticed the puncture wound on her arm. "Go to the principal's office right now!" she continued, while forcefully shoving me several times toward the door.

My back still hurt from the pencil driven into my skin (I checked and found I was bleeding but didn't tell school staff, and certainly not my parents, when I went home). I was in big trouble and was shaking as I was sent to the principal's office for the first time. I was no angel, but I never would have hurt Melissa purposely.

The school secretary had me wait outside the principal's office for a few minutes before he came to fetch me. Scared shitless, I didn't know what to expect. Was he going to paddle me, poke me with a pencil, or what? The principal was a forty-something-year-old White man with a kind look on his face when he opened the door and motioned for me to enter and sit. He quickly said, "Alberto, habla Español?" I was a bit taken aback that his first words were in Spanish. "Sí señor," I uttered meekly in a soft whisper, and then I added, "Un poquito, pero no hablo muy bien" (A little bit, but I don't speak very well). Without passing judgment, he asked me what happened, and I told him truthfully. He believed me, thank goodness! Man, I dodged a big bullet, and I was so relieved when he told me to go back to class, though I didn't want to face that cabrona, Mrs. Bailey, for fear she might stab me again.

The next morning after class began, Mrs. Bailey yanked me by the collar to pull me over to Melissa, whose arm had a small bandage. "I hope Melissa's parents make your parents pay for her doctor's bill," she shouted with a deep frown on her reddened face, adding in front of all of the students, "When you jabbed her, a piece of the arrowhead broke off in her arm." I felt very guilty and sad, though I said nothing and sat down. Luckily no one called home because, had my sister Rita, who treated me like a son, found out what Mrs. Bailey did to me, it would have resulted in her being charged with assault and battery against a teacher on school grounds.

I gutted out the remainder of grade four but hated being in Mrs. Bailey's class all day. She continued being mean, including giving mostly U (unsatisfactory) marks on my report cards. Granted, I was not a good student, but no wonder I didn't like school early on.

The saving grace of being in Mrs. Bailey's class was that I made good friends with two boys, Kenny and Jimmy, both White kids, and Bobby, who was Mexican American. And summer finally arrived—no more Mrs. Bailey! When I wasn't hanging out with my friends or playing in the fields with my dog, there was always a football or basketball game that my older brothers allowed me to join at home, though the rule was "no guarding Al" because I was so much younger than the teenage guys constantly gathered at the Camarillo house.

Those games meant my nickname finally fit again as I lost all of the weight gained the previous year. Those pickup basketball games and 4-on-4 football games also helped me develop into a good athlete as I emulated my brothers Art and Max, who had become outstanding high school football players. Both later headed to college with Division 1 athletic scholarships. Meanwhile, my bookworm brother Ben became the first kid out of the barrio to attend college on an academic scholarship. For the first time in our family, the topic of college came up, with Ben's higher education aspirations having a big impact on us younger brothers.

When I had entered the third grade at Longfellow in 1956, there were likely only a few Black kids in the school. But the faces of West Compton changed dramatically over about five years. When I entered fifth grade in 1958, the ten White students in a class of twenty-nine were now a numerical minority. Twelve others were African American, five were Mexican American, and two were Asian American.

I made friends from different backgrounds in Ms. Caldwell's class. Their African American or Asian American families had settled on the westside the same year as mine, and we stayed friends into junior high. Frank's family moved to Compton from the South in 1956, and they bought a home within a block of our grade school. Neil's father immigrated from China in the late 1930s, and after an arranged marriage, his parents first settled in a majority African American neighborhood just south of downtown LA. They later bought a home in Compton in 1956, but only after being turned away by realtors in Downey, a restricted, all-White suburb northeast of Compton.

Frank and I were classmates again in Mr. Merrill's sixth-grade class. The student composition in our class reflected ongoing changes in the racial makeup of the school and surrounding neighborhoods: well over half of the students were African American, and about 40 percent were White, with a small number of Mexican Americans (maybe 5 to 7 percent) and a few Asian American kids.

Lucky for me, my relationship to school took a big turn in the sixth grade. So, too, did my ideas about the future, though as a twelve-year-old, those thoughts were fleeting. My older brothers' pursuits and Mr. Merrill were responsible for these turnarounds. For the first time I began to talk about college and sports, and the two together. More importantly, I became a reader, for which I thank Mr. Merrill.

A balding, physically fit man about forty years old, he was a cool guy whom I admired and respected. Early in the school year he placed us all into small reading groups and explained, to my disinterest, how reading could help us imagine different places around the world and learn about many different things and different people.

He soon figured out how to reach me, as a student and as a budding athlete. "I have an idea about what you might like to read," he said one morning when we were choosing books for our reading circles. "Have you ever heard of Hercules?" My ears perked up right away. "Yeah," I quickly replied, noting a recent film about the mythic hero that starred bodybuilder Steve Reeves; my brothers had taken me to see it a year or two earlier. "Did you know that there are many other Greek gods besides Hercules?" Mr. Merrill asked, sensing my excitement. He took me over to the class library and pulled a volume about Greek mythological figures off the shelf. "Here," he handed me the book, adding, "take it home if you want," though these books were intended for in-class reading only. I started reading the book in my circle group and that night learned about Zeus, Hercules's father, and about other gods. Man, I was hooked! And as a newly interested reader, I became a better student. Many E (excellent) grades started appearing on my report cards during my final year at Longfellow Elementary and no U (unsatisfactory) grades for citizenship.

Then there was Benjamín Jr., known to our relatives as El Sonny and as Ben by us and his friends. He was the first-born boy of our parents, so held a favored position with Dad. Our father loved his daughters, but his traditional Mexican male gender bias favored the boys.

Ben was a serious, introverted type of guy and was easily overshadowed by Rita—with her dominant personality and her being six years Ben's senior. Although the other Camarillo boys excelled at sports, Ben's studious ways paid off in excellent grades, especially in math and science (I certainly didn't follow in those math-related footsteps). By the time he graduated from Compton High School in 1956, he had earned a science scholarship and been admitted to the University of Southern California.

Attaining a high school diploma was cause for a great celebration among Chicano families. Ben's admission was to a four-year college! Less than 1 percent of Mexican Americans attended four-year universities in the 1950s. Ben was also the first student from the barrio to attend *any* college, meaning that he had no role models or peers to follow from our community.

As an added challenge, though Ben's scholarship paid for tuition, our parents couldn't afford dormitory fees for him to live on campus. So he commuted the twelve miles from Compton to the university every day. The actual distance to campus, compared to the cultural differences, must have made the place seem like light years away for Ben. In part, there were likely no more than five or six other Mexican American students at USC and only a few African Americans. No wonder the university was known in that era as a rich White boy's school, and later the University of Spoiled Children.

Unsurprisingly under the tough circumstances, Ben didn't last long at USC. His scholarship stipulated maintaining a B grade point average. Sadly, he failed to meet that requirement in his freshman year. Ben didn't consider enrolling at any college the next academic year. He worked instead at a drugstore warehouse for a time before being drafted into the army. When he returned from the service, though, he enrolled in Compton Junior College and earned his associate of arts degree. It took him almost fifteen years as a part-time student at California State University, Los Angeles, but Ben finally completed the degree in civil engineering he likely would've achieved at USC in the first place.

However rocky his educational path was, Ben's venture into the unknown world of higher education planted the idea of college in my head. He modeled what being a good student looked like. In part, I admired Ben and the idea of going to college, though at age twelve, I only had a vague idea of what that entailed. I also wanted to be like my brother Art who was a role model in sports, the other part of my life that gelled by the sixth and seventh grades. Harpo was the first in our family, and the first kid from the barrio, to make a name for himself on the gridiron.

All my brothers were tall (about six feet) good-looking guys, and Art was athletic and tough, too. By the time he entered middle school, Art had a barrio reputation as a badass dude you didn't mess with. He was already strong, muscular, and agile. It was a good thing he turned his energies toward football rather than fighting guys in the hood. By his senior year of high school, Art was an all-conference lineman at Compton High and was being recruited by Division 1 football programs, including the University of Washington (though they wanted him to enroll in a community college in the Seattle area before transferring there). He instead opted to stay home and enroll at Compton Junior College where he earned his associate of arts degree and was named a Junior College All-American honorable mention as a tight end. Art then accepted an athletic scholarship at New Mexico State University. But because he didn't like the coaching staff at NMSU much and didn't expect to have opportunities to play, he decided to come back home after one semester.

My brother Max, who graduated from Compton High in 1961 when Art was finishing at Compton College, was also an outstanding lineman on the football team. Recruited by Division 1 universities as well, he accepted a scholarship at the University of Utah along with his teammate Roy Jefferson (Roy went on to a stellar career in the NFL as a wide receiver). Max, like his big brother Art, left the university after one semester.

I shared their football-playing dreams. By the time I started middle school in 1961, my lofty goals were to go to college and to play football, and maybe other sports too. In the sixth grade, I already had shown some athletic abilities. Mr. Merrill also turned out to be a damn good quarterback. During lunch time he would often organize us into passing-only, pickup football games. Those games helped me realize I had good hands as Mr. Merrill turned me into one of his favorite throwing targets. Those many times my brothers said to get Bones's "fat ass out here to play" football and basketball had finally paid off. (When our second son Greg played football at Stanford University and later in the NFL for eight years as a wide receiver, I was sometimes asked by reporters or fans how he had developed such good skills as a receiver. I would always reply, "He's got his mama's hands." But actually, I like to take total credit for all of Greg's skills as a receiver. Greg's mother, by contrast, claims his long career in the NFL was attributable to his smarts for using his mathematical and mechanical engineering skills to outwit most defensive backs, a claim I simply can't dispute.)

To excel in athletics, like academics or just about anything in life, building confidence in yourself is key. I began to see myself as a good athlete by the sixth grade. Chano, an older cousin who lived across the street from us, was already into football and track at the Catholic high school he attended (having also been greatly influenced by Art and Max). When he signed up for a Knights of Columbus all-comers recreational track meet in Compton, he invited me to join in. I signed up for the eleven- to twelve-year-old competition that included events such as the 50-yard dash, high jump, standing broad jump, and football throw. Of the seventy-five or so fifth- and sixth-grade contestants, I won all the events. Man, I was feeling good about my performance. And I received an amazing prize—a coveted Roy Rogers lunch box with a thermos!

As a twelve-year-old, I now understood that I was strong, and fast (at Longfellow Elementary's annual track day, I had already placed fourth in the 50-yard dash and first in the softball throw). Convincing myself that I'd grow taller than all my brothers didn't work, though I often told family that I was going to be six foot two by the time I was fifteen (I was already five foot eight in the seventh grade). Unfortunately, I inherited the height genes from the López side of the family and didn't grow but an inch past age thirteen.

My newly earned confidence in class and in sports made the transition to Walton Junior High School a pretty easy one. The newest of five middle schools in Compton, Walton was built in 1953 next to string bean and other vegetable fields. The middle school campus adjacent to Richland Farms was often referred to by visiting sports teams as the "bean field" school. My brother Max followed Art three years later in attending Walton, but I was the first to start at Walton after our move to Richland Farms. It was the school where they'd discovered their love of team sports, while playing football for the Wildcats.

Of course, I was going to play football at Walton too. That opportunity happened faster than I expected, soon after I started the seventh grade, thanks to the Soviet Union and Cold War politics. The President's Council on Physical Fitness was established during the Eisenhower administration in the late 1950s, but it became widely associated with President John F. Kennedy in 1961 as he grew concerned about Americans' fast-food fad, flabby bellies (especially among men and boys), and TV-induced sedentary lifestyles. He and others believed strong American bodies and minds were necessary to counter the Soviets during competitions in the space race and international athletics. So when I entered Walton, my classmates and I—like our counterparts across the nation—were required to pass a series of physical fitness tests.

Walton staff and the Compton School District decided that team sports should be encouraged at a younger age, so a 7-on-7 flag football program began at Walton in 1961. Each of the fourteen seventh-grade homeroom classes were asked to form a team, and Mrs. Van Pelt's homeroom, my team, turned out to be outstanding. We not only defeated our fellow Walton JHS homeroom teams to win school honors, but the twelve of us selected as all-stars went on to beat seventh-grade teams from the other five Compton middle schools. We were crowned City Champs in 1961. My confidence as an athlete and as a football player took a big leap. My team also went on to win the intramural basketball and baseball championships. And later in the year, I was one of seven boys on the seventh-grade track team, though my ability to compete on par with the best sprinters was beginning to decline.

While I developed as a student athlete during my three years at Walton, and later in high school, I started taking on leadership roles that brought even more important life lessons my way, though I didn't fully understand them at the time. In those years in the 1960s in Compton, I was fortunate to be exposed to both the problems that ethnic and racial differences can create in a diverse society and to witness the best qualities of people who valued forming bonds with others of different racial, religious, cultural, or national origin backgrounds. The friends and foes I met during these years were part of my baby steps in learning how to foster a racially and ethnically engaged, yet diverse, community.

SEVEN

A Different Westside Story

From the late 1950s to the early 60s, my views of racial differences and intergroup relations began to gel as I moved among elementary and middle school friends who were White, Black, Japanese, Chinese, Filipino, and Mexican. Yet as westside Compton transitioned to becoming majority African American, I also encountered racial tensions as struggles over integration played out on and off school campuses, sometimes violently.

The demographic changes came so quickly, while White flight soared. I had no Black classmates in Ms. Vocila's class at Longfellow Elementary in 1956. Three years later, Mr. Merrill's sixth-grade class was mostly African American, and fewer White kids were at the school.

Walton Junior High, between 1961 and 1963, showed the signs of White exodus on the westside being nearly complete, and it matched the speedy growth of all-Black neighborhoods. When I started seventh grade, African Americans formed about 63 percent of 1,100 students at the school. White students were about 20 percent of the student body, and Mexican Americans 16 percent (there were 10 Japanese Americans and 2 Chinese American kids). By my graduation from Walton in 1963, fewer than 60 White students were in the entire school, or about 5 percent of the student body.

In many ways, the changing faces in my social world in the 1960s represented the challenges of getting along across racial lines that had become a national focus; the sometimes-painful lessons experienced during those years helped mold me into being a committed, multicultural citizen. They would influence me one day into being a better educator, leader in ethnic studies in higher education, community activist, and spouse and father.

Entering middle school was exciting because I would meet new classmates and, for the first time, have teammates. Many of the White kids I knew at Longfellow Elementary, one of several elementary feeder schools for Walton, had moved away from the westside during the summer. Some White parents may have been influenced to do so by campus friction. Early in the school year, I was hanging out at lunch time with a friend since the fifth grade. Kenny was a friendly kid, short and skinny, with blondish hair and blue eyes. He became a target for Charles, a bully who was obviously looking for someone to intimidate. Charles was a short, stocky seventh grader like us. He came over to where we were standing next to the gym with one of his African American buddies who was very tall, maybe six foot one, and started to harass Kenny. "What you doin', Patty boy" (a derogatory name for Whites), Charles said with a mean look on his face as he pushed Kenny, who backed up and just looked down, likely hoping Charles and his friend would go away. Charles pushed Kenny again and held him against a wall, so I had to step in.

I had been in many low-level skirmishes in the barrio and at Longfellow over stupid kid stuff. And I had made many Black friends at Longfellow who were now at Walton, so Charles didn't intimidate me. "Why don't you leave him alone, man?" I said, "He didn't do anything to you." Charles punched me in the chest, just hard enough to get me out of his face. I was wise enough not to retaliate, partly because it would have been two-on-one—and because as I looked up, I saw Coach Dick Banton looking through a window at what was going down. I backed off, and Charles and his friend walked away. (Banton was the only African American PE teacher and coach at the school; he became my basketball coach in eighth and ninth grades, and a role model, as a former UCLA Bruin basketball player.)

Kenny didn't make it to the end of the seventh grade, becoming one of so many White students who left Walton by the droves then. I never experienced any harassment again at Walton, primarily, I think, because of becoming known as an athlete with Black friends and teammates.

Over the next year, my friends increasingly became other kids of color. That included ninth graders while I was in eighth grade, especially David, a Mexican American, and Rosario, a Filipino boy, both of whom lived a few blocks from us in Richland Farms. And I befriended the Copp brothers (Larry was in my grade and his brother Roy, a grade ahead at Walton), White kids who lived about ten houses from ours.

My circle of African American friends and teammates also expanded. Beginning with my class, the eighth- and ninth-grade football and basketball teams had been combined, and I was proud to be good enough to start on both teams as an eighth grader.

While my love of sports grew, my interest in girls also slowly began. Reaching puberty in the sixth grade—at twelve I was already showing a faint shadow of a mustache—I still didn't have a serious crush on any girls at Walton. I did have my first date in eighth grade. My friend David, who dressed and looked like a vato from the barrio (greased, combed-back long hair, khaki pants, Sir Guy shirts, and polished black shoes) was really tight with a group of Mexican American kids at the school, many of whom I knew. David set me up for one of our campus dances with the finest-looking Chicana at school—and a ninth grader. Dolores was a short, shapely, very nice but rather quiet girl. I didn't pursue her after our date for lack of chemistry.

Hanging out with David also got me into another scrape with Black kids, but not from Walton. One evening we walked with Rosario over to David's girlfriend's house on the other side of Compton High School, about a quarter mile from where we lived. As we were walking back home, past the hamburger joint across the street from the school, a group of about ten Black teenagers was hanging out there. Mind you, Rosario was a very dark-skinned Filipino kid, and David and I were medium-brown Mexican boys. Just past the hamburger stand, about six of the African American guys turned the corner and yelled out something to us, which I couldn't hear clearly. "Let's get out of here, man," David said, but I responded, "Let's see what they want." Those two ran off, while I turned around and walked up to the group, thinking maybe I knew one of them; it became clear as I approached that they were unknown high school–age guys, though.

"What's happenin', White boy," the lead teen said, as his friends began circling around me. "I'm Mexican, man, I ain't no Yak," I replied, using a word for Whites some African Americans used at the time. The dude on my right punched me in the mouth with enough force to turn me sideways. As I regained balance, I hauled ass and ran. I may have been dumb enough to try to talk, but I wasn't going to try and fight. And that evening, I bet I ran the quarter mile in record time.

I ran over to Rosario's house where he and David had gone. "Why didn't you run?" Rosario asked while opening the door, relief in his eyes to see I was okay. "I made a mistake, man," I replied, still breathing fast from running hard. "I stayed because I thought I might know one of those guys," I said in defense of being such a pendejo. Once at home, the bathroom mirror revealed a welt inside of my bloody lip.

That night brought another hard lesson about differing takes on racial identities and being viewed as an outsider by other groups. I started to understand that a racial divide was forming in Compton, where some folks viewed David, Rosario, and me as White because we weren't Black.

My Black friends at Walton served as a buffer against generalizing this incident into more than it was. Reflecting on it many years later as an undergraduate studying American racial attitudes, I also realized that what'd happened that night at age fourteen reflected a White versus Black divide that was defining cities in the 1960s. The Compton I lived in had become a tale of two cities, separated by race and physical boundaries and reinforced by a culturally promoted racial consciousness of "us versus them."

White realtors during my time at Walton were conspiring to hold the line against African American encroachment into the city's eastside neighborhoods as the westside quickly became predominantly Black (and Brown). The real estate agents collectively pledged not to sell to African Americans beyond the new racial boundary they drew down the middle of the city, using Alameda Street and the Southern Pacific Railroad tracks as the physical barrier separating White from non-White Compton. Such blatantly discriminatory "informal" guardrails had failed previously—with Rosecrans Avenue in the 1930s being the border that Mexicans couldn't cross and with a failed 1940s pledge to "Keep the Negroes North of 130th Street." Now, in the early 1960s, the last stand for the segregationists was based on letting "them," as one former eastside resident recalls, stay on the "Black side of town."

By the time Compton realtors drew the latest attempt at a line in the sand, the school district had already done the same for high school students. The district officials' cover argument was that increasing student enrollment in the city's lone high school called for the construction of two new high schools in the 1950s. Centennial High was built in 1953 in the northwestern part of the city, which happened to be located in neighborhoods quickly becoming predominantly Black; and Dominguez High opened in 1957, somehow receiving approval to be located on the far eastside, where no Blacks resided. Meanwhile, Compton High—in the city center—was transitioning from a majority White to a mostly African American student body by the mid-1960s.

Other suburbs in LA and other California counties, and in metropolitan America in general, were grappling with similar race-related changes during the 1960s as people of color sought better housing and schools after decades of being locked out of White areas. But nowhere were these issues more pronounced than in Compton due to its rapid demographic shift from White to Black.

Why was the White versus Black divide so dominant? In part, although Mexican Americans had lived in Compton since the early 1900s, we likely seemed less of a threat to White homogeneity on the eastside due to our smaller numbers relative to Blacks. Mexican Americans never experienced the same level of antipathy and residential segregation encountered by African Americans, as a result. A history of discrimination against Mexicans, Asians, and Native people was real and still prevalent in mid-century, but the hate directed toward Blacks was of a different magnitude.

Racial tensions elsewhere in the nation also influenced the atmosphere in Compton as efforts in support of the civil rights movement in the South reached a feverish pitch. It was hard to miss newspaper coverage of highly charged racial incidents, such as the Woolworth's lunch counter sit-ins by African American college students in Greensboro, North Carolina, in 1960 and the assault on Black and White Freedom Riders who protested segregated facilities at interstate bus stations in the South in 1961. Even more vivid and real was the televised national news coverage in 1963 that brought to living rooms the atrocities of White policemen using high-pressure fire hoses and attack dogs on non-violent Black protestors, many of whom were high school students, in Birmingham, Alabama. Worse yet were the published photos in September 1963 of the bombed-out 16th Street Baptist Church in Birmingham, where Ku Klux Klan terrorists had killed four little girls and injured others. Later that year, the state's despicable, racist governor, George C. Wallace, stood guard at the entrance to the University of Alabama, blocking the path of the first Black student to register at the segregated college.

Legal efforts to forge paths to social equity started to gain traction in states outside the South, though. After years of challenging racial discrimination in California's housing markets, for instance, Black leaders and their White Democratic Party supporters in the state legislature proposed a far-reaching law that would prohibit discrimination against people of color in private and public housing.

The Rumford Fair Housing Act in 1963 met stiff opposition from Republican state lawmakers and the California Real Estate Association (CREA). As a result, the legislation that passed was greatly watered down through many exemptions. Despite this, CREA launched a ballot measure the next year to repeal the Rumford Act. Proposition 14 won by a two to one margin, indicating that a White backlash to liberal civil rights legislation was alive and well in the Golden State. (Two years later the California State Supreme Court ruled that Proposition 14 was unconstitutional, though, which the U.S. Supreme Court validated in 1967.)

My own exposure to racial tensions became more direct during these turbulent years, opening my eyes to how pure, unadulterated bigotry operates in our society. The first experience in 1961 involved a trip my sister Rita scheduled for the two of us to visit our brother Max in Salt Lake City. He was a freshman at the University of Utah then, and Rita knew he was struggling to adjust. Rita often assumed the role of sister-mother for her youngest siblings. With no children of her own, she cared for us like offspring, giving us lots of love, though sometimes very tough love. I adored Rita like a second mother as she smothered her "baby" brother with lots of attention.

Soon after he'd arrived on campus, Max had gotten into a fight with a White teammate, and he was sporting a cast on his broken wrist when we

visited. Max later recounted to our brother Art how that incident likely related to how the team environment felt for him. Max had been pulled aside
by one of the football coaches who asked about Roy Jefferson, who had been
a Compton teammate and friend, and was among the first Black players
recruited to play at the university. "Does this N-word know his place?" the
coach had asked Max, who must've been troubled to discover he was being
coached by a White supremacist.

After arriving in Salt Lake City, we immediately picked up Max and his
football teammate, Vinny, a dark-skinned Italian kid from New York. Rita
wanted to treat them to the best steaks in town. An old, stately downtown
hotel was suggested. We went to this historic hotel and sat in the restaurant
waiting area for the hostess to seat us—and waited and waited. When Rita
finally asked again about a table, the hostess said she didn't know when we
would be seated.

Rita knew that the hostess was avoiding seating an apparently White
woman with two darker-skinned young men and a boy. "You bitch, if you
don't want our business," she yelled at the older White hostess, "we'll give it
to some other restaurant." We all stormed out.

A few weeks before that Utah visit, my father had decided to take my
mother and me on a Labor Day weekend drive up north to visit his cousin
José in Milpitas, a town near San José. On the second day of our visit, José
decided to show us downtown San José. I was walking several yards in front
of our family group as we strolled along one of the main streets. I had on
shiny light-tan wingtip shoes my mom had bought me for the trip. Behind
me, a man said loudly, "Look at those N-word shoes he's wearing." I turned
around and stared at the guy, who was laughing as he pointed at what I
thought were cool-looking shoes. I didn't say anything to this racist fool,
but I wish I had.

After Max left the University of Utah in 1961, he was drafted into the
army and was later stationed at Fort Sam Houston in San Antonio, Texas.
Rita decided to take a road trip to visit him with my mother and me in the
summer of 1963. Max had a weekend furlough, so after we picked him up
in San Antonio, we drove to a local Ramada Inn to stay the night. With
Max and I in toe, Rita asked the man behind the front desk for a room. He
quickly glanced at us all and replied, "We don't have any rooms available."

An entire board filled with keys attached to room numbers was on the wall behind him. "What are all those keys for then?" Max asked, while pointing to the keyboard. When the man repeated a similar comment, adding that "you should look for a place in West San Antonio" (meaning the Mexican side of town), Max leaned over the counter to grab his coat collar, but Rita pulled him away and calmed him down. Jaime Crow clearly was in play in some Texas establishments. After another failed attempt to find a hotel nearby, we settled for a fleabag motel in West San Antonio, where I encountered some huge Texas-style cockroaches for the first time.

I had only a superficial level of understanding about racism at the time, but I began to realize that some people hated other people simply because they were different. I couldn't have imagined, then, that I would devote an entire career to understanding racial inequality and trying my best to confront it whenever possible. All I knew was that I had a greater appreciation for the orbit of friends I'd made at Walton, who helped me believe it was possible to successfully cross racial divides.

By the early 1960s, my social world mirrored West Compton's changed demographics. All my best friends in ninth grade and nearly all my teammates in football, basketball, baseball, and track were African American. I had started getting involved as a class leader too, and my Walton classmates in social and service clubs were almost all Black. Though I never lost sight of my own ethnic/racial identity, I had a budding interest in R&B soul music and the Motown sound; the dances I learned, the girl I liked, the clothes I wore, and some of the slang I used reflected African American tastes from the culture that had embraced me and that shaped me indelibly.

Just before racial tensions in Compton, in nearby Watts, and in cities across the United States exploded with fury in the mid- and late 1960s, I had become aware that racial differences need not separate and divide us and that embracing people across all dividing lines makes you a better person and a better citizen in a diverse community and nation. These weren't fully formed lessons at the time, but they were pieces of a puzzle that helped shape me later as an adult.

My bonds with Mike, Ruby, Regina, Frank, Melvin, Brenda, Jackie, and many other African American classmates, some since our elementary years together, grew stronger over time. I still had Mexican American school friends at Walton, but I wasn't really close to any. There were only about six Japanese American and two Chinese American kids, including my friend Neil from Longfellow, in 1962 and 63. Among the 340 ninth graders, there were fewer than a dozen White kids, and I was also friendly with several of them, especially David, a football teammate.

Mike was my best buddy and teammate, after becoming good friends in eighth grade when we played on the football and basketball teams together. He was a great guy, and in the ninth grade we did everything together. A shared sense of school spirit and encouragement from teachers and administrators to participate in extracurricular activities gave us reason to join many school groups together. We shared membership in the Bobcats (the school service club), the pep club, and student council, and we were elected student body officers together. Most importantly, we were joined at the hip as teammates in four sports, although Mike was the better athlete. He was the most agile, strongest, and fastest athlete at Walton—and easily won "athlete of the year" at our graduation ceremonies. Although I never visited his home in Watts because it was very far from my neighborhood, Mike came over to my house many times. He enjoyed meeting my family, especially my brothers, whose football-playing reputations at Compton High were still well-known.

Mike's family's journey to Los Angeles was part of the Great Migration. His parents were born in Baton Rouge, Louisiana, and first moved to Portland and then to California in 1947 when his grandfather started work at the Point Mugu Naval Air Station in Oxnard, just northwest of Los Angeles County. Most of Mike's other Louisiana relatives moved north instead to Chicago, along with tens of thousands of other Black folks.

Born in Watts, where he went to elementary school, Mike recalled that "My mother wanted me to have a better education by going to a Compton middle school, so we used the address of my cousin who lived in Compton so I could enroll at Walton." Mike and his older brother Cliff enrolled at Walton together. But where Cliff focused on being an excellent, four-sport athlete, Mike initially fell in with some guys who got into trouble. One day Mr. Banton, our PE teacher and our future basketball coach and mentor, took him aside and encouraged him to find different friends. Participating in sports, Mike said, gave him an avenue for that and allowed him to follow in his brother's footsteps.

I also first met Mike's steady girlfriend Regina in our seventh-grade homeroom. A friendly, talkative outgoing girl, she was also a good athlete. We became good friends in the ninth grade, but it was not until recently that I learned about her harsh exposure to racist Comptonites.

Her parents were Texans who headed to LA after the war in the 40s as part of the Black massive migration for over a decade (African American Angelenos increased from about 64,000 in 1940 to 335,000 in 1960). Like so many African American families who moved to Compton, they eventually bought a three-bedroom, one-bath home in the heart of the westside in 1954 that was near the Compton/Woodley Airport. Before Regina entered Walton, though, she had been enrolled at the newly built Laurel Street School near her home, and then spent third grade at Victory Park School.

That school was located in Victory Park, the last vestige of segregated, White-only housing in the midst of an expanding Black population on the westside in the late 1950s. Opened in 1942, the eighty-acre complex was built by the federal government for workers in war-related industries and for veterans, but it had been sold sometime in the 1950s as surplus property. An all-White homeowners' association was established, and the triplex units and spacious single-family homes in Victory Park had become off limits to African Americans.

Victory Park's "in your face" segregation drew Black community leaders' attention by the late 1950s. After the Compton branch of the NAACP formed in 1957, part of its agenda was breaking the color line there. "Look, no Blacks are going to move in there," a representative of Victory Park's homeowner's group matter-of-factly told members of the chapter, Maxcy Filer among them. "And they meant it," Maxcy recalled, and "we did not [move in]." The only concession made to the NAACP was to allow some African American children, such as Regina, to enroll in Victory Park School.

The Victory Park homeowner's representatives made it clear to the NAACP that the concession came with rules, such as no hanging around school at day's end. Regina stated, "I remember my third-grade teacher always reminding us to go directly home after school." She also vividly recalled the one time she visited a classmate's home in Victory Park. "Robert and I were in the same third-grade class at Victory Park [School]," she told me a few years ago, "and he invited me to his home for cookies after school one day." "Growing up, my mother put a lot of focus on personal appearance," Regina recounted, "and I remember trying hard not to get my dress dirty during recess that day. After school we walked to his house, and he entered through the back door and his mother was right there." The words from Robert's mother's mouth that day are burned into Regina's memory. "When she saw me, she yelled, 'You can't come in here!' Go away and never come back to this house." "Well, needless to say," Regina said, "I ran as fast as I could to get out of there." "In my innocent little mind," she reflected, "I thought because I had dirt on my dress, socks, and shoes was the reason she was upset." Robert told Regina at school the next day that she could never visit again. "This is something that has stayed with me my entire life," Regina confided. "I think it was in high school before I truly realized it wasn't the dirt on my clothes but the absolute racism that existed during that time."

Friends from other westside neighborhoods that were transitioning in the 1950s and the early 60s sometimes shared an almost romanticized memory of a golden age of diversity when White, Black, Mexican, and Asian kids lived in harmony on the same block, at least for a few short years. "I had a wonderful childhood in Compton," my friend Frank reminisced, as he reflected on his neighborhood and the schools he attended after he and his family moved to the westside in 1957. "Everyone got along very well," he recalled, "and I made some wonderful friends that I still have today."

Frank and I met in fifth grade, and we were basketball and track squad mates at Walton, as well as sharing membership in student government. He appreciated the "good life" in Compton especially after living for a time with his mother's relatives in Nacogdoches, a town in far eastern Texas. "While there," he remembered, "I experienced a lot of racism and dealt with the Jim Crow laws of the South." His father, born in Louisiana, was a sergeant during World War II who met his mother, from the so-called Black WACs (Women's Army Corps), while they were stationed in segregated military units at an Arkansas base. After their move to Compton, Frank Sr. worked as a sheet metal mechanic at the Long Beach Naval Shipyard while Janet, formerly a teacher, became a stay-at-home mom for their three boys.

Neil was another class friend in fifth grade and a fellow member of many of the same clubs that Frank and I were involved in at Walton. One of only two Chinese American kids at the school, he also absorbed Black cultural ways through friendships, music, and more. We reminisced not long ago about how race differences didn't seem to matter to us at age thirteen because of our bonds of friendship.

Apparently, school administrators had noticed my cross-cultural relationships as I emerged as a student leader in the ninth grade (I was elected school vice president and commissioner of athletics and served as president of the Bobcats service group). I found that out in March 1963, when Walton administrators used the longstanding National Week of Brotherhood to establish a Mr. and Miss Brotherhood Award at the school for the first time.

The idea of celebrating brotherhood in America was started in the late 1920s by the newly formed National Conference of Christians and Jews; the goal was to facilitate more harmonious interethnic and interfaith relations at a time when immigrants and their children formed majority populations in many U.S. cities. President Roosevelt expanded the focus to a week-long commemoration in 1936, though race relations weren't originally mentioned.

By the early 1960s, Brotherhood Week had gained new meaning given racial strife in the South, the civil rights movement, the assassination of President Kennedy, and the March on Washington in 1963 that included Reverend King's famous "I Have a Dream" speech. "Brotherhood Week . . . is a time of deep appraisal for all Americans," announced newly sworn-in President Lyndon B. Johnson at the kickoff for the national program. "Tragedy is in our land and from the darkness of our sorrow ought to come a new dedication to the ideals of love and brotherhood," he stated:

> Democracy cannot live in hate and fear. Prejudice and bigotry are the advance guard of failure. No better time exists for a searching of our hearts and minds than this National Observance of Brotherhood. . . . In this time, still heavy with sadness, I urge all my fellow Americans to join with me and the National Conference of Christians and Jews in this national community celebration of tolerance, truth and charity toward our neighbors, wherever they live, whoever they are.

LBJ's prophetic words still ring as true today as sixty years ago.

In the midst of Compton's racial transformation and accompanying racial strains, Walton's leadership wisely chose to recognize and celebrate student symbols of brotherhood. I was quite honored to be nominated by students, teachers, and administrators to be Mr. Brotherhood for my positive interactions with students across racial and ethnic lines. Then, the following month, the local Optimist Club chose me as Boy of the Month. When introduced at the luncheon award ceremony, the Optimist Club president noted my membership in Walton's honor society, election to student body positions, work in service clubs, participation in sports teams, and especially my Mr. Brotherhood Award.

Besides enjoying the recognition in general for doing things I really enjoyed at Walton, the Mr. Brotherhood Award ceremony introduced me to my first real love interest. Rubazene (she went by Ruby) and I had known each other since seventh grade, but in the ninth grade our paths crossed almost every day. Friendly, smart, and athletic, she, too, was in student government and involved in service clubs, the pep club, and the honor society. Ruby could instantly make anyone feel at ease, and it was little wonder she'd been chosen Miss Brotherhood. And, Ruby was really pretty.

The night of the Brotherhood Awards ceremony, I wore my first coat and tie—and my parents and Rita attended. The special evening became more so when I laid eyes on Ruby, who looked stunning in a beautiful new dress, white gloves, flawlessly coiffed hair, and a smile that could light up a room. Even my mom said, "What a pretty girl." All I could utter in response was, "Yeah, yeah, she sure is!"

But Ruby had a boyfriend, who was my friend Regina's brother. He was a grade ahead of us at Walton. The odds were stacked against me to lure Ruby away, and I could also get my ass kicked. From what I knew, Richard was generally a nice guy; but he was also a powerfully built athlete at Compton High. Meanwhile, I weighed maybe 120 pounds. I still gave it a shot as Ruby and I got closer, including going together to the formal graduation dance at the end of the year, which involved double dating with Mike and Regina. Our date must have really pissed off Richard because many years later—after he and Ruby married—he half-jokingly told my brother Art (a fellow cop on the Compton PD) that "Your brother tried to take my girl away from me." Yeah, I sure did, but I failed. In more ways than one, partly due to my parents and sister Rita.

When we all graduated from Walton Junior High, all of my friends knew that I wouldn't be attending Compton High with them. Mike and I, sometime during ninth grade, came up with the crazy plan of becoming star athletes at St. Anthony's, a Catholic high school in downtown Long Beach. As Mike recalled recently, we were inspired by my cousin Chano, who'd attended a local Catholic high school and become a star track and football player. St. Anthony's had great football and basketball programs, and we'd visited and met with their football and basketball coaches. They strongly encouraged applying, though they didn't mention scholarships.

So Mike and I were set to enroll at St. Anthony's in the fall. After school let out in June 1963, I continued to see Ruby and hint at my interest. For instance, early in the summer when I traveled with my brother Art and his new wife to visit her relatives in Minnesota, I sent Ruby postcards along the way. But when we returned from Minnesota about two weeks later, my whole world had turned upside down.

"Mom and Dad sold the house," Rita told me, "and they bought a home in Paramount, near Dominguez High School, and that is where you will go to school." My jaw dropped. "I ain't going to that White school! I'll go live with some of my friends," I stated, while taking this blow in, and "I'll go to Compton High instead of St. Anthony's, but I'm not going to Dominguez." Pleading with her and my parents didn't change the scheduled move in August, just four weeks away.

My fifteenth summer was the worst ever. I was sad, mad, and anxious about enrolling in a high school of strangers. The only friend I told was Mike. How could I muster the courage to tell Ruby that I would be attending the segregated White high school in East Compton and that I probably would never see her again?

Later, I learned that selling our home and my going to Dominguez High without any notice was actually part of Rita's plan, which went too far. Being seventeen years older than me, and living at home until her late twenties, Rita saw me as both little brother and surrogate son. She was the dominant personality in our family and held much more conservative views than our parents. In so many ways, she did so much for my parents and siblings, especially for me. But though I loved her deeply, her playing with my life then still hurts.

Her intentional ploy resulted from taking on the views of the conservative work world she'd entered, rather than our parents' views as die-hard

FDR New Deal Democrats. Rita was influenced by the people she'd worked with at the bank for a decade. So, for instance, when it came time for her to vote, she registered as a Republican—wearing "I Like Ike" buttons and such in the 1950s.

After working as the assistant to a vice president at the bank in downtown LA, Rita eventually shifted gears to real estate. Together with her boyfriend—and future husband—she opened a real estate office in Compton in the early 1960s. Harry was White and a former Compton cop who was also super conservative. A Dust Bowl transplant from Oklahoma by way of California's Central Valley, Harry was also racist. So Rita held racist views, not only against African Americans but Mexican Americans and Asian Americans as well.

It turns out that Rita had actually told my parents the White realtors' BS: that when "Negros move into our Richland Farms neighborhood," as my mother recounted years later, "your property value will go down." Somehow, my father believed Rita (who would have made a great prosecutor). She put our home up for sale and convinced Dad to buy Harry's home in Paramount, a neighborhood just on the other side of Compton's eastern-most boundary. Harry was planning to move and, according to Rita, would give my parents a "great deal." How my father, a Mexican immigrant who eight years earlier had been kept out of Lynwood by a racist realtor, went along with the concern that "Negros were moving into the neighborhood" is still a mystery.

I also learned many years later, directly from Rita, the other main reason she wanted my parents to move: "You had too many colored friends, and no way was I going to let you attend St. Anthony's because I knew you would like Dominguez High."

There you have it. She thought I was becoming too Black and was determined for me to go to a White school and to have White friends. We moved, and within three weeks I was going to Dominguez High's football team workouts in the weeks before school started. I didn't know a soul on that team or at the school, so my social world flip-flopped as I mingled with the other side of Compton.

EIGHT

Eastside Racial Tensions

I enrolled, reluctantly, at Dominguez High School and started classes in September 1963. Even though I hadn't been around so many White kids since the third grade, my elementary school exposures on the westside meant I didn't feel too out of place as a Mexican American minority student.

What was strange was suddenly not seeing a single Black kid on campus, considering they made up 40 percent of city residents. None lived within the deliberately drawn Dominguez High boundaries set up in the late 1950s to keep Blacks on the other side of the tracks.

About 95 percent of Dominguez students were White. The student body had roughly 80 Mexican American students out of almost 1,800 (and only 5 Asian Americans). Only a few of these students I'd known at Longfellow and Walton. Yet my school transition went pretty smoothly.

Many of the Mexican Americans came from immigrant families who'd lived on the eastside during its earlier farming years; the mostly White suburb spread around their homes after World War II. Other Chicano families, like mine, lived in working-class neighborhoods in Paramount. This neighborhood to which we moved was located just a few blocks from the high school, and it had been incorporated into Compton school boundaries when Dominguez High was built.

To be Mexican American apparently didn't present a problem for White homeowners and realtors on the eastside as long as the numbers were small. Had I been Black, though, I know my transition story would have been different. It brings to mind an old song by Big Bill Broonzy, an African American blues musician, who sang about race in 1938 in a tune he titled "Black, Brown and White." "If you's white, be all right," the lyrics of the chorus go. "If you's brown, stick around, but if you black, oh brother, get back, get back, get back." I was a Brown kid at Dominguez, so I could stick around, but it was harder for African American students who began to enroll at the school in small numbers during my junior year, and in much larger numbers the year after.

As I struggled to make the best of this new school situation, my mom was doing the same with giving up her custom-built, dream home in Richland Farms. We now had a shitty cookie-cutter suburban tract home with a tiny kitchen that she hated (especially with a washer and dryer stuffed into a corner). Our home was just outside Compton's city limits across the Los Angeles River. The only saving grace was its big backyard and, for me, having my own bedroom for the first time.

About two weeks before classes began, I ran into Ruby on a downtown street while clothes shopping. "Why didn't you call me?" she said sternly, as our last phone call had been about six weeks earlier. "Why didn't you tell me you were moving and going to Dominguez instead of St. Anthony's?" (She'd learned from Regina, Mike's former girlfriend at Walton, about the move.) I uttered a stupid fifteen-year-old boy's response, something like, "Um, I don't know why," before she rightfully stormed off. Two years later, when a regional student government conference brought us face-to-face again, she ignored me. Almost six years later when I reached out, I was so relieved that she wasn't still holding a grudge against me, though we didn't discuss the past.

After the 1963 academic year began, I settled into the school. As with Walton, I'd used football to gain new friends, meeting others in classes, including several college prep courses that my high Walton grades had allowed me to enter. My interest in college was firmly, though vaguely, established by my first year in high school.

Everything seemed good, until about two weeks into the semester, when I received a summons from Mr. Joseph, the vice principal. "Oh, shit," I whispered to myself, recalling the arrowhead incident from fourth grade. "I didn't do anything wrong, so why the hell is he pulling me out of class?"

"Please come in and sit down, Al," Mr. Joseph said, as I tried to hide the up-and-down shaking of my left leg, a nervous habit. The next sentence from Mr. Joseph's mouth floored me, though. "We think you should run for election as sophomore class president," he said emphatically. "Why on earth," I wondered to myself, "would Mr. Joseph and his colleagues want me, a kid newly relocated from the westside, to run for class president?" "We know you were a student leader at Walton and Optimist Club Boy of the Month," Louis Joseph stated.

Although I mumbled something about not being known at the school in response, his encouragement helped me give it a shot. Somehow, I was elected class president for the fall semester, and, as a result, my tenth-grade circle of friends expanded while serving on the student council with the junior and senior class presidents and other student body officers.

Having served in student government at Walton the previous year gave me a new confidence, and I enjoyed being viewed as a leader. It was also fun; continuing in a school leadership position provided another community anchor at Dominguez besides playing football and basketball and running track. My reputation in basketball soared when the varsity coach asked me to join his outstanding team before the California Interscholastic Federation basketball playoffs; I actually got to play as a sophomore. I also earned points at school dances because I could bust some moves learned from my days at Walton, moves that were rare for the eastside.

At one of those dances toward the end of my sophomore year, I began my first real romance. Carol was a cute, spunky girl, the junior class treasurer, and a member of the cheerleading squad. It was true puppy love. We did everything together for about a year, despite her parents being Southern Baptists and her stern mom, a politically conservative Republican. The fact that I was a student athlete helped because Carol's older brother had been an outstanding football player at Dominguez a few years earlier. Her dad was a low-key guy too, who shared an interest in fixing up cars.

Cars were a second love. What would you expect from a kid from the car culture of La-La Land? Throughout my years at Dominguez, I worked weekends at service stations, first at a paternal uncle's gas station in Paramount, and later for a mechanic who owned the ARCO (formerly Atlantic Richfield) station near home on the eastside. As I learned mechanic skills, I stashed away every dollar for my first car. That opportunity came in the summer when Art sold me his wife's car, a well-worn 1958 Chevy Impala into which I poured my part-time earnings so I'd have one of the coolest rides at Dominguez my senior year.

By then, some of the White kids at Dominguez High had become close friends. Ken was a football and basketball teammate I'd known since tenth grade, a huge guy at six foot five, and an excellent athlete as the son of an Olympic champion. Ken Sr., the 1936 Olympic gold medal discus winner, had coached football at Compton College and knew my brothers. (La Jefita remembered Ken's dad from elementary school in the early 1920s, when he used to pull her hair and make fun of her.) Ken Jr. remembered me as an opposing player from Walton. So, too, did my best friend Danny.

That funny, witty, and incredibly loyal friend who it turned out had also attended Rosecrans Elementary was a football teammate beginning in junior year. That's when Danny and I made the varsity squad (the year before I had played on the undefeated, league champion B football team as a 125 pounder, and he played on the junior varsity team). Born in Arkansas, his family moved to Compton in the early 1950s, where they opened Quality Market in West Compton.

After breaking up with Carol near the end of junior year, my time hanging out with Ken and Danny increased, and I gained some girls as best friends. I'd met cheerleaders Janet and Pam in the tenth grade, and we became close buddies senior year. Janet was a student council member, a talented musician, and a super-friendly red-haired girl, as well as my first Mormon friend (as a lapsed Catholic, religious differences meant nothing to me). We were singing partners at the annual talent show and at dances. Janet's mother came from pioneer Mormon Church stock in Salt Lake City and had moved with her husband to East Compton in 1922. Pam's parents were midwestern transplants who had arrived in the late 1940s.

I also had a cadre of friends, mostly girls, from the "smart kid" group who were really sweet, special people. I spent a lot of time with Roberta, Sharon, and Patsy in college prep courses. Sharon, who like Roberta was Jewish, attended the winter formal dance with me. Her family owned and operated Bargain Town grocery store on the westside, where my family had previously shopped. Much later, as in fifty years later, I learned that when Sharon told her father about our school date, he'd commented, "Camarillo? Isn't that a Mexican name?" She'd scolded her dad, replying, "Daddy, I am going to the dance with Al, so don't say anything more about it." I heard similar stories from a few other girls I'd dated at Dominguez many years after the fact. One in particular cut off any possible friendship after her mother forbade her to go out "with that Mexican boy," an explanation she emailed me many years later for why she'd avoided me the summer after graduation. I wasn't really surprised. At the senior graduation party she held at her home, the party chaperone—her mother—shot knife-like stares at me when I slow danced with her daughter.

All seemed good in terms of classmates getting along for the most part in the different groups where I hung out. After all, the White kids from the eastside were not really different from the African American, Asian American, and Mexican American kids I had hung with on the westside in many ways. We all came from working-class and lower-middle-class homes and lived in suburban houses in a community much like communities throughout the LA metropolitan area and beyond. And our parents had all settled in Compton with the same desires: to access good schools and safe streets for their children, affordable homes, and good job opportunities.

My rather naïve perspective as a teen who'd had positive multiracial experiences till then began to change. For instance, a sports-related incident at the beginning of my junior year revealed that race did indeed matter—especially if you were Black. As the varsity football team assembled for the 1964 season, my junior year, one of two African Americans that had tried out had made the team. They were among only about twenty-five Black students at Dominguez High then. And Ron, a senior transfer from Centennial High, the "Negro school" on the westside, turned out to be an outstanding running back and a terrific guy. But early on in our pre-season practice schedule, a teammate since sophomore year, whose locker was next to mine and the leading prospect to be starting quarterback, said loud enough to be heard by teammates nearby, "Hey guys, I'm going to write KKK on the front of my helmet and hit the son-of-a-bitch hard today."

"Are you crazy, man," I quickly said, unsure if he was serious or not. "Why the hell would you do that?" He wasn't the only footballer not thrilled to have a Black kid on the team, and I regret not saying something more forceful, like "You dumb ass racist." But I let it go after he got up and left the locker room since no one responded to his ridiculous idea (he actually was a dumb guy and not a very good quarterback). That day at practice he picked a fight with Ron that the coaches quickly broke up—but some of us knew why it happened.

In time, Ron was voted team captain and earned the respect of most of the White teammates. It didn't hurt that he was by far the best athlete on a really bad football squad. Ron turned out to be a remarkable guy in more ways than one, though, and I came to respect him greatly.

Ron's westside background meant we had an unspoken kinship. And when we surprisingly beat Centennial High, Ron's former school, the way he'd played his heart out was crucial for this lone victory that year. We still were feeling thrilled for beating one of the best teams in the league on our bus ride home when I stood up and said, "Three cheers for Ron!" The team followed by shouting, "Hip, hip, hooray!" I could see in his eyes how much his White teammates' acceptance meant.

Ron was also gutsy off the field, including when he ran for election as the second semester student body president. As one of the first Black students to break the color line at school, I was amazed hearing his campaign speech at a schoolwide assembly. "I know most of you don't know me because I am from the other side of Compton," he said candidly, "and because I am the first Negro to run for school president." I don't remember the rest, but Ron's opener stuck with me for resembling my words when I'd run for sophomore class president. Ron lost the election, but he'd served notice that change was ahead in the formerly segregated high school.

Did Mr. Joseph also summon Ron out of class, like he did to me the previous year, and suggest he run for student government? I'll never know.

Though many students accepted Ron before he graduated in June, numbers seem to matter in bringing out the fear of "different" people. There was no obvious racial strife when there were only a dozen or so Black kids at Dominguez in 1964–65, but after many more students were bussed in the following academic year, the situation quickly changed. As the fall semester came, about 120 Black students were now on campus. It so happens they arrived a month after a human earthquake—known as the Watts Riots— shook the foundations of race relations in California and the nation.

The summer of 1965 began with big decisions for me personally, related to preparing for college athletics. Coach Kane, an outstanding basketball coach with winning teams, called me into his office at the end of the spring 1964 semester with a proposition. "I want you to be the starting guard next year with Terry [a senior, high-scoring guard]," he said authoritatively, "but you will have to stop playing football." As we concluded our brief, one-way conversation, Coach Kane made it crystal clear that I'd likely not play much otherwise.

Fortunately, Kane soon announced he was leaving Dominguez High to become head coach at Long Beach City College. I played football that next autumn *and* was the starting point guard on the varsity basketball squad under a new head coach.

Exactly a year later though, the new basketball coach called me into his office and asked a similar question. "What are your plans after high school?" Coach Tift asked, rhetorically. "If you want to play basketball at the next level," he stated matter-of-factly, "you'll have to give up football to have any chance of landing a scholarship." Coach already knew I desired that, but I loved football even though we had a really lousy team, and the head football coach had already invited me to become the starting quarterback in the fall. I had never played this position before and was intrigued and terrified that I might be an awful QB (worse yet, at barely five foot nine and 140 pounds, I might get my butt beat into the ground because of our weak offensive line).

To my brother Art's dismay, I quit football to concentrate on basketball. The football coach was so furious about my decision, I learned he told my former teammates I was a traitor and that they shouldn't speak to me again.

I also was elected in spring 1965 as Dominguez's student body president, the first person of color in that position. Well into summer, I had thought my duties as president starting in senior year would involve mostly mundane tasks of leading student government at the school such as chairing council meetings, offering welcoming remarks at school assemblies, and the like.

Concentrating on basketball meant a great start to the summer, as I improved my game a lot. In the inter-scholastic basketball summer league, I was one of the leading scorers in the South Los Angeles division, replicating that for the intra-school summer league. I was prepped for a big senior year as a hoopster, despite having a lower caliber head coach than previously and a mediocre team.

But on August 11, 1965, my summer dreams turned into a nightmare. Thousands of people in the nearby community of Watts, which was almost entirely African American by this time, revolted in reaction to yet another case of police brutality. The horrible reputation of the Los Angeles Police Department among Black and Brown folks was decades old by the mid-1960s, punctuated by several high-profile cases that started with the Sleepy Lagoon incident in 1942. General police harassment of African Americans was common knowledge on the streets of South Central LA and Watts, where most of the city's approximately 335,000 Blacks resided, and in East Los Angeles where most of the over 600,000 metro area Mexican Americans concentrated. The tense relationship of the LAPD, with African Americans especially, was like dynamite ready to explode.

What began as a seemingly routine incident between cops and a young Black guy had Watts aflame within twenty-four hours and resulted in the destruction of most of the stores where I shopped years earlier with my mother. On a hot summer evening on a South LA street, Marquette Frye, a young Black man who lived near but not in the Watts area, and his brother were returning home from a nearby gathering. A California Highway Patrolman on motorcycle pulled them over for what he viewed as erratic driving. Marquette had been drinking and failed a sobriety test, after which the officer told him he was under arrest and called for a car to transport Marquette to the local substation for booking. He also called a tow truck to pick up Frye's car.

When Marquette's brother asked the CHP officer if he could drive his brother's car home a few blocks away and was told no, Ronald ran home to fetch his mother to retrieve the car. Black residents seeking relief from the heat on their front porches watched the incident escalate from afar until Marquette's mama showed up about ten minutes later and started scolding her son. Marquette, who had peacefully cooperated with the CHP officer until then, became agitated and struggled with the arresting officer as dozens of residents gathered around the worsening scene. Backup cops arrived quickly, including LAPD officers. The crowd swelled and became belligerent when Marquette's mother tried to intervene on her son's behalf after night sticks landed on his head; she and her other son were arrested and placed in a squad car.

The small group of onlookers grew to about 300 within a few minutes, and more cops were called to the growing disturbance. By the time the police began to leave with the Fryes in custody, there was a crowd of 1,000 people. Someone spit at a cop as he was retreating to his car, and the officer made the mistake of going after and arresting a young man and woman he believed were responsible. Rocks and bottles began to fly as the last squad car left the scene.

The genie was out of the bottle from so many decades of repressed rage. Later that night small groups of young African American men began to throw rocks at cars on the main avenue driven by White motorists, some of whom were pulled over and beaten. The LAPD set up a command post nearby, made dozens of arrests, and believed the uproar was contained.

In an effort to quell the unrest, the LA Humans Relations Commission called a meeting the following afternoon with Black community leaders and local residents. Members of the press were assembled, and several elected White officials and law enforcement representatives were also present. The meeting was a plea for law, order, and calm, but it also served as a platform for some local folks to express grievances, including one young man who said that Whites in adjoining areas were going to be attacked that night. The press, of course, seized on his comments, heightening the fear level for everyone.

That night large crowds formed at the site of the previous evening's incident—and all hell broke loose. Hundreds of LAPD cops were present, and some fires had been lit. Rocks were thrown and later shots were aimed at firefighters attempting to douse the flames. Conditions spiraled out of control quickly as more local residents, mostly young men, hit the streets and began looting and setting more fires. The perimeter of the violence expanded greatly, and the local police lost control.

Widespread violence erupted early the next morning in the downtown area of Watts when a group of about 3,000 people assembled in protest and targeted White-owned stores, especially those viewed as predatory toward local Black customers. Many were looted and set ablaze. The two-block area of the Watts business district went up in flames, and, again, as firefighters attempted to respond, they were stoned, and some were shot at. The police moved in to make arrests of anyone on the streets. With sporadic violence, looting, and fires throughout South LA, the LAPD chief eventually called for National Guard troops.

The five days of violence, fires, looting, unrest, death, and mass arrests were quelled only after a 46-square-mile area of LA was put on curfew and some 14,000 National Guardsmen, together with about 1,700 LAPD and LA County Sheriff's deputies, cleared the streets. According to some local observers, Watts and Southeast LA looked like a war zone. National Guard troops, in full battle mode, set up blockades with signs, at least one of which sent an alarming message to local residents: "Turn left or get shot." To make matters worse, LAPD Chief Parker likened the Black rioters to "monkeys in the zoo."

The toll was devastating: 34 dead, over 1,000 injured, nearly 3,500 arrested, and almost 1,000 businesses and other buildings damaged, looted, and/or destroyed at the cost of $40 million (about $320 million today).

The Watts rebellion was a preview for what would go down in dozens of U.S. cities in the next few years. It would shake the foundations of Watts, Compton, Los Angeles, California, and the nation. It was also an early cry against longstanding police brutality, social injustice, and racial inequality, and thus was a touchstone for the Black Lives Matter Movement.

But these consequences weren't immediately apparent. Compton, for instance, had remained largely untouched by the violence next door because its police heavily patrolled the city's northern boundaries adjacent to Watts twenty-four hours a day. With the blessing of the Compton PD, some business owners on the westside, both Black and White, stationed themselves next to their property with shotguns ready. Many White residents prepared themselves for war, such as the group in Victory Park who established a militia of veterans who patrolled the segregated residential area each night carrying loaded weapons. Fear was also rampant among White Angelenos in general. Gun stores sold out of weapons and ammunition practically overnight.

In the wake of what occurred in Watts, the most explosive and destructive of several racial disturbances in American cities in the summer of 1965, California Governor Pat Brown assembled a group of leaders and citizens to investigate the hows and whys of the upheaval. Looking back, given the tragic legacy of racial inequalities and injustices heaped on the backs of African Americans for generations, the findings held no surprise when the Governor's Commission on the Los Angeles Riots (known as the McCone Commission for its chairman, the former director of the CIA, John A. McCone) issued its report, "Violence in the City: An End or a Beginning?" The McCone Commission highlighted problems such as state violence against Blacks, school failure, unemployment, and other grievances voiced by residents. But the report only scratched the surface of the problems that plagued the Black community in Watts and in South Central Los Angeles.

The Watts Rebellion, Watts Riots, or however we label that chaotic summer uprising, heightened racial tensions everywhere, including the Dominguez High campus when classes started a month later in September 1965—with a significantly higher number of African American kids. The great majority of Black students who enrolled in Dominguez were new to the campus, mostly sophomores who were bussed across town during a time of heightened racial tensions.

The fights broke out very soon after classes began; nearly every morning during breaks for snacks and lunch there were scuffles where hate speech was exchanged and punches thrown between White kids and the Black guys they taunted. Though the fighting was small in scale, the school's administration was worried enough to place the Compton PD on alert. My brother Art, who had joined the police department in 1964, remembers the high school principal's calls about the problems surfacing at Dominguez that autumn semester.

Though I never saw the "Go home N-word" sprayed on a school wall as did other classmates—school custodians quickly erased them—there was a group of racist White kids who resisted the school opening to more Blacks. At the weekly student council meetings, which I chaired during the fall semester as student body president, Mr. Gregory (the administrator and

coordinator of student activities) asked all student government leaders to
watch out for and report any incidents between White and Black students
as tensions mounted.

The school administration soon decided to be more proactive by establishing the Multiracial Council on Human Relations. They asked me, a
seventeen-year-old, to chair the group.

I lacked any experience handling racial tensions, but it made sense because I was school president. But more importantly, I knew many of the
African American kids from my years on the westside, especially the few
who'd enrolled the previous year at Dominguez and had attended Walton
Junior High. And, many of the new sophomore African American students
remembered me as a ninth-grade student leader at Walton when they were
seventh graders. I also had many friends within the majority White student
body and in the small group of Mexican Americans. So, though I didn't
know what to expect, I gladly agreed to help calm racial tensions. Because of
my deep connections to westside African American classmates and friends,
I felt particularly obligated to help those feeling alienated and unwanted on
a new high school campus.

The main council goal was building interracial understanding and,
specifically, tamping down fighting between Whites and Blacks. Yet the
administrative staff advisors to the Multiracial Council were all White, including Mr. Lee (school principal), Mr. Joseph (vice principal), Mr. Gregory
(coordinator of student activities), and Mr. Neill (counselor for the senior
class). (Of eighty-five teachers and administrative staff at Dominguez in
1965, only three were people of color.) My experience of growing up in the
barrio, attending White-majority elementary schools, and as a student
leader at a predominantly African American middle school served me well
as I reached out to classmates and planned activities.

The adult advisors to the council wanted to focus on the boys who'd been
involved in the sporadic fighting. Though I was nervous it would end up as
a name-calling, figure-pointing brawl, I organized an after-school meeting
with a diverse group of boys. I first reached out to the Black kids I knew
from the westside and to the few African American athletes on the football
and basketball teams and asked them to invite some of the younger African
American students to the meeting. Many of my White friends were coaxed

to attend as well, several of whom were athletes. I also reached out to Mexican American friends, particularly some of the vatos, the tough homeboys.

In all, about seventy-five boys showed up for the after-school meeting in the cafeteria. That number surprised me, and it included a small subgroup of White boys that I hadn't invited. They were part of a group that was called the "dumb surfer boys," kids who didn't appear to care much about school or student activities. Some had been getting into fights with Black kids, so I assumed Mr. Joseph required them to attend. They sat as a group in the back of the room, looking disinterested.

I opened the meeting by telling my story of arriving on the Dominguez High campus two years earlier, not knowing a soul but slowly making friends and feeling included. I hoped these comments would help the Black students see that they, too, might feel more included in time. But blank stares filled the tense room. Looking around, I pointed to several former football teammates—Black, Brown, and White—and stressed how joining the team changed things. "At first, we were all competing to make the team," I said, "and sometimes we had to battle against each other for positions, but after a while we became teammates, and it didn't matter what the other guy looked like because soon we were fighting together to win games." Again, the gist of my analogy didn't seem to go anywhere.

I ended with a statement instead of a story. "All of us in this room are students at Dominguez High," I tried to say sternly, "and we have to figure out how to get along better because fighting will only make matters worse." "And," as I concluded with a made-up threat, "Mr. Joseph told me he would bust your ass if any more fights break out, and he'll call in the cops." Finally, the guys were paying attention.

A moment later a Black student I knew from Walton stood up. "We are cool with you, Al, because we know you," he said looking straight into my eyes, "but we know lots of you don't want us here at your school," as he panned the room. "We don't want to fight, but we ain't going to let you push us around." A White kid and a Mexican American kid said something briefly about all the fights, and then the room fell silent.

"Oh shit, what am I going to do now because I don't have any more stories or messages to share," I thought. Thank goodness, Lowry Cuthbert stood up. An outstanding football player, and a Black kid from the westside who'd played on the varsity squad with me the previous year, he was a fierce competitor you didn't want to be tackled by on the field. But otherwise, Lowry was a kind, quiet, sweet kid whom everyone liked.

"Can't we just talk and get along," Lowry said with a straight face and in all sincerity, "and have cookies and milk together?" The room erupted in laughter. Lowry had broken the ice, and the tension eased. As others spoke, the focus was mostly on figuring out how to stop fighting.

I wish I'd told Lowry then how grateful I was for what he'd said (Army Sergeant Cuthbert was killed in action a few years later in the Vietnam War). Remarkably, the fighting on campus appeared to end. I have no idea if the Multiracial Council meeting helped, or if it was that false threat I'd said came from Mr. Joseph. Whatever the reason, calm was restored through the end of the academic year, though I think mostly because White and Black kids just kept distance from one another.

Soon after the cafeteria meeting, I organized a small panel of students to discuss race relations in the library at lunch time; the room was filled to capacity. I remember this meeting vividly, not so much for what was said but, in retrospect, for a totally wrongheaded, stupid remark I made to one of the panelists. I chaired the panel, but the female panelists—a White, a Mexican American, and an African American junior—were picked by administrators and/or teachers.

The panelists' brief remarks were generally about how racial harmony was important; but the African American student astutely mentioned the importance of the 1964 Civil Rights Act and the Voting Rights Act passed by Congress in August 1965. In the Q&A follow-up, this brave girl, who was new to the school, declared how slavery was the root cause of discrimination against Blacks. When she finished, I quickly stated, "Slavery ended over a hundred years ago," so "how do you figure it is still important today?!" She looked down dejectedly while sitting at the table and didn't say another word, clearly wounded by the statement made in a privileged way by the student body president, panel chairperson, and non-Black male. Talk about showing the importance—or ignorance, on my part—of knowing your history!

My asinine, ahistorical comment about the irrelevancy of slavery in 1965 was absurd, and I wish I could go back in time to that day and say to her: "I am so sorry, because you were entirely right, and I was absolutely wrong." (If you, by chance, read this book and remember that race relations panel, please forgive me for my stupidity and arrogance. I have spent my entire career proving you were correct.)

The socially distant calm of campus also meant that African American students rarely chose to attend dances and other school events, likely from feeling alienated on campus. A Black girl who was a sophomore in 1965 recalled her experience as follows: "We felt outnumbered. . . . I remember they never had a Black on the homecoming court at Dominguez until the year after I graduated in 1969 . . . there was a lot of tension then."

Similar tensions occurred throughout the city in the early 1960s. As the number of Blacks in Compton began to reach parity with Whites, the growing local chapter of the NAACP took on the challenge of segregation and discrimination. African American leaders complained to the Compton Unified School District about a lack of representation on the board and no Black teaching staff at eastside schools. Though African American customers were served in the downtown Compton Woolworth's, NAACP members picketed the store, with support from White and Mexican American members of the United Auto Workers union, demonstrating in solidarity with their civil rights movement brothers and sisters in the South.

The NAACP folks also led voter registration drives that began to produce some changes in a city whose local government and municipal agencies had locked them out completely before the early 1960s. Jesse Robinson (a NAACP leader) was appointed in 1963 as the first African American on the board of trustees for the Compton school district, filling a vacancy when Ramón Gonzáles (the padrino of the barrio and godfather to my siblings and mother) passed away.

By 1965, the school board of five men had two African Americans (one as president) and a Mexican American who served as vice president. The first African American member of the city council, Douglas F. Dollarhide (who became Compton's first Black mayor in 1969), was also elected in 1963. And within a couple of years, the first African American woman was elected city clerk.

Integration and change were happening, but resistance remained, especially in the housing market on the eastside. Dr. Ross M. Miller, the second

African American member of the school board, found that out the hard way. A respected surgeon and chief of staff at a nearby hospital, he had inquired before joining the board about purchasing a home on the far eastside of Compton. The White homeowner refused. A White friend purchased the home for Ross and immediately transferred its title. Not long after the family moved in 1964, a cross was burned on their front lawn.

Despite fear levels being higher after the Watts Riots, White homeowners couldn't hold the line against Black movement into eastside neighborhoods, as a result of this block busting and just sheer determination. The White exodus I had witnessed on the westside in the late 1950s and early 1960s turned into what someone labeled "White panic" on the eastside after 1965. Many families of my White friends from Dominguez picked up and moved after graduation in 1966. A fellow student, who was a senior when I was sophomore, later described her parents' fear of Blacks. "When we were at the dinner table every night," Pam remembered her parents saying, "We have to get out . . . everybody talked about it." Pam's family soon moved to the nearly all-White city of Lakewood, one of the most infamous "race-restricted" suburbs in Los Angeles.

My time in Compton was growing short, as my senior year at Dominguez ended in June 1966 (before the eastside became predominantly African American a few years later). I initially planned to apply to UCLA and Stanford University, where my friend Ken had accepted a football scholarship. I asked my basketball coach to send a letter to Stanford's coach, Howie Dallmar, about the possibility of a scholarship.

I had good, but not excellent, grades—and mediocre SAT scores. Stanford wasn't on my original list, but with a not-so-good basketball team, I thought I had a shot. Also, the star player from the Dominguez varsity squad two years earlier was now playing at Stanford. Dallmar responded quickly and kindly in a terse letter that the admission's office review of my transcript determined I couldn't be admitted.

My academic accomplishments were good enough to attend UCLA, however. And though I knew better than to inquire with Coach John Wooden about a basketball scholarship—the Bruins had won the national championship two of the three previous years—I was intent on beating the odds and planned to soon be playing there.

Luckily, I was headed to Westwood with one of the first scholarships ever given to a Mexican American student in the state by the Compton chapter of the Mexican American Political Association, a civil rights and political advocacy organization. The $200 was enough to almost pay for tuition and fees at UCLA for my entire freshman year.

As I said goodbye to Compton at summer's end in 1966, I couldn't have imagined in my wildest dreams how higher education would change me. From the boy who didn't realize the tremendous weight of historical factors such as slavery, I would be so shaped by education that it would impact my social consciousness and my entire adult life.

Downtown Compton, Compton Boulevard looking east,
1915. This view of the commercial buildings on Main Street
(later named Compton Boulevard) in downtown is what
Benjamín Camarillo would have seen when he arrived in 1911.

Four-year-old Albert sitting on the front steps of the "backward house" on Culver Street, circa 1952. This is the photo father Benjamín kept on his nightstand when he was a patient in the tuberculosis ward in a Long Beach hospital in 1951–53.

Camarillo brothers (*left to right*) Ben, Art, Max, and Al, at Richland Farms home with view of farmland in the background, July 1959.

WEST ON COMPTON BOULEVARD
FROM ALAMEDA STREET, 1962

Downtown Compton, Compton Boulevard looking
west from Alameda Street, 1962.

Courtesy of The Gerth Archives and Special Collections,
California State University, Dominguez Hills.

Walton Junior High School ninth-grade graduation dance, 1963. Ruby
Cook (*far right*) is next to Albert Camarillo, and Regina Spicer (*far
left*) is next to Frank Harris. The students in this photo were among
my friends at Walton and together reflected the predominantly African
American student body and population of westside Compton in 1963.
The bonds I shared with these and other friends in West Compton
helped shape my sense about race relations in positive ways.

Courtesy of Regina Cromwell.

ADVISORS — Shown above are the advisors of the multiracial council on human relations and Associated Body president of Dominguez High School. From left to right are Keith J. Lee, principal, Al Camarillo, ASB president and chairman of the council; Howard Neill, senior class counselor; Robert Gregory, Coordinator of student activities; Louis Joseph, vice principal.

Advisors for the Dominguez High School's Multiracial Council on Human Relations, 1966: (*left to right*) Keith J. Lee, principal; Al Camarillo, student body president and chair of council; Howard Neill, senior class counselor; Robert Gregory, coordinator of student activities; and Louis Joseph, vice principal. The clipping is from the *Herald American newspaper*, circa October 1966. The Multiracial Council was formed to help deal with tense race relations on campus after Black students were bussed from westside to eastside Compton to integrate Dominguez High School. As student body president and former westside resident, I was asked by school administrators to chair the council.

UCLA freshman basketball team, 1966. I am
number 45 (*kneeling, third from right*).

At the Walter Payton NFL Man of the Year Award event, Washington, DC, 2010: (*left to right*) Lauren, Al, Greg, Jeff, and Susan. Greg was the Miami Dolphins' nominee in 2009, an award to honor player contributions to community service. Greg's community service work began in 2006, a year after he started his football career with the San Diego Chargers. He and his brother Jeff established Charging Forward for Academic Success, a program to motivate and reward student athletes at Compton's Vanguard Learning Center.

Camp Camarillo, sponsored by Charging Forward for Academic Success at Centennial High School, Compton, July 2010: (*left to right*) Jeff, Greg, and Al. Charging Forward held a football camp for about a hundred high school players from the three high schools in Compton, and it became the model for The Athlete Academy, a nonprofit Greg founded in 2022 to empower high school student athletes in underserved communities in San Diego.

Vanguard Learning Center, Compton, 2009. Pictured are six of
Jeff's former VLC students with Al. This group of students aptly
reflect the demographics of West Compton in the early 2000s.

Courtesy of Misha Gravenor.

California Latino Legislative Caucus Spirit Awards reception, May 6, 2019: (*left to right*) Assemblyperson José Medina, Greg, Al (holding Jaxson), Susan, Jeff, Josephine (holding Jayce), and Lauren.

Camarillo family photo, Father's Day, 2023: (*left to right*)
Avery, Greg, Cameron, Sharon, Josephine, Jayce, Jeff, Jaxson,
Susan, Al, Sloane, Matt, Maya, Diego, and Lauren.

PART II

Pursuing a Social Justice Passion

NINE

Early UCLA Days

Getting lost on my first student visit to UCLA should have given me a sense of what was to come. Two weeks before classes began, I had to take the English "Subject A" exam to determine my placement in a standard freshman English composition course or in what students called "dumbbell" or "bonehead" English. My anxiety about the test worsened while heading to Westwood after taking the wrong freeway turnoff near downtown Los Angeles. I was fortunate not to be pulled over as I sped on Sunset Boulevard through Hollywood, West Hollywood, and Beverly Hills.

When I exited the car shortly before the writing exam was to begin, an old friend, Neil, from Longfellow Elementary and Walton days, happened to park near me, and we walked together to the large lecture hall for the test. It was filled to capacity with about 700 students. I failed the damn test.

Money challenges also meant making choices about commuting, as my parents couldn't afford dormitory costs. But my brother Max, who had been admitted to UCLA as a community college transfer student after his discharge from the army, now lived in an apartment with a roommate, a fellow UCLA senior.

There was no way I was going to drive to campus five days a week for my freshman year on crowded LA freeways. So I had to settle for the three of us sharing a small one-bedroom, one-bath apartment close to the campus in West LA. I couldn't afford a campus parking permit either, so my customized 62 Chevy Impala, which I'd worked on all summer, sat at the apartment while I rode the local bus daily.

A few kids from Dominguez High entered UCLA with me and were the only students I knew among the 27,000 plus enrolled at this beautiful campus nestled among the gently rolling hills of Westwood. Talk about it being different from Compton. The campus bordered the super-rich neighborhood of Bel Air on the northside. Two blocks from the university, peddlers on Sunset Boulevard sold maps to tourists showing the mansions where famous Hollywood celebrities lived. To the east and west of campus were tree-lined Westwood streets with row after row of beautiful, large homes with finely manicured lawns, the likes of which didn't exist in South LA. Westwood Village, next to the campus on its southern edge, was the small, quaint commercial center where students could find a hamburger or sandwich joint mixed in among high-end restaurants, jewelry stores, and clothing shops that catered to affluent locals.

Although only about twenty miles from Compton, the whole area seemed light years away. I had a sinking feeling in my gut from being out of place as I wandered around campus as a new Bruin, searching for the buildings where my classes were scheduled. But at the same time, I was excited to be at this beautiful university, especially when I walked past the new Pauley Pavilion, a basketball arena that was the only campus building I'd previously visited.

Tryouts for the freshman basketball team began the same week autumn quarter opened. There were four scholarship players already selected for the squad, which left eight "walk-on" spots that would be filled by the tryouts. About thirty to forty other b-ballers like me wanted to make the team that would become part of the emerging basketball dynasty of John Wooden and his coaching staff. My goal was to use team membership to gain a foothold in a new setting again. But this was UCLA, and my chances were slim.

Scrimmages were held every afternoon for those of us seeking to gain a spot. We were pitted against the "scholarship guys," which meant my regularly facing up with Fred Gray, a six foot four standout guard from a San

Fernando Valley high school. Although I was way faster and quicker, I had to badger the hell out of Fred, with his seven-inch height advantage, and play a little dirty defense to get an edge and be noticed. I also wanted to show the coaches I was a sharpshooter (I never met a shot I didn't like, though I was always a hot-and-cold scorer).

My strategy paid off, but by week's end, Fred's annoyance with my "fly-paper" defense meant he called me out on the court. We squared off, but Coach Gary Cunningham intervened and sent us to the showers. We later became good friends (even reconnecting years later as teammates playing intramural basketball at Stanford).

Soon after tryouts ended, the team roster was posted on the locker room door, and I felt the thrill of having my dream of playing college basketball realized. Not on the varsity squad, though. Way back then, not even Lew Alcindor (Kareem Abdul Jabbar), who was a freshman at UCLA the year before, was allowed to play varsity ball in the first year because of an NCAA rule.

The freshman and varsity teams practiced daily at the same time on adjoining courts. One interaction led me to be able to claim teaching an NBA legend how to shoot a three-point shot. Some of my former Stanford students, after they learned that I played basketball at UCLA, would laugh when I recounted the following story. The gullible ones responded, "Wow, really?"

It began when we were at practice one day, shooting around before drills began. My claim to fame as a frosh player was an ability to score buckets from long range, primarily because at barely five foot nine, it was suicide to drive to the basket with giants waiting there to reject shots. But there was no such thing as a three-point shot before the mid-1980s. As I prepared to take a twenty-foot shot during warmups, Lew (Kareem) stepped out of the locker room and began to walk to practice. He was about twenty feet away from the basket on the left baseline. "Hey, Lew," I shouted at Kareem, playfully, "we little guys have to shoot the ball from way out here," as I stood beyond the top of the key, "and you big guys just lay the damn ball up three feet away from the hoop." I tossed Kareem the ball. He stopped, pulled up, and shot—swish! All us frosh squad players went wild. Without a word, Kareem quietly turned and looked at me, and with a little smile, that I read as "Take that, you little . . . ," he walked to the adjoining varsity practice court. I never again questioned Kareem's ability to make the long shot, though he rarely did so in college and in the pros. He made one three-point shot in his long, illustrious career in the NBA.

As Kareem, and UCLA basketball under Coach John Wooden, went on to set record after record, I don't think any of us fully understood the lessons of what the "Wizard of Westwood" and his coaching staff were trying to impart. I thought it was crazy, for example, when we were instructed at the first practice how to properly tie the laces of our basketball shoes. But when a coach noted that well-tied laces reduce the likelihood of blisters, it made sense. We were constantly told, as well, that executing drills and plays with precision during practices—over and over again—would pay off with victories over less prepared opponents. In time, I realized this truism worked, whether you were an athlete or a struggling student trying to be better.

As I settled in at UCLA in 1966, I was happy to have a few fellow frosh "Brubabe" players as buddies. Another group of students I soon met, but had no interest in hanging out with, were NROTC "midshipmen" students. Following my brother Max's advice, I'd signed up for the Naval Reserve Officers Training Corps, a program to become a commissioned officer in the U.S. Navy after college. He didn't want me to get drafted after graduation, as he had been by the army after graduating from Compton College. That could've meant being sent to a far-off war in Southeast Asia, a war that by 1966 was escalating.

During the NROTC orientation session the first week on campus, I finally learned their training and course requirements. Besides enrolling in a NROTC-related class every quarter, we had to follow military protocol that included saluting in the presence of the program's instructors, all of whom were active-duty naval officers. I actually thought that would be kind of fun since I'd grown up watching movies about World War II and mimicking salutes. The bad news came with being issued khaki uniforms that had to be worn to campus once a week for field drill exercises. What the hell did I get myself into?!

Besides struggling to declare a major, I struggled to stay current in the readings for almost every course. My study skills were horrible while competing against some really smart students from excellent West LA public schools. You'd think the NROTC program would have offered some tutorials about keeping a midshipman's head above water!

To pay for rent, food, and books, I'd also kept my weekend gas station job in Compton. This allowed time away from the overstuffed apartment, as I went home almost every weekend in between the Bruins away basketball games. That meant enjoying Mama's home-cooked Mexican food, which I really missed, and bringing back a care package of La Jefita's prepared meals for Max and me to feed from for several days.

My social life as a UCLA freshman sucked, though, from being cut off from the dorms' social world. And I often saved money by making a bag lunch, eating by myself somewhere on campus while reading the *Daily Bruin* student newspaper.

One day in the fall quarter, my newspaper habit was rewarded with a feature article about Mexican Americans. Among the many points made by the author, Yolanda Araiza—a Mexican American student at UCLA—was her claim that fewer than fifty Mexicans Americans were currently enrolled at UCLA. Observing my classmates while walking to Pauley Pavilion for basketball practice that day, it sure seemed likely. There were almost no students of color, reminding me of how isolating it had felt my first day at Dominguez High three years earlier.

UCLA was no exception to the rule. Colleges and universities across the nation in the pre-affirmative action era were almost entirely White. Even with UCLA's revenue-producing team sports, in 1966 you could count the number of athletes of color on your fingers and toes. For example, not one Black player was on my frosh basketball team. And, on the soon to be famous, undefeated 1967 national basketball championship team, there were only three African Americans—Lew Alcindor, Lucius Allen, and Mike Warren. With varsity football, only five or six Black students were on the entire team.

UCLA and other universities weren't required by the federal government to provide race data on students until 1968, and my best guess is that there were fewer than a hundred African Americans on campus my freshman year, maybe two hundred Asian Americans, and forty to fifty Mexican Americans. Roughly speaking, that meant Mexican American students made up two-tenths of a percent of UCLA's student body then.

Araiza had been hired the previous summer as a research assistant for the UCLA Mexican American Study Project, the first comprehensive, multidisciplinary study of its type at that time. The findings of this massive study were published in 1970 as *The Mexican-American People: The Nation's Second Largest Minority*. Araiza's task was to interview dozens of Mexican American families in Los Angeles on a range of questions. Her November 1966 article in the *Daily Bruin*, "The Mexican-American's Search for Identity," was obviously deeply influenced by her project work.

Araiza also shared a poignant observation about the generation of young people, like me, born of Mexican immigrant parents. Rereading that opinion piece some fifty-four years later, after a career of helping to build a body of historical knowledge about Mexican Americans and other people of color in the United States, I was struck by her spot-on analysis.

"The problem of identification for the Mexican-American does not end by knowing what to call himself or inventing euphemisms such as Mexican-American, Americasian, Latin-American, and other terms," she stated. "American society," she noted, "the final judge of race and creed, decides who the Mexican is and what he should be called." She referenced our age group as a "generation caught between" the traditions and culture of immigrant parents and the attitudes in a society that prized assimilation and conformity to White norms.

Araiza noted a range of assimilation that characterized our generation, from those who entirely rejected their ethnic background to the assimilated ones, as in "those whose family traditions are less rigid, whose personalities are more flexible and yet are fully conscious of their Mexican heritage." At the article's end, she pointed out the ideal for Mexican Americans at UCLA and beyond: a biculturalism where "a positive combination of the two (Mexican and American cultures) is not only possible, but very probable if American institutions would allow it to be."

Max and I were among those campus Mexican Americans who were "fully conscious of their Mexican heritage" and "highly acculturated." But assimilating into UCLA's dominant culture took time and effort. And it took time for UCLA to provide people of color more opportunities to enroll and for the campus atmosphere to allow bicultural or multicultural students to thrive.

Young people like me, of Mexican origin and under thirty, were by far the largest cohort of Mexican Americans in the Southwest in the 1960s. We came from communities that had one of the highest median family sizes in the nation, close to that of African American families in the South. And, like Blacks during the Great Migration, we were leaving agricultural areas in droves, seeking opportunities in large Southwest cities.

The Mexican-origin population in the United States was estimated at about 5.6 million in 1960, and growing. Five million of these people lived in the Southwest, and I was one of about 1.4 million Mexican Americans in California. The LA area alone became home to over 600,000 of us. All told, we were the fastest urbanizing population in the nation during the 1950s and 1960s. And because no new, massive influx of immigrants had come from Mexico since my father's "revolution era" group, my generation of native-born U.S. citizens represented about two-thirds of the entire Mexican-origin population in the region.

This generation was forced to stand at a crossroads in the 1960s. Would we mirror the millions of children of southern and eastern European background, whose parents had arrived at the end of the nineteenth and the beginning of the twentieth centuries? And who, by post–World War II years, were swimming swiftly in the mainstreams of society? Or, even if we assimilated, would we remain outside the institutional and cultural heart of America—much like African Americans, the nation's largest racial minority that had long suffered from exclusion, inequality, and injustice at the hands of Jim Crow and more?

Since the early 1900s, Mexican Americans did have civil rights and other reform-minded organizations, in California and elsewhere, working to help end racial discrimination in public places such as schools, recreational sites, and the criminal justice system. In the years following the Second World War, White racial liberals joined Mexican American, as well as African American and Asian American organizations, to push reforms further while seeking to dismantle structures of inequality deeply embedded in American institutions. Some of these efforts resulted in monumental pieces of legislation and judicial decisions such as *Brown v. Board of Education* in 1954, the Civil Rights Act in 1964, and the Voting Rights Act of 1965. Without question, movements for racial justice and equality had moved the needle forward by my freshman year at UCLA.

But a much more difficult proposition involved changing the cultural foundations of America so that people of different races, ethnic and cultural backgrounds, gender and sexual orientations, and disabilities could participate in society on equal footing. Those societal changes were needed before people historically viewed as "different" and "unequal" could begin to build pride of identity without denying or camouflaging their ethnic, cultural, gender, and racial identities of origin.

Over time, the ideal of assimilation crept into the organizational agendas and minds of so many people of color. Given the narrow definition of being an American back in the post–World War II years, I believe assimilation came to be viewed as a companion characteristic of the American Dream.

Yet as generations of African Americans and other people of color were striving to gain equal footing, they were stymied by concepts based on perceived racial differences. These dominant ideas, now referred to as "scientific racism," outlined the supposed inherent inferiority of non-Caucasian people. This pseudo-science, which "proved" beyond a doubt that dark-skinned people of the world were inferior to Whites, was first advanced by European intellectuals in the nineteenth century and later became widely accepted by their American counterparts well into the twentieth century.

These ideas about innate racial inferiority formed the bedrock of policies, practices, and social customs that have stained American civilization, providing justifications for everything from the institution of slavery to the racist principle of "separate but equal." Millions of Americans over time carried the burden of this idea of inferiority that favored the practices of assimilation, often while internalizing feelings of self-doubt as they rejected their racial and cultural heritage, and worse.

As a result, some Black leaders and organizations advocated for decades that African Americans must "uplift" themselves to become "respectable" middle-class citizens as a way to be accepted in American society. Countless Mexican Americans, and some of their organizations, did so as well, charting a path with a similar emphasis on discarding immigrant traditions and embracing full cultural assimilation.

The idea of assimilation became infused in the notion of the "melting pot," which was a theory advanced by American sociologists beginning in the 1920s. It gained greater traction after World War II, when the atrocities of the Holocaust in Europe became widely known. The American ideal of assimilating people once viewed as being "different" took on new meaning and greater importance in light of the horrors of the Nazi regime. After all, if the United States had become the beacon of freedom and democracy worldwide, as racial liberals argued, welcoming others (into a narrowly defined definition of Americanism) seemed key. These sociologists claimed that cultural assimilation in America worked—in time, the sons and daughters of European immigrants had become "good" Americans.

What was missing was an understanding of the complex web of racism and the lived condition of people of color. Even if, as an individual, you altered your cultural orientations in an attempt to assimilate into White society, your success was hamstrung by being on the margins socioeconomically, politically, and educationally. The invisible, yet entrenched, color line—representing structural inequality based on race—still was real and pervasive, especially for African Americans.

There were few alternatives in higher education for students of color like me, in the mid-1960s, beyond following the path of assimilation. And man, as an eighteen-year-old freshman, I sure wanted to fit in. Playing basketball helped a lot, and two NROTC students, Randy and Jerry, were among a few friends on campus. But I wasn't meeting any women classmates, despite an abundance of beautiful coeds. I lacked the confidence to ask out girls I hardly knew in my classes, and sharing a small apartment with my brother and a roommate didn't help, making me envious of guys I knew who were dating.

I remember one day toward the end of basketball season when I dropped off a teammate, and he invited me and another player into his apartment to hang out. As soon as he opened the door, I saw a pretty girl taking a nap on his couch, awakening as we entered. "Damn, John," I said to him, "you come home from practice and there is a beautiful girl waiting for you? Where can I sign up, man?" "This is Susan," John replied, grinning as he introduced her as his best buddy's girlfriend. (That was a fateful day in my life.)

Randy and I also became great friends. He was not only a friendly, funny, outgoing NROTC amigo, but our families had roots going back a generation. Randy's father was Mr. Gregory, the coordinator of student activities at Dominguez High, and we got along famously. Mr. Gregory also knew my siblings from his time teaching at Willowbrook Junior High, and at Walton, and then Compton High, where he was an assistant coach when Art played football there. Randy even got rides on Art's shoulders after games he attended. And, like me, Randy was into sports and wanted a new place to meet people outside his dormitory.

So, when at the start of spring quarter freshman year, our good NROTC friend Jerry invited Randy and me to a Friday afternoon party at the Phi Kappa Sigma house, we agreed to visit his fraternity. The three of us were already the NROTC's three amigos. We didn't take the program too seriously and often joked about the "military nerds" in it. We also were clearly the outliers with military protocol, particularly with wearing the ugly khaki uniform with an officer's hat once a week to campus. The uniforms were worn to practice marching in formation on the grass field in front of the NROTC building. Randy, who lived in a nearby dorm, routinely dashed there after NROTC practice to change clothes before he headed off to afternoon classes. I didn't have time to go back to the West LA apartment before basketball practices. So, on those dreaded NROTC uniform days, I had to not only wear the full uniform on the bus to UCLA, but all damn day long, which my basketball teammates loved. Each week when I entered the locker room to change into practice clothes, the guys would immediately snap to attention and salute. "At ease, gentlemen," I would reply, joining in on their fun.

My social world began to open up with Jerry's encouragement; he invited Randy and me to pledge his fraternity. With its reputation as a jock house, it seemed like a good fit and the hazing wasn't horrible—mostly doing fixer-up, cosmetic work on the old, grand, three-story Phi Kap house located just off campus. Finally, I began to meet girls. Another big plus living at the fraternity was that I could work as a kitchen hasher to reduce room and board fees my second year at UCLA. Most importantly, I didn't have to live with my brother and commute anymore.

By spring quarter, however, with time committed to pledging a fraternity and playing as much basketball as possible to prep for the next season, my attention to coursework, and grades, slipped. I had taken the introductory course in philosophy pass/fail. I failed. I beat myself up over it. "Pendejo, look what you got yourself into now!" My overall grade point average dipped below the level to be in good academic standing at the university. With two quarters of failing to meet a 2.0 GPA, you could be dismissed from the university, so spring quarter was a wakeup call for me.

The news from the registrar's office arrived at my parents' home about two weeks into the summer. I was placed on academic probation. Even knowing that was coming, it hurt to read the official letter. "Can you bounce back?" I remember thinking, alone and in silence in my bedroom. I should have told someone, to help with my confidence and for support, but I didn't. I certainly couldn't tell La Jefita, who'd seen too much sorrow in her life. I just knew she had enormous hope for me and my future. Thoughts of my three brothers also came to mind; each had returned home after one semester of college. Even before I started UCLA, my mother had worried that her youngest son would follow the same path.

Self-doubt was new, but it didn't paralyze me. No way was I going to fail out of UCLA and come back home to enroll at the community college. No way would I settle for some type of low-income job, or worse yet, be drafted into the army. No way!

Somehow, I believed I could get out of this academic hole. In the battle between confidence and self-doubt, confidence won out. Though failure was not an option, that didn't mean I had the experience to map a specific way out. I simply knew I had to do better as a sophomore, even while struggling because I hadn't found a subject of real interest, and my study skills were only marginally improved. In an introductory course in political science, I ended up hating the obtuse readings about political theory. The NROTC courses in naval history and celestial navigation were not interesting—why did a future officer really have to know these seemingly useless subjects?

My immediate plan for summer 1967, besides a work-study job on campus, was to play as many pickup games as possible against varsity players at Pauley Pavilion to prepare for varsity squad tryouts, again as a walk-on.

Having watched carefully how talented the walk-on players were on the varsity team, I was convinced I could outplay at least two of them to make the reigning national championship team's roster. As autumn quarter approached, though, my survival instincts took over when considering entering sophomore year on academic probation. Plus, I was preparing to move into full fraternity guy mode living in a house with about thirty other frat boys, most of whom, like me, didn't seem like serious students.

I bit the bullet, cancelling a meeting with Coach Wooden to talk up my value, and didn't try out for the team. I don't regret putting so much time and effort into basketball during my first year at UCLA. For one year, I was inside college basketball at a golden time. And even if I had made the varsity team and played in almost every game—the 1967–68 team demolished all competition, so the few walk-ons ended up playing a lot—I knew there was no future for me in basketball. What I needed more was to muster the limited skills I had to survive academically at UCLA.

TEN

Awakening to Social Activism

How does a rudderless, nineteen-year-old college student find a sense of purpose and meaning? How do you bounce back from a mediocre high school education while navigating a challenging university? It's not easy, but I can tell you how I did it: learn by doing, by experience. Absorb knowledge, not just from books and teachers, but by opening your eyes wide and keeping your mind open to new ideas, new experiences. It is okay to try something and fail—because you can become wiser as a result. Reach out for help when needed, whether it be from family, friends, or professional staff on campus. And get involved, whether in extracurricular or service-related activities on and off campus.

Giving yourself space to reflect on new experiences and knowledge gained will help you relate to your sense of self, family, community, and larger society. And, particularly in times of perplexing social change (as was true when I attended UCLA in the late 1960s—and today perhaps even more), keep asking yourself an important question inherent in a phrase my generation often considered: "If you are not part of the solution, you are part of the problem." Figure out for yourself what the problems are and how you can contribute to the solution. All of this is part of getting an Education with a capital E: a formal and experiential education. If you are lucky, as I was, along the way you will find an academic or a social passion, maybe both.

That's a long, important list. I didn't realize this at the time, but during my sophomore and junior years at UCLA, from 1967 through 1969, I experimented with what I now preach. My Education transformed how I viewed almost everything—including my future.

My intellectual and social justice awakening involved strife as well as soul searching. Family expectations were in the mix. My parents couldn't begin to understand what I was experiencing at UCLA beyond their hope that I would graduate, get a good-paying job, and have a better life. Bottom-liners, they wanted an easier life for me than theirs had been. My sister Rita, by contrast, somehow expected me to join the real estate business that she and her husband had developed. Regardless, my family members expected success because I'd done well in middle school and high school. Same here, but I was struggling to gain an academic foothold.

So there I was, a student at a huge public university trying to figure how to succeed for la familia and myself. For me, UCLA offered both an opportunity to grow as a young citizen of the nation and as a serious student.

The twists and turns as a student included learning lessons about class preparation the hard way. Although I did well enough, barely, to get off academic probation by winter break my sophomore year, I still struggled to succeed, and I had no idea about what to declare for a major or what career to pursue. Getting a zoology degree and becoming a marine biologist had briefly been an idea during freshman year, before I'd looked at the math and science requirements. An opportunity afforded by the NROTC did the same for a short time.

Jerry, Randy, and I had the chance to spend a few days over winter break at the naval air station in Pensacola, Florida, flying aircraft as trainees. After a long flight in an old cargo propeller plane, we were assigned to a flight training squadron in Pensacola. Each of us would fly in the navigator seat of a two-man training aircraft. Our flights involved a live machine gun practice run against a target pulled by another plane, which had the exhilarating feel of being on a super–roller coaster ride on steroids. Randy and I almost lost our cookies—while Jerry actually threw up.

For at least the next six months, I dreamed of being a jet fighter pilot. The idea of flying on and off large aircraft carriers, commanding a supersonic jet, and visiting ports around the world seemed appealing. I wasn't thinking about a military career. Rather, I knew that after a few years of active military duty, former navy pilots were prized as commercial airline pilots. The pay and travel and all of that sounded good to me then, though Jerry was the only one of us who made it to flight training school and wore the uniform of a commercial pilot.

My flirtation with naval aviation lasted about as long as my flirtation with sorority girls as a frat member, but I had fun living in the frat house. In particular, the Phi Kaps attracted many varsity athletes and skilled former high school jocks who played beside me in a really competitive intramural football program; we went undefeated to capture the 1967 all-UCLA championship trophy, the highlight of my days as a wide receiver.

The end of my sophomore year at UCLA proved to be momentous, for many reasons. For one thing, I finally found a course I enjoyed, and maybe even a major to declare. In spring 1968, I enrolled in a history course on post–Civil War America. It opened my eyes to subjects my high school history class had covered briefly and uncritically: Reconstruction and Blacks in the South, European immigration, labor conflict, and a host of other subjects. What struck me, especially, was learning about the utter failure of federal Reconstruction and the rise of Jim Crow in the South. This course made me think about the parents of my Black friends in westside Compton, nearly all of whom were born in the apartheid-like southern states. I did well on the exams, deciding to declare history as a major, though I still had doubts about my scholastic abilities, particularly in upper division courses in a major that required written exams and research papers.

Further inspiration came with a heavy dose of sadness, after learning of the assassination of Dr. Martin Luther King Jr. on April 4, 1968, which rocked the nation and the world. Still struggling with how to process his death while on the way to the frat house a few days later, I saw hundreds of people funneling into Pauley Pavilion for a service to memorialize Dr. King. Thousands of mourners of all races and age groups had assembled that afternoon, and I joined them in listening to multiple speakers extolling the life and virtues of the fallen civil rights leader.

That bright spring day, we participants stood up together, interlocking our hands and arms, and sang "We Shall Overcome." A chill went down my spine as I scanned the huge basketball arena nearly filled with students and guests, most with teary eyes, some sobbing uncontrollably. I felt my sense of well-being grow as part of this group of like-minded people committed to a cause and remembering a noble leader.

The gods of fate and good fortune blessed me at about the same time with a genuine treasure. Toward the end of my second year, I began to hang out with that pretty girl Susan, who had been napping on my teammate's couch freshman year. In time, I realized she was beyond what I had hoped to find in a girlfriend and partner—being intelligent, fun, and so special in many ways.

A graduate of an excellent West LA public high school, Susan had outstanding study skills, which was something I learned from her quickly. She was politically progressive, and though not outspoken in her beliefs, held strong ethical values. We also shared similar family backgrounds: her father was a Jewish émigré from Hungary who came to the United States at age sixteen, and her mother was born in the United States of Hungarian Jewish parents. Her family was loving and close-knit, and she was witty, sensitive, and caring, adding to the chemistry between us. Plus, she loved basketball and sports in general!

There were some obstacles, however. Luckily for me, she and her boyfriend, who had been together since high school, were having difficulty with their long-distance relationship and had decided to see other people. But other guys knew this and were showing interest, including two of my former teammates.

A romantic summer together before our junior year helped convince her I was the right guy for her, and we became inseparable soulmates from that point forward. She taught me, by example, how to improve my study skills and became my editor for all writing assignments from then on.

A foundational part of our relationship was a growing interest in political liberalism and in activism. College campuses across the nation had become hot spots in the late 1960s for vexing issues that were pulling at the seams of American democracy in so many ways. Even if you considered yourself to be an apolitical student, you couldn't ignore those realities at that time.

Multiple factors molded Susan and me into politically progressive students and budding activists. They included the anti-war movement, the United Farm Workers movement, the feminist movement, and the Black Power movement. The Chicano/a movement and ethnic studies movements on California campuses, in my case, also shaped me to the core, as my intellectual awakening was underway in understanding history and the complex web of race relations interwoven into the tapestry of American institutions and culture.

A huge impact, and a huge challenge for me personally as it gained momentum on higher education campuses by 1968, came from the growing sentiment that something was terribly wrong with the war the United States was waging in Southeast Asia. Even as I attended NROTC classes and training, my eyes were open to the perverse nature of warfare in general, and to the horrendous actions of the U.S. military, in the name of Americans, to save democracy from the spread of communism. By 1968 and 69, peaceful protests against U.S. military involvement in Vietnam had spread nationally, with hundreds of thousands of protesting young people like us mobilized into taking a hard, moral stand against the war.

The history of governmental involvement in Vietnam began in the 1950s, when the United States had provided military advisors, first to the French colonials and later to the newly formed South Vietnam government. This was in an effort to stop North Vietnam from uniting with this poor, small Southeast Asian country as a communist nation. In the middle of a Cold War against China and the Soviet Union, the U.S. strategy of "containment" of communism and fear of a "domino effect" in the region prompted President Lyndon B. Johnson to turn up the flame, turning a Cold War into a hot one. After the Gulf of Tonkin incident in 1964, when a North Vietnamese torpedo boat attacked a U.S. Navy vessel, President Johnson, following the advice of his generals, escalated the war by bombing targets in the north.

Student groups mobilized anti-war "teach-ins" and staged protests over the next two years, as more Americans began opposing the expanding war. By 1967, the United States had about 500,000 military personnel in Vietnam, and the number of Americans killed surpassed 15,000, with over 100,000 wounded. Part of the disillusionment stemmed from this war being broadcast live (for the first time). Every night, televisions projected ghastly images of battle scenes and tabulations of the day's dead and wounded. By 1968, you were almost forced to take a stand for or against the war. The tide of public sentiment against the war was fast rising, and most Americans began to believe that President Johnson and the U.S. military had lied about winning the war, especially after 1968 when North Vietnam launched the successful Tet Offensive against U.S. and South Vietnamese troops. As Martin Luther King Jr. and many other notable American leaders added their voices to protesting the war, President Johnson made the surprise announcement in March 1968 of not seeking reelection. Anti-war and other protests still gained momentum, such as violence erupting outside the Democratic National Convention in Chicago a few months later.

While the war, and the pace of student protests, escalated, more young men were faced with the prospect of being drafted. Many students, especially men, now had even more reason to protest. Luckily, my dreams had died the previous year about flying jet fighter planes. In part, I'd learned that U.S. Navy pilots based on aircraft carriers were bombing North Vietnam every day, and many were routinely being shot down. But (as a draft-dodging measure), I was still enrolled in the NROTC and being prepped to become an officer. To find a way out of this commitment so that I could protest more fully, I had to develop a plan—or I should say, one was developed for me after a visit to the UCLA student infirmary.

In the summer before my sophomore year, I developed a bump on the tip of my spine that made it painful to sit down or lie on my back while sleeping. A UCLA doctor diagnosed the problem as an abscessed pilonidal cyst, which was lanced and drained, and he told me about the high risk of it abscessing again.

About a year later, I consulted with a young law student who served as an anti-draft, anti-war counselor to young men of my age. "Do you have any medical disabilities?" he asked and followed up with a question about any surgeries. I said no, and then added, "I had an out-patient procedure not long ago for an abscessed cyst on my tailbone." He quickly confirmed the diagnosis in an excited tone, adding, "You are one lucky guy," with a broad, toothy smile. He handed me a slip of paper with a name and address on it of an anti-war physician, who wrote a medical report about my disability that disqualified me from serving in the military.

I was, indeed, a lucky guy. My medical problem allowed me to receive a coveted 4-F classification from the Selective Service System, a medical deferment from the draft. After I told the NROTC program of my condition, they asked me to see a military doctor at a nearby base; he agreed with the classification and told me I was unfit to serve.

Bingo! I felt like building a shrine to pay homage to the gods of pilonidal cysts. Fortunately, I never had to contemplate using any plan B options after graduation: (1) claiming conscientious objection to the war; (2) moving to Canada; or (3) chopping off part of my right index finger used to pull the trigger on a rifle. Susan and I attended protest rally after rally, the most memorable one being when we drove to San Francisco's Golden Gate Park where 100,000 people gathered in a massive peaceful protest to the war in November 1969.

It was a site to behold. Throngs of people of all ages and all backgrounds were packed in, shoulder to shoulder, on the park's huge green on a glorious Saturday afternoon. We sang anti-war songs, recited anti-war slogans, and listened to speaker after speaker denounce the war. Everyone was there to express opposition to what we considered an immoral war, creating an inspiring energy, as part of protests held across the nation in hopes of influencing policymakers in Washington, DC.

Our political sensibilities against the war increased as did our critique of the U.S. industrial-military complex and a government intent on winning what millions of Americans believed was an unjust war. Susan and I also joined with thousands of students at UCLA and other University of California campuses in a truly unprecedented student strike that shut down the entire UC system during the spring quarter of our senior year. I was nearly arrested as the LAPD descended on campus to quell the protests and force us out of the administration building we had taken over and occupied. Along with hundreds of other students, I played cat and mouse with the police as they chased us to new locations across campus. In the midst of this, La Jefita called me one evening, having seen television coverage of the UCLA protests. For months I had shared with her my opposition to the war, and she mostly agreed with my opinions. What concerned her most was that student protestors were being beaten and arrested. "You aren't part of that group of students rioting at UCLA, are you?" she asked. "Of course not, Mama," I quickly replied, despite my luck at not being arrested that day.

Susan and I also joined protests and boycotts in 1968 in support of the United Farm Workers Union (UFW) strike against grape growers in California's Central Valley. Supporting the UFW opened our eyes to yet another example of injustice and inequality at a time when I was beginning to learn more about historic inequities in American society, especially those that burdened people of color.

I was aware of the union, formed in 1966 by Filipino and Mexican American farmworkers in Delano, and that it had mobilized farmworkers and launched a strike against the state's growers of table grapes. I learned, however, that for decades California labor leaders had tried many times to build a viable union for the poorest of the poor among American workers— the people who harvest our food. I was even more inspired as I came to know more about the UFW, its leadership and its efforts to fight for fair wages, benefits and dignity for forgotten workers—the great majority of whom were of Mexican origin.

Leaders César Chávez (whom I met several times in the years ahead) and Dolores Huerta (who became a friend) had learned grassroots organizing skills while at the Community Service Organization. It was a community-based Mexican American civil rights and advocacy group formed in East LA after World War II. This experience proved useful for building the first viable labor union for farmworkers in American history. Facing overwhelming odds against incredibly wealthy and powerful farm owners, the UFW attracted support from a broad swath of the American public during a protracted struggle to gain union recognition and succeed in a strike that few expected to prevail.

In 1968 the ongoing UFW strike against Giumarra Vineyards (the largest U.S. grower of table grapes) entered a critical phase when Huerta and Chávez launched a national and international economic boycott of grapes to pressure the intransigent company to come to the bargaining table. Susan and I learned about this while strolling along Bruin Walk. One of the many booths for student organizations and political groups was draped in a red flag bearing a black eagle with wings shaped like an inverted pyramid. The people behind the table were not students. They were farmworkers sent to UCLA, and to other university campuses and cities throughout the nation, to gather support for the grape boycott. We signed up for a house meeting and soon heard more about the plight of rural folk who experienced inequities and burdens hard to imagine for kids like me who grew up in the suburbs, even as a poor barrio kid.

We soon began passing out leaflets outside Safeway stores to try to convince shoppers—some curious, some supportive, and some who threw the leaflets back at us—not to patronize their stores while they continued to sell table grapes. We also attended many rallies and joined marches. The boycott prevailed in the end by hurting the grape growers financially and forcing them into negotiations with the union to settle the strike in 1970.

We expanded our politicization as a result of the boycott and became lifelong UFW supporters. In fact, our children still joke with family and friends that they didn't know what a table grape tasted like growing up— we'd banned them from our home.

Especially for urban Mexican American students in college and high school in the late 1960s, it was easy to be drawn to the crusade for farmworkers' rights. Both Chávez and Huerta were Mexican Americans of humble origins, committed to equality of opportunity and advocating for social change through peaceful, nonviolent means and acts of resistance. How could you not be inspired?

Supporting the UFW cause and actively participating in the anti-war movement as juniors and seniors at UCLA into 1970 had a profound impact on us in many ways. The horrendous massacre by Ohio National Guard troops of four students peacefully protesting the war at Kent State in early May of that year pushed this discontent to new heights. There were also other movements around the same time that broadened my vision and understanding of social issues in the United States. Academics now refer to a "second wave" feminism in the late 1960s, but it was known then as the women's movement or women's liberation. It was enlightening for me to begin to understand how male dominance and gender discrimination reinforced ideas about the "separate spheres" for men and women, and how the perceptions and attitudes that propped up male-centered ideologies had oppressed women in our society for way too long. The feminist movement helped me see my gender-based biases and made me a better person, a more informed citizen, and a better partner for Susan as we moved along the path of life together, always on equal terms.

Besides being shaped as an adult by the social movements encountered in Westwood, my path of discovery at UCLA had brought me the love of my life, leading to a marriage of over fifty years, three incredible children, and seven beautiful grandchildren. In my entire life, I have never met a person who is more positive, nurturing, and loving than Susan, qualities known to everyone lucky enough to cross her path.

We were influenced by the social movements we encountered, which helped change the ways we viewed ourselves, our families, our communities, and our society, while giving us a sense of purpose as young people. We learned to walk on activist paths at UCLA, with aspirations to push the United States to becoming a better, more open, more equal, more just, more democratic, and inclusive society. Were we idealistic as twenty-year-olds? You bet! Did we think we could change society? Why not try, as best we could?

As my interest in understanding the dynamics of race and ethnic relations in America grew, my educational search also led me to become part of the dawning field of ethnic studies and to find the Chicano/a movement. My journey at UCLA was sharpening in focus and direction, informing the path for what would become my life's work.

ELEVEN

Authentic Freedom

As a little kid in the barrio, I'd hear family and friends call each other "Chicano" at times. But as a college student in the late 1960s, the term took on a whole different meaning. Becoming conscious of myself as a Chicano wasn't a lightning bolt one day—like some epiphany. Instead, it was a process that began in those later years as an undergrad.

While talking to a dear friend and Stanford colleague Claude Steele (a social psychologist renowned for his work on stereotype threat), we reminisced about the impact of those years. We were sharing memories of our college days, and laughing, for example, when he recounted his efforts to try to fit in as one of the rare African Americans in the White culture of Hiram College in Ohio in the 1960s. "When the Black movement came along," Claude added with a serious look on his face, "we didn't have to force ourselves to assimilate any longer. We could be Black and be proud. It was freedom."

Claude's choice of that word, "freedom," struck a chord with me. I sat in thought for a moment. "You're right, Claude," I replied, "it was freedom." It was liberating to take pride in who we were as people of color. I had never articulated it that way before, but when the Chicano/a movement found

133

me, and I, it, it was freedom. It was psychological, social, intellectual, and political freedom. It was about being allowed to gain a sense of ethnic-racial pride I had never before felt. It was about the freedom of having curricular opportunities that gave purpose to my UCLA studies and a path to a career in higher education. It was a freedom to tackle equity matters in a way that built from past movements for civil rights and social justice, but that nurtured a younger generation of people of color to rise up while carving out spaces for themselves in post–civil rights America. And it was a freedom that, personally, gave substance and greater meaning to my evolving political consciousness.

My personal march toward a broad political consciousness had started with the anti-war movement and the farmworkers movement; it was fueled by courses during my junior year that enlightened me about U.S. history. A particularly influential course in spring 1969 was "Racial Attitudes in America." It had been offered in response to the racial unrest that had exploded in dozens of cities the year before as Blacks rebelled in response to the murder of Reverend King. Coordinated by historian Gary Nash (who later became my graduate school professor and then friend and colleague), this course dove into how racial attitudes were embedded in the ideas Americans held about people of color and also permeated our institutions. It introduced me to what social scientists and some historians were beginning to call "structural racism," or "institutionalized racism." Learning all this was like having a light bulb turned on inside my head, or like a badly nearsighted person being given corrective lenses for the first time and marveling at the clarity of full sight. I was now beginning to acquire knowledge and perspectives on many issues related to racial inequality that I had already decided were inherently wrong on moral and ethical grounds.

Such coursework at UCLA fed my thirst for knowledge. The books I read and lectures I heard helped me to understand, for example, why the institution of slavery, founded on racial oppression and subordination of Black people, was so powerful as an economic, social, and political system in the South. It also became clearer to me why so many African Americans, long segregated in the nation's cities, were protesting their marginalized status. Understanding structural racism also explained how the federal government could justify interning all Japanese Americans during World War II, not only on the basis of a perceived national security threat but from longstanding prejudice against Asians. This course helped me make sense, too, of Mexican American farmworker struggles in California's Central Valley as yet another economic system built on the backs of poor people of color. And closer to home, I better understood what had happened in Watts in 1965 and why my hometown of Compton had struggled with race relations.

For the first time, I was beginning to comprehend—in a serious, analytical, and critical way—my own lived experience, my family's history, and the city I called home. And the more I learned about the history of race in America, the more emotions came up about the consequences it had on the lives of millions of people over many generations. It was a strange and new experience for me to read about an episode of brutal segregation against a group of people and almost feel their pain.

I am grateful that my journey toward intellectual freedom and search for racial justice was funneled in constructive directions as a college student, which I was beginning to understand was a privileged status that most young people of color lacked. I also gained a more realistic perspective on inequity in the criminal justice system, and why young people of color without my privileges might vent their pent-up anger in destructive ways, often paying a heavy price from a society that had long punished those who contested racial and class boundaries.

The course on racial attitudes at the end of my junior year also provided an opportunity to do my first research project on the educational problems encountered by Mexican American youth, an issue I had become passionate about the previous year. The paper's topic was inspired by what became known as the East Los Angeles "walkouts" or "blowouts," of March 1968.

For over a week in what was then the largest mass protest by Latinos/as in American history, more than 20,000 students in East LA and nearby high schools walked out because of deplorable school conditions. I initially learned about the protest while at Susan's apartment with her roommates having dinner. We huddled around a television when the local nightly news headlined the story, with graphic footage: thousands of students from predominantly Mexican American schools had marched out of classes and onto the city's streets to protest the unequal education they believed they received in eastside schools. I frightened everyone when I jumped to my feet and

starting cussing at the LA County Sheriff's deputies who were shown club-
bing and arresting students.

As shocked as I was to learn how bad conditions were at Wilson, Roosevelt, Lincoln, Garfield, and other schools, I was riveted by seeing the news
coverage of students, all just a few years younger than me, defying authority
and peacefully demonstrating. The walkouts were a clarion call for social
and institutional change and were instrumental in the development of the
Chicano/a student movement, as hundreds of thousands of viewers like me
would likely never be the same. Looking back, I also know today that the
walkouts were, pure and simple, a reaction to the dirty work of Jaime Crow
over many decades in local schools.

The issues front and center in the minds of student leaders of the segregated eastside schools were the terribly under-resourced facilities, many of
which were dilapidated. Equally devastating, the dropout rate at the mostly
Mexican American eastside high schools averaged a staggeringly high 50
percent. The Los Angeles Unified School District notoriously directed
poorly trained teachers to East LA and South Central LA schools, where
most Mexican American and Black students were enrolled. Students also
complained about being routinely tracked into the non-college curriculum.

The student protests were crystalizing events for many reasons, seeded
by caring community members in earlier interactions. For several years
before the 1968 protest, community organization leaders had sponsored
small gatherings of Mexican American youth from East LA to encourage
their involvement in civic issues. Two of these gatherings, in particular, provided the impetus for student mobilization. A few older Mexican American
leaders on the LA County Commission on Human Relations organized
a conference of mostly high school students at Camp Hess Kramer, a re-
treat facility in Malibu run by a Jewish organization. Camp counselors there
facilitated conversations for students to gain a better sense of themselves
individually and collectively; inevitably the conversations led to discussions
about problems at students' respective schools and poverty in their East LA
barrios.

A priest of an eastside Episcopal church in Lincoln Heights established
another venue for local youth—the Social Action Training Center. Father
John Luce and the center director supported the UFW and placed high value

in equipping young people with knowledge and skills to improve themselves and their communities. Student activism took many forms, including creation of a newspaper, *La Raza* (the race, another term for people of Mexican descent), that became an organizing vehicle for budding activists and an information source for the East LA community.

A few Camp Hess Kramer conference students and others involved with the Social Action Training Center formed a small organization originally called the Young Citizens for Community Action (ultimately changed to the Young Chicanos for Community Action). They held meetings in a little coffee shop on the eastside and, at first, morphed into a group known as the Brown Berets. Modeled roughly on the Black Panther Party founded in Oakland in 1966, the leaders of this youth organization played an important role in the walkouts.

The seeds of Mexican American student activism were also being planted then by a few college students at local campuses such as California State University, Los Angeles, at UCLA, and at other colleges. These students were among the first to have been admitted under new affirmative action admissions programs. A handful joined with a group of high school students from East LA to discuss plans for a public demonstration of their dissatisfaction with the educational inequality they experienced every day. The tactic of walkouts and marches followed the effective approach used earlier by Chávez, Huerta, and the UFW, and by civil rights crusaders before them in the South.

Not only were the high school student leaders counseled by several college student peers, who were students at nearby colleges, but by some teachers, most notably Sal Castro, a social studies teacher with roots in East Los Angeles. As the walkouts continued day after day and spread to other area high schools, parents and community residents joined the student leaders in pressing for demands before the board of the Los Angeles Unified School District.

Given the dramatic evidence the walkouts provided of a deeply entrenched racial inequality in so many institutions, they inspired my research paper for the "Racial Attitudes in America" course the following spring. Like most students, I would typically have submitted a paper of the recommended page length for an assignment (ten in this case). My paper, which turned out to be the first stone laid in my future as a Chicano academic, ended up being thirty-six pages.

But this topic was a way for me to combine my social justice passions with my newfound intellectual passions. I started out by combing the limited research then available on Mexican American school failure and wrote a critique about how the dominant White middle-class cultural and value orientations negatively affected how educators, in stereotypical fashion, viewed Mexican American students. I acknowledged how opportunities for Mexican American and African American students were stifled by a lack of resources and "raw prejudice." Given my heritage, I focused on how the harmful idea of racial integration through assimilation caused Mexican Americans to "surrender our cultural integrity and identity and pass into that which we are not." This included covering how White cultural values permeated public education and the great importance educators placed on cultural assimilation, often resulting in Mexican American children feeling inferior, lacking self-esteem, and having a lower motivation to pursue education.

My paper indicted the powerful forces of cultural conformity in public education, and in society in general, while critiquing what was becoming termed "culturally pejorative" or "cultural deterministic" academic research that ignored these realities. It fit with an approach that liberal and progressive academics began using in the 1960s to reject so-called cultural deficit explanations for why Mexican Americans and other people of color experienced school failure at much higher rates than White students. And the work reflected my growing sense of identity as a Chicano, influenced by Black Power advocates and by other students like me.

My paper was enthusiastically received by my teaching assistant, who shared it with his friend, the chairperson of a newly formed Chicano student group on campus. I gladly gave him permission to do so, wanting others to read it. By 1969, I was also calling myself a "Chicano" instead of the hyphenated term "Mexican-American," which had gained cultural popularity after World War II (my elders' generation, however, still called themselves Mexicans or Mexicanos),

"Chicano" was not a new term, and the change was far more than a change in terminology. Differences of opinion exist about the historical origins of the term, but we know "Chicano" surfaced sometime in the early twentieth century in many Mexican-origin urban barrios and rural colonias in the Southwest, including my barrio in Compton. What matters is that it was an organic, in-group term—chosen by the communities involved rather than non-Mexicans who learned about it in the 1960s. In Mexican-derived communities, it was only used within your circle of family and friends.

At a time in the late 1960s when other college and high school students of color were connecting to the Black, Asian American, and Native American student movements, I was swept up in the emergence of the Chicano/a student movement. Similar identity changes were happening in the feminist and gay/lesbian movements into the 1970s during these years of great change in American society.

Regarding students' tendencies to seek better ways of being in the world, I am reminded of the wise words of farm labor leader César Chávez about becoming known as Chicano. He stated that "[Students] should not be mere imitators. They must learn to think and act for themselves, and be free." The knowledge that came with education and participation in movements of social change allowed me that freedom to gain a healthier identity.

Some Mexican-origin people preferred to use other identifiers: "Latin American," "Spanish American," "Hispano" (mostly in New Mexico), and "American of Mexican descent" were commonly used. Some of these choices clearly were meant to deflect negative associations with the term "Mexican." Although my generation was initially more apt to use "Mexican American" (sometimes hyphenated), it had the challenge of becoming identified with an assimilated cultural identity as an American.

As more and more young people embraced "Chicano/a" as a new politically and culturally infused self-referent, it created tensions among the older generation who rejected this term. That didn't stop its slow impact on social consciousness, as universities across California and the nation increased the small number of students of color in 1967 and 1968, and nascent student organizations took shape. At UCLA and several other Southern California colleges, as well as campuses in the San Francisco Bay Area, Mexican American students formed organizations such as the United Mexican American Students and Mexican American Student Confederation. These fledging student groups began to develop regional conferences for discussing issues experienced on their respective campuses and in their communities. This increased politicization prompted calls for greater organizational unity and for name changes.

By 1969, after various student groups held a conference at the UC Santa Barbara campus, and after the Chicano Youth Liberation Conference met in Denver that same year, organizations that had used "Mexican American" changed their titles to fit the use of "Chicano" by the larger confederation of student organizations that went under the banner of "Movimiento Estudiantil Chicano de Aztlán" (Chicano Student Movement of Aztlán), or MEChA.

As part of this transition, many students (like me) began to claim pride in our Mexican cultural traditions and history. We openly celebrated what made us different from White cultural norms and vehemently opposed the views of some social commentators and academics that our group was being too traditional and culturally backward.

This change in self-identity was hugely uplifting for me. Although I'd known about my Mexican roots, I felt free, for the first time, to celebrate and appreciate with pride the cultural, ethnic, and racial background of being Mexican in America. But part of our newfound Chicano/a identity included emphasizing our *mestizo* roots (of Indigenous people and of European mixed-race origins), particularly early on. A reference to Aztlán—the mostly mythical ancestral northern homeland of the Mexica or Aztec people before they migrated south to establish Tenochtitlán, the current site of Mexico City—was a symbol of our professed Indigeneity. Back in the 1960s there was no such thing as a DNA analysis, but some of us foregrounded our Mexican native background and rejected our Spanish/European connections. There was a disconnect for me, however, because my Indigenous ancestry was Tarascan from Michoacán (the Tarascan empire, the Purépecha people, were enemies of the Aztecs).

Broadly speaking, all Mexican-origin people in the United States and Mexico are the product of over three hundred years of racial amalgamation in Mexico between Spanish colonizers and Native people. We acknowledged our *mestizaje* (mixed-race heritage) while downplaying our Spanish roots. After all, placing our newfound pride in mestizo and Indigenous roots came easier than acknowledging the colonial legacy of Spain in the New World. The Spaniards were the White, European oppressors.

Over time, as I learned more about the history of Central America, its colonial Spanish past, and the making of modern Mexico, the dichotomies I had drawn earlier between all things Spanish and all things Indigenous grew more nuanced. And though at first I rejected the concept of cultural assimilation politically, I realized, eventually, that I was an assimilated person.

The political reorientation of becoming Chicano/a was as powerful as the cultural aspect. The term *Chicanísmo* embodied both. Some people refer to this word as an ideology or a lifestyle, and it surely was so to those of us caught up in the excitement of reshaping our ethnic/racial identity as students. Chicanísmo defined us as members of a larger group of Mexican-origin people in the United States who shared a common history, common culture, and, perhaps, even a common destiny. By 1970, the Chicano/a identity movement gave rise to a renaissance in the arts and humanities that we young Chicanos and Chicanas consumed voraciously.

Nowadays, many would recognize that this term tended to homogenize the Mexican American people and their experiences and to deemphasize the political, cultural, and ethnic/racial identity differences within this diverse population. Regardless, especially as young adults, Chicanísmo allowed for an exploration of the Mexican American experience, past and present. We were equipping ourselves with critical political perspectives and, importantly, a forward-looking mission to become agents of social change and social justice for the betterment of our people. "Self-determination" was a term Chicanos/as often used, as did other students of color who had become newly radicalized by what they learned and by what they observed in society.

As a freer, more aware twenty-year-old, I had a new clarity about my personal identity and my mission in life. Beginning in my senior year at UCLA, this path would open wider while connecting me to the dawning field of ethnic studies and to a greater appreciation for all that my hometown had gone through in recent decades.

TWELVE

A New Lens on Compton

I had spent little time in the city where I'd grown up with a rainbow of friends since graduating from high school in 1966. That changed within five years, when I returned to Compton as a graduate student in American history to do research on my birthplace. This big leap came about when my passion for understanding history emboldened me to seek guidance from some key instructors at UCLA my senior year. Their support helped this son of working-class immigrants with almost no formal education to become the first Mexican American to earn a doctoral degree in U.S. history with a specialization in Chicano history. That early step would ultimately lead me on a path that included building ethnic studies research centers, becoming an expert witness in court cases about underserved communities' voting rights, and helping to establish the foundation for public school students in California to learn about Mexican American history and ethnic studies.

The start of this tale of the transformative power of higher education begins earlier, though. It came about as a result of a new chapter in education when the U.S. government, after being pushed and prodded by racial justice advocates and liberal-minded policymakers in the post–civil rights years of the late 1960s, required colleges and universities to open their doors wider to advancing the education of so-called historically underrepresented minorities. With those higher education gates slightly ajar, a handful of faculty of color and their White colleagues made it possible for a very small group of students of color (like me) to take advantage of college's life-changing opportunities. These changes also paved the way for new courses and areas of research in higher education, including ethnic studies.

I was in the right place and time for all these new developments in higher ed. I was equally fortunate to become intimately involved in this new field alongside its founders, while researching how the first suburb in the nation to be managed by a predominantly Black leadership became an example of the American Dream denied.

———

He paced back and forth at the front of the classroom, inhaling deeply from his cigarette. Smoke wafted from his lips as he prepared to make his next point. A student today would probably make a cell phone call to the campus police to report a violation of university policy. But in 1969, I sat in that room mesmerized by Juan Gómez-Quiñones's lectures.

I had enrolled in the first Chicano history course at a University of California campus in the autumn quarter of 1969. Even if I had known that Juan was still a graduate student then (due to a paucity of faculty who could teach the subject), I wouldn't have passed on the opportunity to learn about the history of my own people. This course unlocked a new world of knowledge for me as I learned about the history of Mexicans in the United States. I wanted more.

For the first time in my undergrad career, I gathered the courage to speak with a teacher during office hours. Juan's office was located in the History Department, and in what students called the "waffle building" for its shape. Ralph Bunche Hall—named after the UCLA alumnus, the amazing diplomat-scholar and the first African American to receive a Noble Peace Prize—sat on the beautifully landscaped northside of campus.

The elevator door on the sixth floor of Bunche Hall opened to a long row of small, ordinary-looking offices. As I approached Juan's office, I noticed the door was slightly ajar. I poked my head in as I knocked on his door with a sweaty hand, nervously shared my name and that I was a student in his course. A no-nonsense kind of guy, Juan gave me a quick glance and then turned his head back to his desk, while asking, "What is it that you need?" Despite my unease, I explained the team-taught course taken the previous quarter on racial attitudes and how I found it to be particularly important. Bringing up my lengthy research paper related to the education of Chicano students, I noted wanting to do more research in Chicano history and that one of his course readings on post–World War II political and community leadership had piqued my interest.

"So, you are interested in leadership," he replied, swiveling in his chair to look at me again before turning toward his desk to continue writing some notes, for what seemed like an hour instead of a minute.

Before I prepped to tiptoe out, he turned back around. "Here are the names and telephone numbers of some older Chicano leaders. Go to East LA and interview some of these *veteranos* (experienced organizers) who formed the first community and civil rights organizations. Go speak with Bert Corona, Tony Rios, and these other leaders and then let me know what they tell you," Juan said. "Thank you, professor," I said as he handed me his notes, "I will be back soon."

The oral history interviews I later conducted with those veteranos were fascinating. They shared detailed stories and perspectives about their work in labor and community organizations far beyond the scant information already known. These interviews introduced me to what social scientists call field research, or oral history for historians. This work became the basis for my interests in graduate school, too, as Juan quietly took me under his wing. Several follow-up meetings later, I became his first undergraduate student advisee, and a year later, his first graduate student advisee, as my future as a Chicano historian was unfolding.

It turned out that Chicano history, as a new field of scholarship, was carved out by Juan at UCLA in the early 1970s, and I got to be there with him from the chaotic beginning. For Juan was juggling a large load of responsibilities.

Born in Parral, Chihuahua, Mexico, in 1940, Juan and his father came to live with his paternal grandmother and grandfather in the East Los Angeles community of Boyle Heights soon after his birth (and his mother's death).

As an only child, he grew up in that barrio but learned Spanish and gained a binational identity from regular visits to family in Parral. He also picked up a strong working-class consciousness and political orientation from his grandfather, a diesel engine mechanic and labor union member.

Educated at parochial schools in East LA, Juan graduated from UCLA with a BA degree in English in 1962. He was admitted to its Latin American studies program next, receiving an MA in history and anthropology two years later. He then entered UCLA's PhD program in Latin American history with a specialization in Mexican history.

I first met Juan after he left for a one-year teaching position in history at San Diego State University, returning my senior year as a lecturer in the History Department. Besides the Chicano history course in which I had enrolled, he was working to complete his doctoral dissertation and serving as chair of a committee (in 1970–71) to develop what became the UCLA Chicano Studies Research Center. Not until several years later, when I began teaching as a new faculty member at Stanford—also without the dissertation completed—did I come to fully appreciate all that Juan had on his plate while I was his first advisee. Moreover, Juan blazed the trail, over five decades, for hundreds of students who followed in his pioneering steps as a Chicano scholar activist.

Besides his academic work, Juan was a student activist who helped found the first Chicano student organization at UCLA and was a key player in the broader Chicano student movement. Juan, who died in 2020 at age eighty, was also among the leaders who drafted *El Plan de Santa Barbara*, a blueprint for addressing issues affecting Chicanos/as in higher education in general. The document laid the groundwork for establishing Chicano studies programs at universities.

Juan played a critical role in my intellectual and academic growth by bringing me into the orbit of his work at the dawn of Chicano studies at UCLA. And, with one other historian on campus whom I also met in 1969, he encouraged me along my career path. In addition to Juan's course, I had enrolled that fall in Norris Hundley's "History of California." Getting used to earning mostly A's by then, especially in history classes, I was disappointed with the B I'd gotten on Hundley's midterm exam. So, I mustered courage again to head to a professor's office hours; this time, I planned to plead for a higher grade, something that in the previous three years would've been unimaginable.

I queued in line behind a few other students standing outside Hundley's office in Bunche Hall. Finally, a woman at a desk in front of a long, loaded bookshelf curled her raised finger in a motion for me to enter. I did so slowly, wide-eyed from the walk involved through a gauntlet of many shelves stuffed with books (I later learned that Hundley edited an important academic journal and had inherited the huge collections from his predecessor in that role).

"Hello there, young man, please sit down," Hundley said with a gesture at a chair in front of his desk, and a broad smile on his kind-looking face. "How are you?" he asked from behind the desk stacked high with manuscripts and books. "I know you are in my California history class, and I hope you are finding it interesting." His course had about ninety students, so I wondered how he recognized me. I replied in confirmation, using a "Yes sir" that quickly brought a grin to his face.

Sensing my nervousness, he guessed that I came from California and asked where from. "Camarillo—are you Mexican American?" This time I simply said, "Yes, my father was born in Mexico," and confirmed that he had immigrated about sixty years earlier.

Norris obviously knew something about Mexican American history. The way in which he helped settle my nerves that morning in his huge, library-like office led me to ditch complaining about my midterm grade—and influenced how I approached teaching and mentoring in the years to come. I instead told him that I really wanted to do well in his course and improve from the midterm. His immediate reply was, "If you get a higher grade on the final exam, I'll give you the benefit of the doubt and assign you that grade." I thanked him, shook hands, and left his office psyched about our conversation and my plans for acing the final exam. As I turned to leave, he smiled again and said, "Come by anytime you want to talk about the course." "What a nice man," I thought while exiting Bunche Hall that afternoon.

I earned an A in Norris's course, and more importantly over time, I earned his faith and trust in me as an emerging historian. Norris became my unofficial co-advisor for the remainder of senior year, and an official co-advisor the following year as I began the doctoral program. Like Juan, the newly tenured professor was a pioneering scholar who saw potential in me as an aspiring historian, shepherding me through graduate school and beyond. They took a gamble on me by recommending me for admission the next year in the university's PhD program in U.S. history.

Born in 1935 to a Catholic family in Houston, Texas, Norris C. Hundley Jr. was the eldest of six children. His father, who was from Louisiana, worked as a pharmacy salesman initially and then in the oil fields near Houston. Norris's mother, a nurse, was a native Texan. Like so many other Americans nationally, Norris Sr. packed his family up from their working-class neighborhood to move to California after the war, pursuing better opportunities in the petroleum industry.

Norris attended elementary school in Alhambra, about eleven miles east of LA city center. By middle school age, he had opted to enroll into a Catholic junior seminary. He decided to leave the seminary at age sixteen, though, and attended San Gabriel High School, where he met Carol Beckquist, the love of his life. His yearning for more education led to attending a nearby community college and later being admitted to Whittier College, about eleven miles from his family home. An excellent student, Norris graduated from there in 1958 and received his PhD in U.S. history at UCLA in 1963. After teaching at the University of Houston for a year, he and his young bride Carol returned to UCLA in 1964 for Norris to accept an appointment as an assistant professor of history.

When I met Norris in fall 1969, he had recently received tenure and was on his way to a thirty-year career at UCLA, including serving as editor of the prestigious *Pacific Historical Review*. He was savvy about the history of Mexican Americans in the Southwest and keenly aware of the legacy of racial segregation and discrimination that people of color faced, and that I was a rare Chicano student on campus. He also knew and worked against segregation's ruinous effects on African Americans in the South. He had traveled with other UCLA faculty to Selma, Alabama, in 1965 to show support for the voting rights of African Americans who contended with enormous White resistance.

I didn't know about his support for racial justice when I first visited Norris's office that warm autumn day in 1969. This partly explained, I suspect, why he was so kind and supportive of my academic interests. I soon learned firsthand about his commitment to advancing opportunities for students of color. I was among his first PhD students, and the first Chicano student he mentored, with several more to follow over the next two decades. I will always be grateful for his mentorship and friendship, which lasted until his passing in 2013 at age seventy-seven.

With Juan's and Norris's encouragement, I applied for and was admitted to the doctoral program at UCLA in fall 1970. I attended summer session to finish my undergraduate major degree requirements; six weeks later, I began graduate school. I got a mixed response from my parents when sharing that I would be in school another five or six years. My humble and quiet father shook his head and responded, "Ay, pobre mijo, por qué?" (Oh, my poor son, why?). "Él quiere ser profesor" (He wants to be a professor), La Jefita interjected supportively. With that, my dad nodded approval, though it was clear he did not understand why I needed this.

The first research seminar I enrolled in brought the opportunity to retrace Compton's recent history. It was a course in the "new" U.S. urban history, one of the subfields of American history blossoming in the early 1970s that aligned with my interests. The "new" part reflected the fact that, for the first time in the historical study of U.S. cities, the topics of race, ethnicity, immigration, working-class people, and women took center stage (as opposed to focusing on elites, politics, institutions, and mostly White men). A new social history was on the cusp of being forged, revealing the stories of people that had mostly been ignored in traditional American history. This approach was often described as history from the bottom up, rather than from the top down.

The history of the United States was being reinterpreted and expanded by my generation of men and women historians; we devoted ourselves to writing about and teaching subjects previously considered less important, or ignored altogether, by most scholars. The developing emphasis in ethnic studies on the critically important issues of race and ethnic group status specifically guided my work.

Compton really needed a historian-in-training to take the time to visit there in autumn 1970. To trace the demographic origins of the barrio in which my parents were among the pioneering families, I had to rely on information included in Compton city directories. That was because U.S. Census data before 1970 did not even bother to count Mexican Americans (the first and only time Mexicans were enumerated as a separate "race" was in the 1930 U.S. Census).

I spent one morning every week for about three months visiting the Compton Public Library and the city's Chamber of Commerce to use their non-circulating city directories and other historical collections.

The Compton Library, a branch of the LA County libraries since 1913, was a small, old Spanish-style stucco building in an area that would soon give way to the wrecking ball and the development of a new county courthouse, police department, and other public structures. It sat just two blocks from the downtown area, to the west of the former Red Car railroad tracks. The Chamber of Commerce building was directly east of downtown next to one of the city's three banks. I spent many hours at both locations, occasionally taking breaks by strolling along Compton Boulevard and its downtown shops, and making a brief visit to my old barrio, located about three-quarters of a mile north of downtown.

The signs of decline were everywhere, though residents' interpretations of the realities varied. "Compton is not the same anymore," the Chamber of Commerce employee lamented, while escorting me to the room where the directories were shelved. "Almost everyone has moved away," he added, "and our beautiful old downtown looks shabby now." That he was now the sole employee in the building suggested that business in the city was in decline. But while I agreed with his statement that Compton had visibly changed, I also understood that this White man's take that "almost everyone" had moved away was code for White Comptonites.

He was right that, even in the five years I'd been away from the city, the demographics of Compton had shifted dramatically. I'd seen the earlier signs of those shifts in my childhood years of the 1950s, when Compton's African American population increased swiftly on the westside (in 1951, 90 percent of Compton's population was White). By the time I attended Walton Junior High in 1960, the city was racially divided between a Black majority on the westside, the segregated White eastside, with the Mexican American barrio in between.

Although in 1950 Blacks made up only 5 percent of Compton's population, they comprised about a third of all residents by 1960. None lived on the eastside at that time. Then came the 1965 uprising in Watts on the northern boundary of Compton. It had taken more than a decade for African Americans to achieve majority status on the westside as I was growing up, but in only a few years Blacks became the eastside majority. The efforts of real estate agents to fight this withered by the late 1960s as Whites abandoned the city in droves. The avalanche of departures on the eastside included nearly all the families of White students who'd attended Dominguez High with me.

By the time I began researching the city in 1971, Blacks accounted for more than 71 percent of all residents, and Mexican Americans, about 13 percent. By 1970, the city's White population was below 10 percent. Their decline was obvious when I walked the few blocks from the Chamber of Commerce building to downtown; the people I saw on Compton Boulevard were mostly Black folks, with a few Mexican American strollers and White store owners. In fact, by 1970, Compton had become the first city west of the Mississippi River to claim a Black majority population.

While some people lamented these changes, prolonged efforts of residents of color had changed the demographics of the city's leadership in a way that mirrored Compton's population changes. This formerly restricted White suburb was also the first in the LA metro area to elect a Black mayor. Finally, after so many years of being entirely shut out of the city and being contained on the westside during the 1950s and early 1960s, Black community leaders proudly claimed to have reached the promised land. Twenty-five years earlier, when Bernice "Mama" Woods and her young family were among the trailblazers buying a home in an all-White Compton neighborhood, she could not have imagined the changes in the city by the early 1970s, when the city had become a municipality mostly run by African Americans.

While Woods had advocated for decades for the education of Black youth, local NAACP leaders such as Maxcy Filer had fought in the late 1950s and early 1960s to breach the color line through wide-ranging "firsts"—the first Black cop, the first Black fireman, the first Black member of the board of education, the first Black city council member, etc. Affectionately called "Mr. Compton" by many community members, Filer worked hard for the betterment of his people. He mobilized voter registration drives in the city in the 1960s and for years hounded White city officials to hire more African Americans. "I started going, about 1954, to the city council meetings at Compton City Hall," he proudly recalled, looking back on the opportunities he helped blaze for Blacks in Compton. "Most times, I was the only Black in there," he remembered, "Then I started going to the planning commission, the personnel commission, all of them . . . and then other Blacks started going." Filer and his NAACP friends "started talking it up," he said, about how "we've got to attend these things, we've got to do this, we've got to do that."

The wins started coming, and by the 1970s, Maxcy Filer was, in many ways, the new face of Compton. In 1963, Filer helped orchestrate the campaign to elect Douglas Dollarhide as the first Black on the city council, and in 1965, Doris Davis became the first African American to be city clerk. Two years later, Dollarhide was part of the Black majority elected to the city council. In 1969, with his righthand man Filer as his campaign manager, and with support from other NAACP members, Dollarhide was elected the first Black mayor of Compton.

Dollarhide's family, like Filer's, had been part of the Second Great Migration of African Americans who came west after World War II. His father, born into slavery in Texas in 1863, moved to Oklahoma, where he and his wife Daisy raised twelve children. Douglas, born in 1923 in a small, rural town east of Norman, Oklahoma, was the youngest. A veteran of General George S. Patton's Third Army in Europe during World War II, Dollarhide had served in the all-Black, segregated transportation unit vital to the success of Patton's military operations in France and Germany.

Like so many tens of thousands of African Americans who headed to California mid-century, Douglas Dollarhide moved with his young wife to LA in search of greater opportunity. They moved into Compton in the late 1950s, where he became a sales manager at a local car dealership. He soon joined the local NAACP and became one of its leaders, a steppingstone to being elected as the first Black city councilman.

Dollarhide's election as mayor in 1969 marked a turn of the "racial table" in Compton. The Black majority, and its leaders, assumed control of the city in every way—from city hall to the police department to staffing in city government jobs and public schools. For so many African Americans in Compton in the early 1970s, it must have seemed like the end of the long, winding search for progress and equality. Black teachers were now teaching their children in a district run by Black administrators. The first Black police chief in a California city, Thomas Cochee, was hired by Dollarhide in 1974.

The question that history has answered is whether Compton, following the White exodus years, could remain a thriving Black suburb in America. From outward appearances during the early decades, perhaps it could. Working-class and lower-middle-class Black families had bought homes in the city during the 1950s and 1960s and had achieved a big chunk of the American Dream. A small but influential group of African American professionals—doctors, lawyers, and businessmen—also called the city home.

Those families included that of Phillipa Johnson, who at age seven had arrived with her parents from Brooklyn, New York (in 1954). Mrs. Johnson was a registered nurse and her husband was an accountant, settling in Compton with bright hopes for the future. Phillipa recalled, nostalgically, those years when the city "seemed really safe. There were sections of Compton that had professional people. Neighbors looked out for each other, [and] you didn't have gangs at that time."

Other residents included well-known professional athletes, such as John Roseboro of the Los Angeles Dodgers baseball team, and world-class track and field stars Charlie Dumas (the 1956 Olympic high jump champion, the first to clear seven feet) and Ulis Williams, nicknamed the "Compton Comet." Williams, a classmate of my brother Max at Compton High, had been a gold medalist in the 1964 Tokyo Olympics and was one of the fastest 400-meter runners in the world in the early 1960s.

However, by the time Phillipa graduated from Compton High in 1965 and attended college, the seeds of the city's decline were sprouting. Below the surface of Black social mobility and political success in the city of about 78,000 people, huge problems loomed that worsened through the 1970s and laid bare the fragility of this suburb, which the media increasingly called a "Black city."

I spotted some of these problems the minute I'd returned and walked along the downtown area in 1971. "For Rent" and "For Lease" signs hung in the windows of several empty retail stores along Compton Boulevard. The Yellow Cab taxi stand next to the old railroad tracks was now gone. The tracks where Beegie, Luli, Popito, and I once placed rocks, to see the Red Car's wheels crush them, were now eerily silent and rusted over. Also gone was the lunch counter café, inside the Compton streetcar passenger waiting station, where I once enjoyed milkshakes while listening to the hum of passing Red Car trains. The streetcars were scrapped in 1963, and the Southern Pacific Railroad stopped using the tracks to haul freight at night in 1965.

I was saddened to see the city of my youth showing signs of neglect and abandonment. Although I could not fully understand all the factors that led to Compton's decline until I returned many years later, for many Black residents of the city in the 1970s and 80s the first sign was the loss of retail businesses in downtown Compton. They spoke to a downward spiral of the city's economy and, most importantly, its tax base. The exodus begun by White residents had been followed by an exodus of White-owned small businesses by the early 1970s. There was no small business class among African Americans to fill the void. By the mid-1970s, the only two remaining national brand stores on Compton Boulevard—J.C. Penney's and J.J. Newberry—had announced their closures, taking away many local jobs.

It didn't take long for Mayor Dollarhide and the new Black political leadership in Compton to realize the uphill battle to keep the city from tailspinning into an abyss. Partly, they dealt with the legacy of earlier Compton leaders' decisions. For instance, in wanting to keep the town a bedroom suburb, earlier leaders had rejected annexing adjacent industrial and manufacturing zones that could have boosted the city's tax base. That resulted after World War II in a heavy reliance on taxes from residential property owners and the relatively small pool of downtown businesses to fund Compton's schools and municipal services. After the devastating earthquake of 1933, when the city depended on municipal tax bonds to rebuild the city's infrastructure, Compton's property taxes had already climbed to the highest among all cities in LA County.

As the city's population mushroomed, Compton's over-dependence on home property taxes couldn't keep pace with the rapid growth of its student population. Nowhere else in California, during the 1940s and 50s, did public school enrollment grow faster than in Compton. The toll on the education system was evident by the 1960s and grew much worse as the tax base plummeted by 1970, by which time the city's budget was bleeding red.

By the time Black students became the majority, the city once known as a stable blue-collar suburb with good schools showed obvious signs of stress. That included increasingly high pupil-to-teacher ratios and larger numbers of poorer kids. Only one other district in LA County spent less per pupil than the Compton school district.

In the wake of most working- and middle-class White families departing Compton by the late 1960s, hundreds of middle-class African Americans and Mexican Americans followed suit. Many of the Black families moved to adjoining suburbs like Carson, which no longer had restrictive real estate covenants and realtors trying to protect the color line. Much lower property taxes awaited them in this newly incorporated city with new housing tracts. Others moved to more distant, newer suburbs in Riverside County or to cities just west of Compton. Those included Inglewood and Hawthorne (which, ironically, had been known in the 1930s as a "sundown" town for having signage warning Blacks to move on before nightfall).

Meanwhile, all the indicators of poverty began to characterize more and more of Compton's neighborhoods, especially on the westside. The city's unemployment rate doubled between 1960 and 1970. There was a growing number of welfare recipients, families headed by single women, and an increasing dropout rate among students. And, for the first time, rates of felony crime placed Compton just behind the much larger cities of LA and Long Beach. To make matters worse, evidence of gang activity had begun emerging among youth.

As crime became the city's single-most pressing issue, its leaders allocated more funding for the Compton Police Department, further eroding scarce resources away from other pressing needs. With increased policing of the city came more issues of police brutality. Mayor Dollarhide and city council members realized that Compton was adrift. To try to shore up the tax base, the mayor requested permission from an LA County commission to annex adjacent unincorporated industrial areas, but the commissioners turned these requests down (some believed, on the basis of Compton's identity as a Black city). Regardless, by the early 1970s, hope had disappeared for outside investment in Compton's economic redevelopment.

After going back to Compton in 1970–71, I had wondered if the city could have evolved differently. The visits and related research as a graduate student gave me a new perspective on Compton, influenced by what I'd been learning about urban racial inequality and social justice. My hope was the city would recover economically and become a model for Black suburban life in America. But this hope, and the aspirations of so many Black residents, continued to fade over time.

THIRTEEN

Uncovering a Hidden Past

Returning to Compton to take a snapshot of its economic and other changes aided my understanding of the complex factors at play in a city with shifting demographics. And the resulting write-up about the history of Compton's barrio, which became my first published article, served as a springboard for deepening my analytical skills as a graduate student. Yet my graduate school days were as much about putting the history of my family and community in a larger context as they were about defining my life as a young man and possible academic.

The historical search was about uncovering the hidden past of Mexican-origin people in the United States. It was a search to understand the long, troubled history of how racial inequality impacted the lives from the distant past to the present. It was a search to see how a "new" history, part of a "new" ethnic studies, could possibly reshape our societal understanding of the past.

At the same time, I was searching for answers about whether a career as a history professor was right for me, and whether work as a historian/educator could provide a platform to advocate for racial equality in and outside of higher education settings. It was a search, on personal as well as professional fronts, for my future. Susan, my partner and soon to be spouse, stayed next to me throughout the uncharted journey while pursuing her own career, supporting me at every turn.

The first year of graduate study turned out to be a whirlwind that included writing two long original research papers. It left me exhausted, especially after starting the graduate program so soon after completing an undergraduate degree. Developing grad school papers required learning to write more critically and succinctly, while posing original historical arguments and using a variety of sources to bolster my claims. This extremely difficult transition to writing like a professional historian was satisfying— well, it was so *after* I finished the papers.

More than a hundred doctoral and master's degree hopefuls had entered UCLA's U.S. history graduate program with me in 1970. Yet by year two, the grueling coursework requirements had reduced the class size dramatically. You had to be thick-skinned to survive. For instance, a paper I wrote in one of my first courses, taught by a visiting faculty member, was returned with the cryptic comment: "You need to learn how to write better." With the help of Juan Gómez-Quiñones and Norris Hundley, I survived as a bruised—but not beaten—first-year grad student.

Norris Hundley saw to it that my future papers would be better by spending many hours applying a sea of red ink while tearing content apart, inside and out. What else should I have expected from the editor of a premier history journal, though my gratitude didn't keep me from complaining about all the red ink involved (which always brought a smile in response). For at least a decade after I left UCLA, Norris continued to edit my articles and book manuscripts. I applied the same diligence in later years to the written work of hundreds of advisees; I, however, wielded a black pen.

Having been bit by the history bug helped sustain me through these trying graduate studies. In addition, working with Juan in the early days of establishing a new field of history was exhilarating and motivating. I felt part of something potentially big, something important. What we would write as historians in the early 1970s would build the foundation for this new area of knowledge. To put it into perspective, at the time I first entered UCLA in 1966, only a few books on Mexican American history even existed in the campus's huge main research library (which housed over a million volumes).

As we acknowledged, there were a few pioneering scholars in the 1930s and 40s who had written about Mexicans in America, activist writers such as Carey McWilliams and Ernesto Galarza, as well as scholars such as George I. Sánchez, Manuel Gamio, and Paul S. Taylor. But our work was inherently different. Our efforts included a general struggle to have Chicano history accepted widely in the discipline of history and in academia in general. With Juan as El Jefe, I helped cultivate this new history that we hoped would take root and, in time, blossom.

The focus of our studies also differed. We dared to envision a new narrative that included and centered, for the first time, Mexican-origin people in the history of the United States. Today that could seem silly, but in the early 1970s, we had to argue the position that understanding the history of Chicanos in the Southwest—the region's largest minority—was fundamental to understanding the history of the West and Southwest and the states within these regions. Not only that, but we had to confront and break the power of the stories many historians had bought into about how Mexican Americans operated in the world. Existing social science research on Mexican Americans held, more often than not, that we as a group were culturally backward and largely unassimilable.

Worse yet, the history of Mexican-origin people had been whitewashed by what Carey McWilliams coined the Spanish "fantasy heritage," a glorification and romanticization of things Spanish rather than Mexican. Sometimes I look back to those early years of forging a new Chicano history and wonder how a population of about 5 million people could be so misunderstood and overlooked in the history of my home state, the region, and the nation. I need only remind myself about how the virus of Jaime Crow infected society in general, including the circles of higher education. We had not only been largely excluded from attending college, but our history had been excluded.

In the early 1970s, Juan and a few other faculty at universities in California and Texas, and a small but determined group of graduate students like me, set out on what became a decades-long effort to recover this lost past and to establish an intellectual and curricular beachhead for the study of the Mexican American experience. You could count on one hand back then the number of Chicano/a faculty committed to developing the field of Chicano history. Like Juan Gómez-Quiñones, they had trained in Latin American history before making the switch to U.S. history. Rodolfo Acuña at California State University, Northridge, who published the first textbook *Occupied America: A History of Chicanos* in 1972, and Carlos E. Cortés (who became a dear friend) at UC Riverside, were among them. So were a few White historians that had trained in Latin American history and helped define Chicano history early on, most notably my good friend David J. Weber at Southern Methodist University.

Our work was cut out for us—in some ways, it was even more of a challenge than what faced the young generation of historians carving out a "new" African American history. That is because an older generation of African American pioneer scholars, some of whom attended historically Black colleges and universities, had formed an important intelligentsia by the early twentieth century. The contributions of legendary Black scholars such as W. E. B. Du Bois, Carter Woodson, and St. Clair Drake were enormously important keystones for foregrounding Black studies in the late 1960s, 70s, and beyond. These scholars were joined by a group of progressive White scholars who wrote about slavery and Reconstruction and the consequences for Black Americans. We Chicanos/as had nothing comparable to HBCUs, and with a few notable exceptions, had been barred entry into higher education until my generation.

With practically no scholarly base to draw on, our challenge was enormous. On the other hand, the new generation of African American and Mexican American historians, like our few counterparts who were developing Asian American and Native American history, had conceptual advantages in at least two important ways. Most of us were part of a new intellectual movement committed to understanding the historical and contemporary status of communities of color from interdisciplinary perspectives. These perspectives included being unabashedly critical of U.S. institutions when appropriate and deemphasizing mainstream concepts that focused on cultural assimilation, integration, and conformity.

We vehemently critiqued the cultural explanations that scholars and other authors had advanced for many decades to explain why racial minorities were poor, why they lived in ghettos and barrios, and why they could not expect to be part of "mainstream" society (aka, White society). This was part of a larger commitment to developing scholarship that would further racial justice and equality for the communities of color of which we were a part. For my generation of new scholars, the different subfields of ethnic studies created avenues to claim ownership of our past and to establish an intellectual voice to influence social thought and social policy. These twin objectives were incredibly lofty, yet we were motivated by a thirst for social justice and for broader inclusivity in academic realms.

Such efforts began more broadly when students and some progressive faculty at San Francisco State University, supported by local community members, blazed the trail for ethnic studies in 1968. After protests and a strike by the Black Student Union and other students of the Third World Liberation Front, the state university's administration agreed to support the development of a College of Ethnic Studies that had departments organized around Black, Asian American, La Raza (Latino), and American Indian studies. Over the next several years, students and faculty at universities across the nation, including UCLA, similarly advocated for and helped establish departments, research centers, and programs of ethnic studies.

In part, students of color of my generation clamored for public and private colleges and universities to provide a curriculum that included issues centered on race and ethnic status so that our learning experiences reflected the lived experiences of our elders and ourselves (as White students had inherently received for generations). We wanted the inspiration that comes from learning from faculty who looked like us, a rarity for students at non-HBCUs. In effect, we sought recognition at historically White institutions of higher education that our histories mattered—that *we* mattered.

With all that was going on, campuswide and in my own intensive start to graduate study, I was feeling burnt out by the end of the academic year. I had luckily received a one-year fellowship from UCLA to cover tuition and fees. It included a small stipend for living expenses, a real godsend. Otherwise, my demanding coursework would have been affected by having to work part-time or serving as a teaching assistant in undergraduate history courses.

Consuming though my academic training was, I enjoyed thinking like a historian and sharpening my powers of observation, on campus and off. I now viewed people and places around me through historical lenses, especially after moving away from the UCLA campus in my senior year as an undergrad.

I had moved to Venice Beach that year, after becoming acquainted with the place while being a volunteer tutor for Mexican American kids at a local elementary school there. It was only ten miles from Westwood Village and UCLA. I found a funky, eclectic, inexpensive place to live, initially in a tiny studio apartment just a few steps away from a beautiful beach.

I decided to remain in Venice Beach before starting graduate school and moved to a slightly larger one-bedroom flat for $110 a month (this community was popular among grad students, with by far the cheapest rents at the time in West Los Angeles). My flat in the early 1970s was in an old building about 200 feet from the waves of the Pacific Ocean. Venice Beach stood out in stark relief to the much more expensive city of Santa Monica next door.

The community where I had tutored the year before was a small, historic Chicano barrio located not too far from the run-down canals of the city. Yes, Venice Beach was designed by its developer in the early 1900s as a beach resort community of LA, complete with navigable canals and a business area whose architecture had been modeled after its namesake Italian city. But after decades of neglect by the city of Los Angeles, the Venice I lived in was called the "Slum by the Beach." The canals that hadn't been filled in or paved over by then were cluttered with litter, and the water, covered in nasty-smelling green slime.

I learned from long-time residents that back in the 1950s beatniks had once flocked to Venice Beach bars and other business establishments where poor bohemian poets and artists gathered. They had been replaced by counterculture hippies, poor graduate students, and thousands of low-income people.

This made the beach community a fascinating racial/ethnic, class, and intergenerational mix of people. The little gem of an apartment I rented on Ozone Court was in an old, neglected 1920s-era fourplex. Tiny, well-worn bungalows and duplex and triplex units lined the walkway on both sides of it. Instead of a street, these charming walkways led neighborhood residents to the beach. Next door to my building was a retirement home for elderly Jews, many of whom were Holocaust survivors, who had made Venice home in the post-war decades because of the low-cost housing. Our Ozone Court walkway ended at Ocean Front Walk where an old hotel, a remnant of the once lively resort town, had become a single-room-occupancy apartment building.

On the first floor at the back of my building was a friendly group of four young hippies who looked like they'd come from central casting for a Hollywood movie—long-haired and barefooted, they were devout vegetarians who always smoked weed. Below my apartment was a friendly, fifty-something couple with midwestern accents.

Susan, who spent lots of time there with me, loved this diversity too. After graduating with honors in psychology from UCLA, she was working as an assistant teacher at Fernald School, the K–12 school affiliated with the university's Department of Psychology for children with learning disabilities.

Susan had decided to apply for graduate study to pursue her social work interests and learned in spring 1971 of her admittance to the University of California, Berkeley's School of Social Welfare (one of the premier schools nationally). Not surprisingly, she was offered a full, two-year fellowship there because of her remarkable undergraduate record and relevant teaching experiences at Fernald School.

When she accepted, we faced the prospect of being apart. But I desperately needed a break from my PhD studies. Although I enjoyed life as a budding academic, I still didn't know if teaching was right for me. So I decided to take a one-year leave of absence from the program. With Juan's and Norris's support, my plan was to go with Susan to Berkeley, teach at a community college, and then return to UCLA the following year.

Naïve about what community college teaching involved, I applied for, and was soon offered, a one-year position at a Bay Area community college. The position required teaching five different courses per semester, one hell of a heavy teaching load for anyone, especially a novice. Plus, the search committee chairperson had mentioned I'd be required to teach an introductory lecture course in European history, for which I had no training.

Juan came to my rescue by finding me a one-year, part-time position teaching Chicano history in the Department of History and the Chicano Studies Department at UC Santa Barbara. Better yet, I didn't have to formally apply for the position. Juan's recommendation was good enough, in part because almost no one else was trained to teach those courses. I also had the option of teaching a summer session course for the Chicano Studies Department before starting part-time in September. Sign me up!

My lecture courses were scheduled on Tuesday and Thursday afternoons, so I devised a plan to live in Berkeley Fridays through Mondays and to hit the highway very early on Tuesday mornings to prepare for class; I'd then drive back Thursday nights. My time on Highway 101: five hours and twenty minutes, making me brag that I knew every damn twist and turn in its pavement. The 70s song, "What You Won't Do for Love," comes to mind when I remember the miles I put on my VW bug that year.

My days in Berkeley were spent writing lecture notes and going to the university library to continue reading in American history in preparation for my return to UCLA the following year. I also discovered a park near our apartment on Berkeley's northside where some good, but tough, pickup basketball games were being played, including by some talented African American guys. Throughout my first year of graduate study at UCLA, I had continued to play full court pickup games at Pauley Pavilion. I wanted to keep up my basketball skills while getting some exercise after a full day of working out the mind.

When I first hit the Berkeley city courts, though, no one wanted a short Chicano dude on their team. That changed shortly after I finally got on the court for some 3-on-3 games. After my team won three straight games, a young Black guy asked me, with a curious look in his eyes, "Where'd you get your game, man?" I mentioned Compton and UCLA, and he shouted out to the others, "Hey fellas, this brother played for UCLA!" The UCLA basketball dynasty was in full glory in the early 1970s, and my affiliation soon meant I never again had to wait to get in a game.

My experience as a visiting lecturer at UC Santa Barbara also paid off. At age twenty-three, I loved teaching and interacting with students. Though I was only two years older than the seniors in my courses, I soaked up being "the professor." The question I had about committing to life as an educator was unequivocally answered.

I also made some good friends, some for life. I had taken over teaching Chicano history at UCSB from Pedro Castillo, a history PhD student who was studying that year with faculty at UCLA. I also became friends with a small cadre of other Chicano graduate students, particularly with Luis Arroyo, a MA degree student who later joined the PhD program to work with Juan Gómez-Quiñones. Luis became part of our small group of Chicano graduate students forging the field of Chicano history with Juan in the early years.

Another big, unintended benefit of the break year was check-ins with my grad school advisors about upcoming academic requirements. During a session with Norris, he pushed me to think about possible topics for a doctoral dissertation, though that final training stage was two years away. He suggested a project on LA's Chicano history until I explained that other graduate students had dissertation projects planned about the eastside. "OK, then, how about Santa Barbara?" Norris shot back. "Maybe," I replied, though I doubted this old Spanish/Mexican city had the same relevance as the mecca for Mexican immigration in the twentieth century. Santa Barbara was a small, tourist-oriented city known for its Spanish Days Fiesta.

On my non-teaching day at UCSB, I ventured to the downtown public library and historical museum to check it out further. I also poked my nose into county and city archives, soon learning that there were many local Spanish-speaking Santa Barbareños who traced their roots to settlers of the Spanish and Mexican eras. Some, staff at the historical museum said, still lived in the old adobe homes built by their ancestors located in what was once the heart of the original pueblo not far from the "mother" of the California missions. Along with this pleasant shock, I learned about a sizable Mexican-immigrant community in the lower eastside of the city, where a barrio existed that dated from the early twentieth century.

I soon realized that Santa Barbara's Spanish/Mexican community had remained less socially and politically marginalized than other Mexican pueblos in California in the wake of statehood and the Americanization of the area after 1850. I reported these findings to Norris and Juan, who gave the green light for the dissertation topic, with plenty of time to collect historical materials in Santa Barbara over several months.

Susan and I continued to live in Berkeley for a second year until she completed her master's degree. Having spent four years together by then, we decided to get married. Her mother Margaret—an incredibly special

woman, whom I loved dearly—made a generous offer about wedding ar-
rangements. She would pay for a traditional wedding or for a small, family-
oriented ceremony, with the remaining money to travel to Europe for the
summer. The travel option was a no-brainer for young people who came of
age during the counterculture era of the late 1960s.

Our small ceremony involved family and a few of Susan's lifelong friends.
I felt really fortunate to become a member of Susan's family and to claim
Andy and Roberta, her siblings, and their families, as in-laws. We wrote our
own vows, stood under a Jewish-style wedding canopy (*chuppah*), and were
married in a non-religious ceremony by a long-haired, progressive Unitar-
ian minister. Once we had exchanged vows and been declared married, we
kissed and, altering an old Jewish custom for good luck, we both stomped
on wine glasses (traditionally, only the groom stomps). To add to the bicultural aspect of the ceremony, as we walked down the aisle to the reception,
the music of a Mexican mariachi band was supposed to play. There was no
music, however—the mariachis didn't show up. Still, we shared one of the
happiest days of our lives with our families before heading overseas for a
ten-week trek across Europe.

Our summer-long travels in 1972 through ten European nations closely
followed a well-known budget travel guide, Arthur Frommer's *Europe on $5
a Day*. It was still unforgettable, though we occasionally spent more than $5
each, to enjoy a room with private bath facilities—a real luxury!

We returned to Berkeley for Susan to complete her master's degree, and I
returned to UCLA's PhD program that fall. For support, I was fortunate to
have received one of the first Ford Foundation Graduate Study Fellowships
for Mexican Americans (the start of my decades-long association with the
foundation and its unprecedented support programs for "underrepresented
minorities" in higher education).

I enrolled in courses with several faculty, mostly reading courses in
preparation for the awe-inspiring, dreaded comprehensive examinations
that graduate students must pass to receive their degree. Like the old Willie
Nelson song, "On the Road Again," I was back to taking Highway 101
again, but this time, I could only visit about once a month for the next fourteen months. That's how deep my nose was into reading about three to four

books per week in U.S. history and in my secondary field of Latin American history. The eight-hour comprehensive written exam in U.S. history and a three-hour oral exam in U.S. and Latin American history would be grueling (with many entering classmates from 1970 not making it through this vision-blurring stage).

By the time Susan received her degree, she had accepted a position in psychiatric social work at Orange County's Department of Mental Health Services and the child psychiatry department of UC Irvine's School of Medicine. We moved back to LA in summer 1973 and rented a small home in Long Beach, about halfway between her Orange County job and UCLA.

Spending my days reading for the "comps" that summer was intensive but pleasurable. I sometimes spent hours at the beach, just three blocks away, reading the books and articles assigned to me by my faculty committee. At day's end, I'd shoot hoops in the back alley where we lived, with the odd combination causing a neighbor to finally ask what I did for a living. I don't think she understood my explanation.

No sooner had I passed the comps early in the fall than I returned to researching the history of Santa Barbara for my dissertation. Although doing this type of research and writing a book-length study is typically a solitary experience, I was fortunate to join a small group of Chicano/a studies grad students and faculty in Southern California to help form the National Association of Chicano Social Scientists in 1973. Later named the National Association for Chicana and Chicano Studies (NACCS), we held lively annual conferences to share our research. At the local level, we also formed NACCS chapters, or "focos," where smaller groups of mostly graduate students met to discuss readings and to share our dissertation work. I established many lifelong friendships at these interdisciplinary foco gatherings held at UCLA's Chicano Studies Research Center, and I came to appreciate the interdisciplinary perspectives NACCS involvement provided.

Meanwhile, the transition from researching to writing a doctoral dissertation in the fall came somewhat easier for me. By then, I had already published two articles and, with Pedro Castillo from UC Santa Barbara, had co-edited a book on Chicano social bandits (historical figures such as Joaquín Murrieta and Tiburcio Vásquez). I had quickly and seamlessly developed three draft chapters of the dissertation in about four months when I started receiving calls and follow-up letters to apply for faculty positions in Chicano history at UC Santa Cruz and at UC Santa Barbara.

My writing came to a halt while preparing for job interviews and campus visits in 1974. My journey in search of a deeper understanding of my people's history, which had begun as a junior at UCLA, had now brought me to the threshold of a major next step. As a twenty-five-year-old, I didn't know the path would take an even more unexpected turn and be life changing.

FOURTEEN

Affirmative Action Baby

In November 1973, I received an unexpected call while at my desk at home, struggling to begin a new draft chapter of my dissertation. I picked up the kitchen phone to be introduced to John Wirth, who said he was a faculty member in the History Department of Stanford University. "The History Department is planning to hire an assistant professor in Chicano history," Wirth said, then cut to the chase. "We want to know if you are interested."

After a silent moment of shock, adrenaline began surging through my veins, and I uttered an enthusiastic "Yes." We had a brief conversation about meeting up soon, but my mind had trouble getting beyond the words "Are you interested in the position?" I hung up and returned to my desk to process this.

"Man," I said to myself out loud, "Stanford invited me to apply for a faculty position."

Exhilaration and anxiety fought for attention. I had heard about and actively applied to the other Chicano history positions at University of California campuses as a no-brainer because of my interests. But this was an unadvertised position at Stanford—one of the leading universities in the nation, if not the world.

After a quick call to Susan to share the exciting news, my elation turned to anxiety. I was only twenty-five years old! I had only three first draft chapters of my dissertation written! Was I ready for a regular faculty position, especially at an elite private university?

Trying to rebuild confidence, I thought, "Yeah, I'm ready. I can do this."

The American Historical Association's annual conference was to meet in San Francisco the following month, so Wirth invited me to campus to meet with him. Given my previous attempts to join Stanford, my confidence waned off and on. I was over the fact that the university's basketball coach had written in 1966 that my grades weren't good enough to qualify for undergraduate admission, as UCLA had been great to me. But then, three years later, when Susan and I drove to San Francisco for an anti-war rally, I had a dispiriting visit with the chair of the History Department about graduate study.

This was my first glimpse of the campus—known as the "Farm" because the founders (Leland and Jane Stanford) had built the university on their Palo Alto horse ranch. The campus, nestled amidst beautiful undeveloped foothills and surrounded by lush open spaces and trees everywhere, still had wide-open pastures where horses grazed.

Walking across campus, it struck me how different it looked from UCLA's modern architecture or any other university I'd seen; here, the old buildings shared a warm, uniform look of sandstone block walls and red tile roofs. The History Department remained in its original location on a corner of Stanford's historic Main Quadrangle.

Entering it didn't help my nervousness, as it oozed history. Although the hallway wainscoting showed obvious signs of decades of wear, it was made from majestic redwood. The ornate handrails on the stairwells were of wrought iron, making the interior look even less inviting. "Has this old, musty place been renovated since the 1890s when it was constructed?" I wondered.

Professor George Knoles, a U.S. historian, chaired the department. I knocked on his door, and the kindly, bald old gentleman invited me in for what proved to be a very brief visit. I explained my interests in the history of American racial attitudes and Chicano history.

"What kind of history?" he asked.

I didn't know if he was hard of hearing and hadn't heard me, or if he didn't know what "Chicano" meant.

"The history of Mexicans Americans," I added for the old fellow, who I later learned was just a few years from retirement.

Knoles wasted no time responding. "Oh," he said, "Young man, you should stay at UCLA unless you want to study nineteenth-century slavery with Carl Degler."

I was pissed off by his comments, and for the second time, didn't apply to Stanford. No problem, I later rationalized, as UCLA had opened up academic opportunities for me that were far better, anyway.

Yet the sting still lingered. On a chilly December day, five years later, John Wirth invited me to Stanford for an "informal" lunch. I wondered if I would end up facing a "three strikes and you're out" situation. As I left cold, fog-shrouded San Francisco and headed to Palo Alto, I thought I'd dressed appropriately for the expected lunch at an upscale restaurant—a turtleneck sweater (fashionable in the 70s) was under my thick corduroy sport coat. Wirth instructed me to meet at the Center for Latin American Studies, which he directed, and which was in a quaint old building just off main campus. My arrival was warmly greeted by John who was dressed very casually. We were joined by a young colleague, Jim Leckie, who I learned was the second Chicano faculty hired at Stanford a few years earlier. Jim was wearing jeans, a wrinkled short-sleeve shirt, and sandals. "Is this how faculty dress at Stanford for an academic interview?" I thought, as we walked to John's car.

"We're going to lunch at Zott's," John said, before driving us there. "I think you'll like this place."

Instead of heading toward downtown Palo Alto, we took a road in the opposite direction, finally turning onto a small, winding road headed toward the foothills. For a guy used to Compton and Los Angeles highways, the back roads of the Stanford campus looked more like a drive through Yosemite National Park.

After ten minutes, we reached an old, run-down hamburger and beer joint, with a large gravel parking lot. It looked like a hangout for the Hells Angels more than a restaurant, including the long table, carved with names and messages from hundreds of customers over many years. As I soon learned, Zott's started as a mid-nineteenth-century Mexican *cantina*. John clearly wanted this young faculty prospect to feel comfortable with Jim's presence and all, as we ate hamburgers, drank beer, and chatted. Despite the fact that I was melting under my turtleneck sweater and corduroy jacket, it worked.

When I got invited back in late January for a "formal" interview, a young Chicano lecturer in the Department of Spanish and Portuguese picked me up at the airport. Being a member of the search committee, he offered up the encouragement that "This position is yours, if you want it," as we drove to the university.

I was relieved by this rare share. After weighing offers I'd received from Santa Cruz and Santa Barbara, I made the easy, and best, decision of accepting Stanford's offer.

I may have had two earlier strikes against me there, but now I hit a home run. Well, not quite, but at least I was on first base at the Farm.

I am an "affirmative action baby," and I am damn proud to say so! I state that half-jokingly, for affirmative action has been continually under fire, though few may know about its origin as a key tool for opening opportunities for people of color and women.

I first heard the term in 1991 when reading *Reflections of an Affirmative Action Baby*, a book by Stephen L. Carter, a professor at Yale Law School. Carter was among the first Black intellectuals to write about the political and social fallout of affirmative action policies after they became hot button issues in America's emerging culture wars beginning in the 1970s. Since the last third of the twentieth century, affirmative action has been a lightning rod to agitate political conservatives.

Unfair racial preferences! Reverse discrimination! Promotion of the unqualified over the qualified! Perversion of the idea of meritocracy! Violation of White Americans' constitutional rights! Political pundits and conservative politicians have made such denouncements against anything and everything that affirmative action represented. The policies of the federal government and how they were implemented at the local or state levels were questioned time and time again in courts of law and the court of public opinion.

The culture war battles have distorted the intent and meaning of the original policies. Plain and simple, these policies were about creating opportunity. The policies were aimed at helping Americans who for many generations had been denied access to jobs simply because of their race/color, ethnic/ national origin, and gender. Affirmative action policies were intended, first and foremost, to address the historical inequities faced by millions of African Americans. Latinos, as the nation's second largest minority, were also included. Despite the first policies focusing on employment, admission of "underrepresented minorities" to colleges and universities soon followed.

Broadly speaking, most people associate the origins of affirmative action policies with President Lyndon B. Johnson. Yet the essence of affirmative action, as policy, first surfaced in employment-related policies in 1941. African American leaders planned a massive march on Washington to protest discrimination against Blacks in defense industry jobs. With war clouds on the horizon, President Franklin D. Roosevelt bowed to pressure and signed an executive order to establish the Fair Employment Practices Committee (FEPC). Though the term "affirmative action" was not included in the language of the FEPC, FDR's executive order set a precedent for future presidents who strengthened and expanded anti-discriminatory policies during the 1950s, 1960s, and after.

An executive order issued by President Eisenhower in 1953 added language about non-discrimination in federal contracts, but the term "affirmative action" was not explicitly included in policies until the administration of President John F. Kennedy. His executive order in 1961 stated that employers must "take affirmative action to ensure that applicants are employed and that employees are treated [fairly] during employment without regard to their race, creed, color, or national origin."

The Johnson administration and his Great Society domestic agenda rightfully included women as a protected class of Americans under these policies. What most Americans don't know is that Richard Nixon's Republican-led White House deserves credit, though, for expanding affirmative action policies in the early 1970s.

The ideas behind the policies were premised on decades of civil rights advocacy by African Americans and other people of color and their White allies. They argued that generations of exclusion from opportunities heavily blunted the chance of success for most people of color, making the American Dream out of reach for most. Access to jobs and education served as hallmarks of that dream, resulting in policymakers focusing action on these two issues as a way to foster equal opportunity.

Fittingly, sports metaphors are commonly used by advocates. "Level the playing field," some say, or others say, "Let us start at the starting line, instead of always behind it." As a former athlete, a more colorful sports analogy often crosses my lips about affirmative action: "Just give us a damn chance to get into the game."

What is too radical or unreasonable about that ask—to simply be given a chance to achieve some measure of racial and gender equality? I like to think of the affirmative actions I benefited from as a student in the late 1960s, and the targeted hiring that happened in the 1970s, as tools for prying open doors of opportunity just a bit so some of us could even get into the game. These policies were modest and incomplete solutions to massive, longstanding national problems of systemic racial inequality.

As a historian of race, I knew how unequal economic and educational opportunities had stunted the progress of poor White Americans and people of color. I also understood how male dominance and gender privilege had thwarted women's chances for far too long. Affirmative action was an effort to chip away at racial and gender inequality, and I felt honored to benefit from affirmative action at overwhelmingly White universities.

Stanford had recently launched its first efforts to racially diversify the faculty when I came on board in 1975. I had just turned twenty-seven when Susan and I moved to the San Francisco Bay Area to start our new lives there. Though I was a rather naïve new professor while teaching my first courses in spring 1975, there was no doubt that the stakes were extremely high for me at this prestigious, private university, or that I had to deliver on the promise that colleagues saw in me as a young historian.

"I have to succeed," I promised myself, "I must succeed." But this promise wasn't just for me and my family. It extended to my whole community and for others who would follow the mostly unpaved trail into higher education. Many affirmative action recipients like me turned around and helped bring others onto the playing field.

I also had a little angel I imagined sitting on my shoulder, regularly reminding me that "I'm at the faculty starting line at Stanford, and I'm going to run this race as fast as I can." Actually, I was still a little behind the starting line, given my hiring as an "acting" assistant professor. Not until I finished my dissertation and received a formal PhD would I be considered a "real" assistant professor.

This requirement meant that, after finishing my first quarter of teaching at Stanford, I entered the summer grind of completing the remaining thesis chapters and then revising the whole manuscript for submission to UCLA. I had Norris's and Juan's input to help, and I vowed not to return to campus in September as an "actor." My single-minded focus partly stemmed from the fear brought on by having Chicano colleagues who hadn't completed their degrees in a reasonable amount of time. They lost similar appointments. No way was I going to follow suit.

Part of making it at Stanford also involved planting roots—not only on campus but in our first home—using money that Susan's job mostly allowed as a small down payment. Perhaps it was destiny leading us to buy a home in a small, mostly White neighborhood known as University Heights in west Menlo Park. Or, perhaps, we were steered there by our realtor.

Referring to a home we viewed instead in the east Menlo Park area, the cordial, middle-aged real estate agent had said, "In this other neighborhood, your neighbor might be a waitress in a 24-hour diner or a policeman."

"But you will see on the way to the Stanford Avenue home, in an area known as the 'Carmel' of Menlo Park," the White woman added, "there are much nicer homes." Setting aside her class hang-ups, it appealed to us that many residents in the small University Heights neighborhood worked at the university, and it was within walking distance for me.

That said, the rustic, little mint-green home we could afford was a super fixer upper. Once called an "artist's chalet," I could imagine lots of sweat equity to bring out the potential of this run-down little home with a vaulted, wood beam ceiling in the living room and an upstairs landing that'd be a perfect location for a study.

Susan was not so easily swayed. "The brick fireplace is painted pink and magenta!" she gasped as we entered the home. Then there was the living room carpeting that "looks like an old-fashioned movie theater lobby!" She sighed as we moved to the next room—the kitchen—with red and black low-pile carpet. Man, the homeowner must've been colorblind. The high-light, though, was a paper towel dispenser fastened to the kitchen ceiling.

Despite the unique interior design features of this home, Susan and I purchased the property for a whopping $45,000, accepting the "as is" provision of the sale; but we paid a steep price when, a week after move-in, the sewer line backed up. An old pipe had collapsed, and our bank account nearly did so too, to pay for the installation of a new sewer line while Susan looked for a job to restart her social work career. To reduce the financial damage that included barely affording home mortgage payments early on, I spent a weekend digging a huge trench in our front yard for the new line.

It didn't take long for me to realize I was an oddity in the University Heights area at the time (in 1970, Menlo Park was 80 percent White). When a neighbor driving past our home spotted me digging the sewer line trench, he stopped and shouted out. "How much do you charge for yard work?"

"This is my home," I said, drenched in sweat with my shirt off during the heat of the day. "Oh, sorry," he said, as he pulled away quickly, with an embarrassed look on his face. Presumably, he'd assumed me to be a Mexican laborer working in the neighborhood, whereas in Menlo Park's Belle Haven neighborhood, located on the eastside across the Bay Shore Freeway, residents were overwhelmingly people of color.

The color contrast was also evident in the History Department. I was the only Mexican American on faculty there, alongside an African American historian hired in 1969, who was its first tenured person of color (Kennell Jackson) and another UCLA alum, Clay Carson. Clay had arrived at Stanford six months before me and focused on modern African American history. I looked up to Clay as one of the few advanced grad students of color in UCLA's PhD program, and our relationship had another connection—he was the brother-in-law of Susan's best friend since childhood. In effect, Clay and I brought "U.S. race studies" to the History Department (Clay went on to found Stanford's Martin Luther King, Jr., Research and Education Institute).

There wasn't much time for me to dwell on my newfound status at Stanford, as I had to become a hermit to complete my dissertation that summer. With Susan as the main editor and speed typist, we labored day and night to finish and submit the thesis to my committee at UCLA so they could sign off on it. My degree was officially conferred in December, and I received a huge ($500!) bonus from Stanford for doing so. A party with both of our families present put an exclamation point on completing the PhD degree. With pride in his muted voice following throat cancer surgery, my father said, "Gracias a Dios, hijo." Benjamín was happy his youngest son was finally finished with school! So was I.

Some good news shortly followed. The History Department at UCLA nominated my dissertation for a prestigious national award for the best doctoral dissertation in the United States on a topic of American history. I didn't win the Allan Nevins Prize but was thrilled to have UCLA faculty recognize my research and writing as being worthy.

Being on campus in 1975 also brought the excitement of teaching such smart undergraduates. Chicano/a students, in particular, were thrilled to have another Chicano professor on hand, especially one offering courses on the Mexican American experience. From 1970 to 1975, Stanford hired its first few Chicano faculty, all male, and, with one exception, all assistant or acting assistant professors. For example, the other Chicano studies specialist was novelist Arturo Islas, who had received his doctoral degree at Stanford and taught courses on Chicano literature in the English Department. We became good friends and allies alongside the other new Chicano hires.

To acquaint myself as a newcomer to Stanford's huge campus, I occasionally strolled from the Main Quadrangle to other areas. I was struck not only by the beautiful architecture and many undergraduate dormitories (over 90 precent of undergrads lived on campus), but the many wide-open spaces. Those included a pristine golf course and a lake, stunning amenities for someone who'd only experienced public schools.

To traverse the immense acreage—Stanford is spatially the largest university nationally, and second largest globally—students relied on thousands of bicycles. I quickly learned to avoid walking anywhere during the ten minutes between class sessions from fear of being run over. Near misses and minor collisions were common.

It was a far cry from the bicycle unfriendly hills of Westwood in so many ways. However, at least the students of color here, though small in number, were visible.

Had I been a Stanford undergraduate ten years earlier, the chances of meeting a Chicano/a or Black student would have been remote. In 1962, for example, seven Black students were in the freshman class, including Sandra

Drake, who became a colleague in the English Department soon after I joined the Farm.

"Stanford was a very insular world, a western, California white world," she recalled not long ago in a *Stanford Magazine* article, "that seemed to be made up of valedictorians from every high school in the state." "At Roble [a student residence hall]," she added, "it felt like there were 199 blonde giants and me. It was culture shock." Although she attributed no malice to the Stanford classmate who came up to her one day and announced, "I've never talked to a Negro," the comment reflected the student body composition before affirmative action made inroads in the late 1960s.

Roger Clay served on the university's board of trustees and an advisory board for a teaching and research center I helped found in 1996. A dedicated public interest attorney from Pasadena, he was also a Black member of the freshman class of 1962 and had similarly isolating experiences to my early days at UCLA. "I didn't expect a lot of Black people to be at Stanford," he recalled, "but I expected a few. Several weeks would go by," he said, "when I didn't see a[nother] Black person on campus."

Roger's experience was mirrored by Frank Sotomayor, who had even fewer Chicano/a students beside him when he arrived in 1966. Frank grew up in a Tucson, Arizona, barrio, and was admitted to the MA program in the Department of Communication after completing an undergraduate degree at the University of Arizona. Just two or three Mexican American students were part of each entering freshman class during the 1950s and early 1960s, only increasing to around fifteen by 1968.

"I enjoyed my courses and meeting classmates from across the country," Frank wrote in a recently published book about Chicanos at Stanford (*The Dawning of Diversity: How Chicanos Helped Change Stanford University*), but "I felt a cultural loneliness, not only from being away from home but also from not knowing or even seeing another Mexican American on campus." His sense of isolation from other Chicanos changed some after attending a Catholic religious service on campus and meeting Luis Nogales, a first-year law student, and Luis's roommate, Frank Ponce, a student in the MA program in English.

Their conversations soon turned to the few minority students on campus, and in particular, an article in the student newspaper, the *Stanford Daily*, in which Mexican Americans were not even mentioned. With a fourth Chicano undergraduate, they did a little research on the Spanish surnames included in the student directory and wrote a letter to the dean of undergraduate admissions asking for an explanation.

The numbers they had recorded confirmed their informal observations. "We tallied 36 such students, both undergraduates and graduate students, and rounded the total up to 40," Frank Sotomayor wrote. "Out of a student population of 11,311, that amounted to only one-third of 1 percent."

As a future journalist, Frank wrote a professional letter to then-dean of undergraduate admissions, Rixford K. Synder, which stated, "We are anxious to see that the invaluable opportunities Stanford has to offer are made more accessible to students of all minority groups." The May 9, 1967, letter went on to state: "We feel that these students can make significant contributions to the academic community and—perhaps more importantly—they can take from Stanford an educational experience that will be beneficial to their own groups and to society in general." The punch line followed: "We believe that if Stanford is to fulfill its role in developing leadership among Mexican Americans, it will need to improve its methods of attracting qualified students from our ethnic group."

Though Rixford agreed to meet with the group, Frank's eloquent, diplomatic letter fell on deaf ears. Frank's writing skills eventually landed him a job at the *Los Angeles Times*, where his accomplishments include helping win the Pulitzer Prize Gold Medal for Public Service in 1984.

With the rise of governmental interest in affirmative action-related matters, though, data collection became required the next year by higher education campuses regarding how many "underrepresented" or "targeted" minority students they'd admitted. It spoke volumes about the invisibility of students of color at Stanford. From data submitted in 1968 to the U.S. Department of Health, Education, and Welfare, Stanford's undergraduate student body was about 95 percent White.

The near absence of Black and Chicano/a students at Stanford began to change after 1968, as it did at other colleges and universities, thanks to affirmative action policies. They were ground zero in what became, over time, a profound shift in undergraduate admissions.

Structural changes on campus were partly in response to the flashpoint brought about by the assassination of Martin Luther King Jr. in spring 1968. I hadn't been on campus long before I heard about the infamous "Taking the Mic" incident. The university administration had held a forum to honor the slain civil rights leader. A group of Black Student Union leaders unexpectedly walked on stage, took the microphone from the university provost, and announced a list of demands, including admission of more Black students.

The university responded with a study that included recommendations for "special consideration" for admission of more Black, Mexican American, and Native American students if they met "basic requirements of academic excellence and personal achievement." This was the start of Stanford's affirmative action in undergraduate admissions, which caused Black and Chicano/a student numbers to begin to increase slowly in 1969.

By the time I arrived six years later, Stanford had joined most universities in also grappling with how to incorporate more people of color within the ranks of its faculty and staff. This question of racial diversity and inclusivity soon became a huge part of my volunteer work on committees at the university.

That focus was one of the things pulling on my time as a new assistant professor. In this position, I quickly learned the meaning of the phrase "publish or perish." If you wanted to achieve the job security that tenure provided to higher ed professors, the message was clear from day one: "You better not waste any time getting your work published."

Yet, as remains true today of faculty from underrepresented groups, your rarity also adds to student expectations on your time. The challenge as a new faculty member was striking a balance between making progress on my scholarship while being equally committed to teaching courses to and assisting undergraduate and graduate students.

I was soon overwhelmed by the many students who enrolled in my courses and sought me out as informal and formal advisor. During my first full year of teaching in 1975–76, about half of all Chicano students at Stanford enrolled in my lecture courses and seminars. There were roughly 350 Mexican American undergraduate students on campus that year, comprising about 6 percent of the student body. An equal percentage of African Americans was present then, and perhaps the percentage of Asian Americans was about 8 to 10 percent (that undergraduate data wasn't reported at Stanford until 1982). Native American students represented less than 1 percent.

Many of the Mexican-origin students appeared likely to need as much inspiration and guidance as I could muster at the time. Nearly all the Chicano/a students I came to know well during my initial years at Stanford were the first in their working-class families to attend college. Most received financial aid. Stanford's "need-blind" admissions policy made it possible for any student to attend the university who was admitted, regardless of the steep tuition. This impressive undergraduate financial aid policy was a godsend to so many students and families.

As part of student outreach, Susan and I routinely attended dinners at which I gave talks afterward in the relatively new Casa Zapata (the Chicano ethnic theme dorm named after the famous Mexican revolutionary). During the first decade of increased enrollment of students of color, some students requested, and the university established, such theme residences as the cultural and social hub for those who may be struggling to adjust to life on a predominantly White campus.

The Office of Residential Education had long used theme dorms at Stanford to promote extracurricular educational and cultural programs in a variety of areas. For example, some dorms already had been established with academic themes, such as American studies, or were organized around European foreign languages. Students wishing to participate in these programs had priority, but other students lived in these dorms as well. Four ethnic theme dorms began in the 1970s and were populated based on a policy of restricting the number of students from any one group to no more than 50 percent to facilitate intergroup interactions. This was also intended to prevent what some feared would be residential ghettoization or self-segregation of students of color.

Assisting with the important extracurricular and social/cultural programming in these ethnic theme dorms were resident fellows (often faculty, but sometimes a senior staff member). Resident fellows lived in apartments or cottages at the student residences and served as a resource, an "informal" mentor, and a watchful eye.

I thoroughly enjoyed visiting with students at Casa Zapata or the other theme dorms and giving talks after dinner. It gave me a chance to see the students outside of classes and meet those who hadn't enrolled in my courses.

One talk focused on the 1943 Los Angeles Zoot Suit Riots and became an annual fixture in Casa Zapata's residential education programming for nearly three decades. Although most students, it seemed to me, enjoyed my visits to their dormitory, not all were grateful early on. My first presentation to a small group of Zapata House students was about my research, and it evoked a less than flattering response.

"That was really boring," a Chicana student at Casa Zapata shared, with brutal candor.

"I'm glad you liked it," I replied facetiously, about the talk about my first book project that I had been invited to give by Arturo Pacheco, Casa Zapata's resident fellow. The pre-med student who thought I was boring was probably right, as I was a novice then at presenting informal history talks to undergrads in general. I improved with time and continued to enjoy visits with students whenever possible, vicariously getting a little dose of the student dorm life that I'd missed out on as an undergraduate.

The faculty visits were key to supporting a Chicano presence on campus, with only a few of us there in the 1970s. Despite our youth, my Chicano faculty friends and I fully understood what was at stake, both for us professionally and for the well-being of Mexican American students at Stanford. We didn't discuss it per se, but we were an experiment, both on campus and in the larger society. People like us, first gen brown-skinned working-class Chicanas and Chicanos, had never before had the opportunity, as a group, to teach at a university. It was new, it was special. Sometimes it was a little frightening. The future was unknown, but somehow, someway, we were determined to make this experiment successful.

We were all in our twenties and thirties, and we were inexperienced. Yet we were committed to being available to increasingly diverse students on campus and to serving on multiple university committees, typically as the lone minority representative. We also had our eyes wide open, knowing we had to buckle down and publish articles and books to stay at Stanford much longer. As for me, I knew that publishing one of the first books in the "new" field of Chicano history was critically important for my future, and for this field of study to gain traction at Stanford and beyond.

FIFTEEN

Opening the Higher Ed Door Wider

"You have to work twice as hard to get half as far."

These words of James Gibbs Jr., the first tenured African American professor at Stanford, were the best mantra for professionals of color like me, during my first years there. Like Gibbs who came on board in 1966, I was working twice as hard as most peers, though I was too busy to think about it much.

Along with the amazing position of being at such a great university came enormous responsibility to make the most of opportunities, for the larger betterment of Mexican Americans and for people of color. I first needed to overcome my youth and inexperience and learn the ropes as a new professor, in order to take advantage of the efforts of Jim Gibbs and others who helped open the door for me. Although I never told him this, I often thought about Jim as a great role model for my career in general. A Harvard-trained, good-looking man in his mid-forties, I met Gibbs, the dean of undergraduate studies, shortly after coming to Stanford.

Jim was a highly respected citizen of the Stanford community, an award-winning teacher, and a leader in his department and field of anthropology. In my estimation, Jim was superman. I had initially been impressed and heartened by his position. Even more impressive: he helped found the Department of African and African American Studies in 1968 (the first of its kind at a private university) and mentored many first-generation African American students at Stanford.

How on earth did Jim Gibbs achieve all this in his first decade on the Farm? I came to believe in and adopt his "work twice as hard" approach. And I was mentored by him, alongside many other young minority faculty members trying to find their place at the university.

I learned the details of his successful blueprint over time, which he summed up regarding mentoring junior colleagues in a 2011 oral history interview, long after his retirement: "Keeping the right balance between their teaching and research and community activities" was the key, he said. But "for minority faculty in particular, myself included," he added, "there was always the tendency to want to work to make the university a better place."

For me and other faculty of color, making Stanford a better place meant carving out, for the first time in the history of this great university, a place for minority folk. Though the number of students of color had topped 10 percent when combining Blacks and Chicanos by the mid- 1970s, faculty of color were scarce.

There were comrades in arms that I discovered in time for this work—many women and White male colleagues who shared the objective of diversifying the campus. Most were young, socially conscious, newly hired faculty who had also been deeply influenced by social movements of the 1960s. Many were also among the first generation of scholars devoted to establishing new fields of study in their disciplines.

Despite the camaraderie this provided, I still had a steep learning curve to navigate the complex university, learn to juggle multiple responsibilities, and secure tenure in a six-year time frame. My situation wasn't helped by not being very good, initially, at saying no to the many, many requests that came my way.

Through phone calls and more formal invitations sent via a memorandum, I was asked to serve on many committees, advisory boards, and the like. Within a few years, I served on the faculty advisory committee of the Chicano Fellows Program (the quasi-Chicano studies program), the Urban Studies Program, and the newly established Center for Research on Women.

And I was a faculty advisor for a program that supported innovative, social justice-oriented undergraduate student research.

I always said yes. Late-night work, weekends without breaks, and less leisure time with Susan was the price. I did so early on from believing the projects were all important—and because it was gratifying to be in high demand. But this drain on time, though very difficult, was okay with both of us until babies came along later.

As one of only a handful of Chicano/a faculty at Stanford into the 1980s, I served, at some point, on every Chicano-related committee. For instance, there was the Chicano Community Concilio (council), a group of students, staff, and faculty that helped plan educational and cultural activities for students; it was especially important because it proposed the creation of El Centro Chicano, the Chicano/Latino student cultural center established in 1978.

Even in my own department I served on several committees, and I was called to chair an inaugural faculty affirmative action committee; but as an assistant professor, I had no clout whatsoever. It wasn't until I'd made my way further up the faculty ranks that I learned much more direct ways to successfully prod for more positive responses.

I was treading water, but at least I didn't drown. Other men and women of color who came to teach at Stanford, and other faculty friends in higher education, experienced a terrible toll on their lives. Susan and I were deeply troubled when some friends divorced because their relationship broke apart on the competing rocks of home and work priorities. We were scared when others were denied tenure and packed up their children and belongings to leave California without job prospects. Others left the university before their tenure alarm clocks rang for fear of rejection—sometimes they left academia altogether. Worse yet were the few cases of friends whose careers faltered when health declined.

Despite the many demands, I never lost sight of striving to keep a happy home and the "do or die" consideration to keep research and publication a priority. I had been doing all the committee work, teaching a full load of courses, and other responsibilities, but I needed devoted time to turn my doctoral dissertation into a book (as expected for most humanities and social science faculty at research universities). The solution came when the

National Endowment for the Humanities Research Fellowship program and the National Chicano Council on Higher Education/Ford Foundation Fellowship program provided funding to complete research to write my first book.

This help came at a perfect time. Like most universities, Stanford only offered assistant professors three-year appointments; if you successfully passed muster, you were then reappointed. By the end of the initial appointment, a departmental faculty committee evaluated tangible progress made on your research and writing, plus evidence that you were at least a "good" teacher. To not pass this first evaluation with flying colors signaled that your consideration for tenure, in less than three more years, was in jeopardy.

No way was I going to jinx the evaluation, regardless of commitments to committee work (euphemistically called "university service"), teaching, and mentoring. The fellowship funding allowed me to take a leave of absence for an entire academic year to finish the research and complete my book manuscript.

I needed a publisher as well—a well-respected, or better yet, prestigious one. The stakes were enormously high because Stanford's tenure bar was too. Jim Gibb's informal mentoring became invaluable, as was support and advice from a few senior White colleagues in the History Department. They were all world-class historians and leaders in their fields who took me under their wings.

These "gentleman scholars" had been on campus twenty-plus years, and they and their wives welcomed Susan and me into their homes. With me being their first Latino colleague, I think they consciously reached out to make me feel more comfortable and included. Sometimes, though, I think they primarily liked me because they enjoyed Susan's company even more.

These scholars from more genteel times sometimes offered informal mentoring and advocacy. For example, the chair of the department initially had wanted me to teach two lecture courses my first quarter on campus. "Johnny" Johnson, one of the most respected Latin American historians of his generation, stepped up and convinced the chair to make it easier for a new faculty member by having me teach small group courses instead. Don Fehrenbacher, a Pulitzer Prize–winning author, offered sage advice on publication strategies and suggested to the department chair that more research dollars be allocated to support research on my book project (after other universities started inquiring about my joining their faculty).

Then there were Gordon and Louise Wright, two of the most genuine, lovely people we had the pleasure of knowing. Gordon was a quiet man, and the premier historian of France in the United States. He was a kind and gentle soul with a liberal social compass. Louise was a wonderfully energetic and friendly conversationalist who routinely hosted dinner parties at their home on campus. She was also an early activist advocating for university-supported campus childcare, which Susan and I benefited from tremendously in the years ahead.

Sometimes even casual conversations with these colleagues had huge payoffs. Louis "Lou" Spitz, a world renown Renaissance historian, and I crossed paths one sunny afternoon in the courtyard outside the history building. "How is the writing coming on the book?" he asked. It was a timely question, with my continuing appointment as an assistant professor under initial departmental review.

"I completed the manuscript," I replied with big grin on my face, "and now I'm looking for a publisher."

Lou quickly shared that his editor from Harvard University Press would be on campus the next week. "I'll ask him to schedule a meeting with you." That meeting led to the publication of my first book with Harvard's press, a big boost to my tenure prospects.

Early on, I could not have imagined following in the casual mentoring footsteps of these historians. But my sentiments changed after realizing the power of their softer style of networking that built bonds of mutual trust and respect. The social graces and kindness of these gentlemen scholars and their spouses were qualities Susan and I wanted to emulate "when we grew up."

———

"We have to wait until I finish my book," I said to Susan, as we started to talk in the late 70s about having children. She was enjoying success in her career as a school social worker, so her nod in agreement came with a "But when will that be?"

I knew I had to give birth to my first baby beforehand—my book. To not publish it by 1981, the year of my tenure evaluation, would mean I was dead meat. I would be looking for work at another university.

That knowledge didn't mean I ever really felt the great fear that gripped many colleagues when it came to gaining tenure. Was it confidence? Partly. Was it because I am generally a calm person? Partly. I was lucky to have an incredibly supportive spouse. Was it because I had good mentoring and was laser focused, when need be? Sure thing. All of these helped me envision being on the other side of the tenure gauntlet, with the security gained at Stanford allowing me to more fully carry out the things that were most important in my career and life.

I had a passion. I was on a mission: to establish a toehold for a new field of scholarship and teaching—Chicano history and ethnic studies. I never lost sight that I was among the few of my generation—as a Mexican American, as a person of color—to be granted the amazing opportunity of working at a university that was prestigious and that served as a model for the direction of other higher education institutions.

While a love for what you are doing can be an overwhelming, all-consuming power, mine was not that kind of passion. It was way more subtle, but a passion welded firmly into my character and professional mission. I didn't know where this mission would lead me, but I knew that if I could succeed at a place like Stanford, I could make something with my life and career that would create opportunities for others who followed. I knew in my heart and mind, and from experiences I'd gained in youth, that opportunity can change your chances in life, especially for those whose choices have been blunted by racial and economic inequalities beyond their control. I also knew, personally and as a historian of the Mexican American experience, that social and institutional change is an intergenerational project. I was at Stanford because the generation before me, and the one before them, sacrificed and struggled to open doors that had been mostly closed to them.

Deepening my resolve—and my mission—happened after some momentous life events. One was when Benjamín T. Camarillo, my father, died in 1978, about six months before our first son, Jeffrey Benjamín, came into the world. My father had been living on borrowed time from a diagnosis with throat cancer at age seventy-two. Smoking most of his life finally caught up with him. He had surgery to remove his larynx, and though his voice was then gone, he had a few good years left before the cancer returned and killed him at seventy-six.

I am so truly grateful that I'd recorded his oral history—his voice—a year before that surgery when I was a first-year grad student at UCLA. Benjamín had been a mere child when he immigrated to the United States and had taught me the lesson of hard work as he struggled to make the most of his life and to build us a better future along the way.

He succeeded within the limits of his opportunities and the norms of society, regularly reminding me that "Educación es muy importante, hijo." For a man who didn't spend a single day in a classroom, he sure got it. My educación at UCLA was where I first learned that history could have a powerful influence on the way we think and behave. The death of my father made me more conscious about intergenerational change and the power of opportunity through education.

My book served as an educational outreach vehicle as part of my mission. Published within a year of my father's death, *Chicanos in a Changing Society* was dedicated to Benjamín and Rose, a labor of love dedicated to people I loved. And the book, subtitled *From Mexican Pueblos to American Barrios in Santa Barbara and Southern California, 1848–1930,* was the first of its kind in the "new" approach to Chicano history by one of the "new" field's historians. It was a big deal that Harvard University Press published it, and that it came out well before the so-called tenure clock chimed for me.

Books have a way of legitimizing new areas of study, so in that sense, the publication was also part of a watershed moment. Soon after its publication, I was invited by UC Berkeley's Department of Ethnic Studies to join two of their own faculty with similar new works in an event to showcase our books. The department held a forum in which about 700 students and some faculty packed into a large lecture hall. Sharing the stage with me were Ronald Takaki (considered one of the fathers of ethnic studies) and Mario Barrera, a friend I'd known when he was previously at UC Irvine. The Berkeley forum gave notice that ethnic studies had *arrived,* and it was here to stay.

Just as importantly, books have a way of legitimizing people's lived experiences, especially for those whose histories have been obscured, or worse yet, forgotten. The highlight of publishing for me was feedback received from some old-timers who came to a book signing event in Santa Barbara.

"Muchísimas gracias, profesor," said a smiling, gray-haired man, with deep wrinkles in his brown face, immediately after my book talk in 1980. Tears welled in his eyes as he held the kind of prideful gaze that my father would have, and he shook my hand. "Mil gracias para su libro, gracias para la historia de nuestra gente" (Thank you very much for your book, thank you for the history of our people). This *viejito*, this old Mexican man who had lived in Santa Barbara for most of his life, thanked me for writing about his community, his history. Other folks, young and old, from the local Mexican American community offered similar comments at the event, sponsored by colleagues in the Chicano Studies Department at UC Santa Barbara.

To top that off, I had a wonderful, vivid dream soon after returning home from these book outreach events. My subconscious mind one night transported me back to the late nineteenth century, where I walked through the historic pueblo of Santa Barbara. Small adobe homes, more than a century old and worn down from use over generations, lay scattered along the winding dirt path. I recognized in the dream that this was the first segregated Mexican barrio in a historic California town that had already become majority White.

In my dream, I saw a group of men, women, and children in front of their adobe house, warming themselves over an open firepit. They were speaking Spanish as I approached. One of the men, an older fellow, stood up and stared into my eyes.

"Todo lo que dices, mijo, es verdad" (All that you've said, my son, is true), he said. He sat down again. I nodded in silence and walked away, content that the history I'd written about Mexican Americans in the Santa Barbara area was accurate and appreciated by the people.

As I became a more seasoned teacher and historian, I better appreciated how understanding history can transform lives and help institutions change in positive ways. It certainly continued to do so for me.

A peculiar, fascinating thing happened as I matured as a historian. Sometimes when I write about historical events, an almost indescribable feeling sweeps over me. The "good" stories of individual or group success, accomplishment, and progress over adversity bring me elation and happiness. Though momentary, the feeling is real. With painful, difficult, and hurtful stories, a heavy weight hits my heart for a while.

The latter was true while writing a lecture about Japanese American internment during World War II and reading some first-person accounts. Sorrow struck me full force, and I had to stop writing for a few minutes because of the anguish. Tears came when I thought about the kids, the entire families who had been hauled off to concentration camps in horrible, remote locations simply because they were Japanese. This pain soon mixed with an anger, almost a rage, as I thought more about the injustices heaped on these patriotic Americans, most of whom were U.S. citizens. In reflecting on the Japanese American friends I had at Walton Junior High in Compton, I realized how clueless I'd been then about what their parents and grandparents had experienced.

Early in my years at Stanford, I learned to channel these visceral feelings of anger and frustration in constructive ways, such as advocating for affirmative action, especially in matters of faculty hiring. When I came on board in 1975, for example, there were only about eight other Chicano faculty at the university (all assistant professors without tenure, except one). We constantly strategized to find ways to increase our small numbers, gathering at least once a month in meetings scheduled by Cecilia Burciaga, assistant to the university's president for Chicano affairs. Cecilia routinely spoke with school deans and department chairs across the university on our behalf. Two or more of us reached out repeatedly to these and other campus academic leaders (not a woman among them at the time). We dutifully followed their suggestions and did our homework: identify new PhDs, compile names, gather resumes of prospective candidates, and submit them for review. The feedback was almost always the same: they weren't "Stanford material" (a euphemism for less than qualified), they weren't ready, or they weren't a "good match for our faculty." We did this over and over again, usually to no avail. We were always pissed off from these types of responses, but we didn't relent.

As the newest addition to the Chicano faculty in 1975, I was introduced immediately to the discussions about affirmative action hires and the frustrations so common within our small group. We were all affirmative action hires, so we cared deeply about this university initiative. There were a few successes, but many more failures and disappointments. We decided to focus our efforts in areas of greatest need. The law school was one of our priorities. The first Black and first woman professor had been hired just a few years earlier in the law school, so we thought the timing was good for suggesting the first Chicano professor. We found a potential candidate we believed was exceptional. We submitted his resume and met with the faculty colleague in charge of the school's faculty appointments committee. He said something to the effect of, "Maybe in a few years someone will come along who we will consider, but not this candidate." It took lots of self-restraint to hold back expletives after hearing such responses, but they flowed from our mouths when we met to debrief. So many times, we all agreed, our arguments to promote diversity through affirmative action appointments fell on deaf ears.

Lo and behold, however, a year later we learned that the candidate we had suggested to the law school was approved. We were shocked and elated. This newest Chicano professor, Miguel Méndez, had a distinguished thirty-year career at Stanford and was a key part of our Chicano/a faculty group for decades.

I learned an important lesson from this example, one that I put into my toolbox and used throughout my career, especially years later in my final leadership position at Stanford as special assistant to the provost for faculty diversity to help appoint faculty of color across the university. It was also a lesson learned from studying history and the actions of people committed to social change. Persistence and advocacy, combined with compelling arguments and passion, are some of the ingredients in a recipe to promote change. Turning frustration into productive action doesn't always work, but when it does, it fuels the passion.

Some might say this is a passion of a bleeding-heart liberal. Others might claim I am too close to my subjects and too intimately tied to the history I study. Maybe so. I'd like to think that my attachments to historical issues and advocacy for change sharpen my resolve to understand the past as a historian and make me a more passionate teacher. I'd like to think they make me a better person and a better citizen.

At the core, my passions are about fairness, equity, and justice. A commitment to these principles drew me into dealing with many issues in the decades ahead, especially once my roots were more firmly planted after receiving tenure.

Being reviewed for tenure at any university is a long, byzantine process. If you are denied after six or seven years, your faculty appointment is effectively terminated. You have one year to prep to move on. With being granted tenure, you are guaranteed lifelong employment, which can seem antiquated and strange to outsiders. They are right. What other occupation besides being a justice on the U.S. Supreme Court provides employment security for the rest of one's career? It is what it is, however, and to succeed at a university, you must secure tenure.

The tick of my "tenure clock" wasn't too horrible before my review in academic year 1981–82. I had confidence that I could jump this barrier based on the circumstances that had lined up in my corner. I had some good fortune that also turned my way.

In January 1979—well ahead of schedule—I had completed the final editing of my book manuscript for Harvard University Press. Susan and I rejoiced knowing that my book baby would be born a few months after our first real baby. She was six months pregnant with our first son, and we were thrilled. I set the manuscript on our fireplace mantle one Monday night, readying it for mailing the next day.

I was feeling great the next chilly morning after sending off the big package with my manuscript. The next time I saw the content, later in the year, it would be as a beautifully bound hardcover book. My good feelings ended abruptly late that morning when I received a frantic call from a neighbor that our home was ablaze and that she'd just called 911 for us. I rushed home to find our home still smoldering as the firemen were mopping up. The entire front part of our home was destroyed, and most of the other rooms—including the almost-finished room additions and personal belongings—were smoke damaged.

The firemen told us the blaze originated in our old furnace, located no more than three feet from where I had placed my book manuscript the night before. The book gods must have been looking out for my welfare, because my manuscript could have been a pile of ashes. After a few nights in a motel, I found us a home to rent nearby. Six months later our home was rebuilt, and we proudly moved back in with our four-month-old baby boy, Jeffrey Benjamín.

My book was published in late 1979, almost a full year before my tenure decision was scheduled. The gap allowed time for some buzz to generate about my work, which didn't hurt. Over the next several months, the *Los Angeles Times* and other California newspapers lauded the work in reviews. Even more important professionally, the first reviews of the book in historical journals were overwhelmingly positive. I was invited to many universities to give "book talks" as I soaked up the accolades from colleagues and students. Things were looking hopeful for tenure.

Some administrative changes also provided a surprising boost of confidence before the formal review, while allowing me to help further campus diversity goals. The appointment of Donald Kennedy as the new provost of Stanford in 1979 presented the Chicano faculty with a new opportunity to voice our many concerns. A highly respected member of the faculty and former chair of the Biology Department, Kennedy had returned to campus from Washington, DC, where he had served as commissioner of the federal Food and Drug Administration during the second half of the Carter presidency. Within a year after Kennedy was appointed provost, he became the next president of the university following the resignation of longtime Stanford president Richard Lyman.

The Chicano faculty had a very fruitful meeting with Kennedy shortly after he was named provost. We aired our many grievances about the small number of Chicano faculty (only eleven us at Stanford in 1979, and all male). We noted the frustration of being repeatedly rebuffed by department chairs after approaching them with hiring concerns about potential Chicano faculty. We also raised issues with Kennedy about increasing the number of Chicano/a undergraduate and graduate students and staff. He seemed genuinely interested in our concerns and vowed to help, and he voiced an open-door policy whenever we wished to speak with him again.

My initial respect for Don Kennedy grew rapidly. Soon after the release of my book, El Centro Chicano, the newly established student cultural activities center on campus, held a book publication celebration packed mostly with students. He was among the few faculty and staff present, despite an incredibly busy schedule as provost. I was impressed by this public statement of support for Chicanos/as at Stanford.

In addition, Kennedy (who would soon move up to being president) met early on as provost with a group of Chicano/a students. Their grievances echoed one of our key complaints voiced earlier: the small number of Mexican American professors. The students also complained about how few Chicano studies-related courses were offered in any given year (only four of us taught them). To my surprise, soon after the meeting, one of the students shared with me a comment Kennedy had made. The students had raised their concerns about a Chicano faculty member who'd just left Stanford for fear of being denied tenure. The students were worried that other assistant professors, including me, might do the same (though three of our group had achieved tenure in recent years).

"I am sure Al will receive tenure," Kennedy told the students, "and if he doesn't, the department and deans will hear from me." I was shocked about Kennedy's reported comments. Provosts usually don't say such things. But Don was not content with the status quo, acting based on his instincts and experiences to change the university in important ways.

Moreover, when the Chicano faculty came up with a plan to move the needle forward in Chicano studies and faculty hiring at Stanford, Don immediately agreed.

"Let's do it!" he said to us up-front. Wow, again, I was shocked. The proposal was to establish a research center to facilitate faculty and student research and training in Chicano studies. A few public universities had developed such centers, including UCLA, but not a single private, elite university had yet done so. In a way, this was our first test of the new provost's true willingness to support what would become an important institutional anchor for Chicano studies research.

As I was leaving the meeting alongside Jerry Porras, a dear friend and professor of organizational behavior in the Graduate School of Business, he turned to Don and asked why he so willingly agreed. The provost, who was trained as a neurobiologist, looked at me and said, "Al's book. If this is the type of work the center will promote, then Stanford should support it."

My jaw was about ready to drop, but I managed to smile instead. The provost actually had read my book! Although his career focus had been far removed from ethnic studies, Don was an activist scholar whose career experiences meant he appreciated the value of new, interdisciplinary studies in higher education. He was also committed to institutional change.

He and other colleagues had founded the program in Human Biology in the early 1970s. This innovative interdisciplinary teaching program for undergraduates was hugely popular by decade's end because it equipped students with multiple perspectives and knowledge to understand the many factors that shape human health and welfare in modern society.

Universities typically move very slowly and deliberately when developing new programs and centers. But that wasn't true under Kennedy's watch. Within nine months of our first meeting about a Chicano studies research center, Kennedy had put in motion all the pieces to launch the new Stanford Center for Chicano Research (SCCR). Guess who was asked to serve as director, despite only being at Stanford for four years? I knew I was up to this huge challenge and opportunity when offered it. But there was a big problem—I was still an untenured assistant professor in early 1980 when the center was established. Focusing the needed attention on it without having the security of tenure could be a deadly career combination.

Kennedy was named the eighth president of Stanford in 1980 and had appointed a co-founder of the Human Biology program, psychologist Albert Hastorf, as his provost. I raised my concern with Don about directing a new research center as an untenured assistant professor whose review wasn't scheduled until fall 1981. He asked me to meet with Hastorf.

"Well, young man," Al Hastorf said, "I agree with you about not taking on the position as director without tenure. Let me speak with Peter Stansky to see if we can accelerate the tenure process." Peter was the chair of the History Department. Early tenure reviews for faculty were uncommon and not recommended because university leaders don't like to create precedents that other assistant professors might wish to follow.

Peter Stansky had been a strong supporter of my work, and he consented to the provost's request that my tenure review start earlier, though he did not form a tenure review committee right away, given the quick notice. By the time I assumed directorship of SCCR, my tenure review was well underway, and all the markers looked positive. My work in support of building Chicano studies at Stanford and beyond could proceed.

At age thirty-three, I was likely the youngest faculty member ever to be named to direct a research center, but I was eager to hold my first academic leadership position at Stanford. Soon after I took up my position, I received tenure. I had no way of knowing where this work would take me, but it was an exciting time for me, my Chicano faculty colleagues, and for our students. The door to Stanford, and to higher education in general, was opening some more, and it was now our generation's responsibility to help open it even wider.

SIXTEEN

Building Families

"Welcome to the Stanford family," an older history colleague quipped, shortly after I received tenure. I certainly knew what he meant, and I was grateful to be more than an untenured sojourner. It took some adjusting to accept those references though, which in my earliest years at the university had come across as really elitist. But as I came to know the campus community better as an insider, and especially after Susan and I started our own family, I began to appreciate more what it meant.

The happiest days of my life were the births of our children. Jeff was the first in 1979, and Greg came along three years later. Our daughter Lauren was born in 1988. They are wonderful and talented, and they are the loves of our lives.

Creating a happy, functional, and cohesive family unit, personally or otherwise, I came to learn is founded on many essential building blocks. Abundant, unconditional love serves as the centerpiece of the foundation. Susan and I had been lucky to have experienced this type of love growing up, so it was easier to give others the same. A reciprocity, respect, and partnership you build with your spouse/partner in sharing and juggling family responsibilities is equally important. And, as our children matured, we tried to figure out ways to share important values and behaviors such as empathy, compassion, fairness, and integrity—by example rather than by giving lectures.

As I was learning to be a parent in the 1980s, I was doing the same as an academic leader at Stanford and beyond. Besides using some of the same ingredients for building a strong, caring, and cooperative nuclear family, I tapped into what my elders in Compton had taught me about how support from others, especially in times of need, strengthens connections between individuals and fosters community cohesion.

Building institutions within an institution like a university requires similar thinking. I made some mistakes as an academic leader on campus as well—and learned from those errors. I realized early on, for example, that asserting unilateral authority in decision making can be viewed as ego-tripping, and that, when possible, it works better to consult and build consensus around important issues. The huge amount of time I poured into my "Stanford family" brought rewards that compensated for the growing pains.

Stanford, when I became tenured, was struggling to find ways to fully incorporate its newest members—people of color. To give credit where credit is due, the university's earlier diversity-related efforts had increased the number of undergraduate students of color. In 1980 they now accounted for over 20 percent of the freshman class (about 350 of 1,560 first-year students), a huge upswing from ten years earlier.

I had more opportunities, both in and outside of the classroom, to get close to and hear about the concerns of being minority members of the Stanford family from hundreds of African American, Chicano/a, and Native American undergraduate students into the early 1980s. In part, I was not long removed from my undergraduate experience at UCLA and could still identify with their circumstances. And they identified with me.

In addition to courses in Chicano history that were natural conduits to meet hundreds of Chicano/a students over two decades on the Farm, I had dorm-related and other opportunities to build special bonds with students from other backgrounds, likely gaining entry to communities of undergraduate students of color in ways other faculty missed out on.

Besides being among the Chicano faculty regularly invited to give talks and attend cultural events at Casa Zapata (sometimes with my family in tow), I also interacted with students at El Centro Chicano, the cultural center on campus. The resident faculty fellows and student staff (resident assistants) at Zapata were especially key to cultivating a caring environment for students. "It's my home away from home," a student once mentioned to me. "It is my Stanford familia."

Not long after I arrived on campus, some Zapata residents who'd heard that I'd played basketball at UCLA recruited me to play on the dorm's intramural team. And I was soon drafted to quarterback Zapata's intramural flag football team.

"Los Casuals" (the Casual Ones) they cleverly called themselves. The students, mostly from Los Angeles, gave me a nickname: "El Camino Al," taken from the main street that borders the university, El Camino Real (the historic route that linked the Spanish/Mexican missions in California). My intramural football career and the chance to finally be a QB lasted only one season before Susan urged me to hang up my jersey. I usually came home after games limping and banged up. But I continued to play intramural basketball for several years.

My involvement with intramural basketball came thanks to one of my undergraduate Chicano advisees. Mike knew I'd played with Los Casuals the previous year and asked me to join his team, which turned out to be exclusively Native American students.

I hadn't yet taught or met any Indigenous students at Stanford before then. Before 1970, the number of Native students on campus could've been counted on two hands; that year, about twenty-five students were admitted. They soon began to organize the Stanford American Indian Organization (SAIO).

Many struggled to adjust to a campus culture far removed from their lived experiences, with the SAIO actively advocating to make a home for them at Stanford. Over time, the successes included convincing Stanford to rid itself of its "Indian" mascot—stereotypical to the core, and one of the most demeaning features of campus life for many Native students. The university abandoned the mascot in 1972. Like other organizations of students of color, SAIO called for establishing an American Indian Cultural Center, which opened one year before my arrival on campus.

From my undergraduate and graduate coursework at UCLA in U.S. western history, I knew about the diversity of tribal societies, the long, troubled past of broken treaties, and the tragic stories of forced relocation of Native peoples to reservations in the nineteenth century. I'd also read about the efforts of the so-called Indian boarding schools of the U.S. Bureau of Indian Affairs that had ripped Native kids from reservations and sought to "Americanize" them by stripping away their tribal languages and cultures. And, as a student of American urban history, I knew about the efforts of the federal government, beginning in the 1950s, to relocate Indigenous people from their reservations to cities, yet another attempt to detribalize and acculturate them.

As I came to know the Native students on the intramural basketball team, I learned just how diverse their experiences were geographically and otherwise. They came from unique places and perspectives. At least two hailed from tribal reservations in the Southwest while others were from various cities and towns in the American West. One, Albert, was an Alaskan Native from Anchorage. Most seemed rather shy around me at first, but as we became teammates, they loosened up around "The Professor," yet another nickname.

My connection to African American students in the late 1970s came about after a Black student in my course on U.S. urban history learned of my Compton origins. He invited me to dinner at his dorm, Ujamaa House, the African American theme residence that was suggested to the university in 1968 soon after the "Take the Mic" demonstration. In 1974, this ethnic theme dorm moved to its current location and two years later was named Ujamaa, a Swahili term for familyhood or extended family.

Nestled within the beautiful Lagunita Court residence complex, Ujamaa consists of a quaint, Mediterranean-style dorm built in the 1930s. I was immediately impressed by the sense of community among the residents, who had many cultural and extracurricular educational programs. Mirroring Casa Zapata for Chicano/a students, I learned from students that "Uj," as many called it, also felt like a home away from home, reinforcing important aspects of Black culture they associated with their family and neighborhoods. For others, it exposed them, for the first time, to lessons in African American history and culture. It also provided a place of comfort for many in an institution where being seen as minority was a daily experience.

"I don't have to be 'on' at Uj," an African American resident said to me several years later, when I asked why she'd opted to live in that dorm for the three of the four years she attended Stanford. I knew immediately what she meant.

Being "on" is code for being on alert, particularly as a Black person among Whites. It is a common experience among underrepresented people of color in predominantly White settings, and something I experienced as a student at UCLA and later as a faculty member. The "on" switch is activated when, as a person of color, you perceive that you are being watched and evaluated by Whites. This feeling of being observed as "the minority" can be exhausting, especially when young and in an unfamiliar setting with few others who look like them.

For many residents at Ujamaa, Casa Zapata, Okada House (the Asian American theme dorm), and at Muwekma-Tah-Ruk (the "house of the people" in the language of the Ohlone), these spaces allowed them to turn off the "on" switch for a while, to take a break from learning to cope. The ethnic cultural centers also functioned as such havens.

At such spaces, and with Stanford's increasing commitment to diversifying its student body, more students from different ethnic/racial and socioeconomic backgrounds were interacting with one another. Sometimes the interactions were wonderfully positive and even inspirational to observe.

I was witness to some of that beauty when I began to see undergraduate student life at Stanford from a personal perspective. The director of the Office of Residential Education called me to ask if Susan and I would consider becoming resident fellows (RFs) in one of the new undergraduate student dormitories in a large complex the university planned to open in 1982. We were intrigued by the opportunity. It also had a financial incentive because after having our second child, we were considering either moving to a larger home or adding onto our little Stanford Avenue house. Renting out that home for two years while living on campus would certainly give us additional needed cash for either option.

We signed on as RFs at Murray House, one of three small "independent" dorms that housed fifty-eight undergraduates. It was a non-themed dorm with sophomore to senior students. Located on the far westside of campus at a former horse pasture near the historic Stanford Barn, Murray House provided a wonderful temporary home setting.

One of the core ideas behind residential education is to provide undergraduates with connections to faculty outside of class. Faculty and staff who serve as RFs in most dormitories work with a group of student staff as part of that engagement, while coordinating educational and extracurricular programs for residents. RFs also broadly oversee the policies of the Office Residential Education and residents' welfare.

Serving as RF exposed me to a broader swath of undergraduate students. It was also an opportunity for Susan to work closely with Stanford students. Murray House was an attractive, three-story structure, and our RF cottage was a small but cozy two-bedroom, one-bath apartment semi-detached from the main dormitory. Our two little boys had a nice backyard to play in, and Jeff, from age four to five, had the run of the entire place for two years. We loved it.

"Jeff, it's time to come back to the apartment," I frequently announced on the dorm's intercom system because he was always playing with students in the hallway, upstairs or in the lounge. "He's upstairs," a student would reply into the intercom, "We'll send him right down." Sometimes a group of students would stay to chat with us when done escorting him back to our apartment.

Meanwhile, our baby Greg was the center of attention for many students, especially those missing younger siblings at home. By the time he was one, we usually placed Greg in his playpen with lots of toy balls in the middle of the dining room during meals. When he wasn't being fussed over by the students who wanted to hold him, the Murrayans loved playing catch with him.

In year two at Murray House, Greg, now a toddler, would call to the students "guck" (he couldn't yet say "catch") a signal he wanted to play ball. Practically every meal we would hear students saying, "Guck it, Grego" (his nickname at the time), "Guck it," as he stood waiting at the edge of the playpen to catch the ball. Many years later, several of these Murray House students joked that Greg wouldn't have been a wide receiver on the Stanford football team and, later, in the NFL if not for them.

It was special for me to see the diversity of students in our small Stanford dorm seemingly getting along well together. They studied together. They socialized together. They sat together at meals. Some became dear friends to each other. A few became spouses.

Our Murray House experiences led to some wonderful friendships. Marty, one of our dearest friends for forty years, was our Murray House staff resident assistant. And those residents who connected as "older siblings" with our two little boys became part of our extended Murray House family (many of whom are now close to sixty years old). We still enjoy close connections. I also had the pleasure of teaching some of their sons and daughters during my last years on faculty.

Although the students at Murray House mirrored the ethnic and racial diversity of the undergraduate student body in general, I knew of lingering problems some students of color encountered at the university. Members of the Chicano/a student community occasionally shared disturbing stories of being pulled into uncomfortable conversations by other students.

"Are you at Stanford because of affirmative action?"

"Do you ever feel guilty that you were admitted to Stanford and took someone's place who was probably more qualified?"

"You are the first Hispanic I've ever met. You speak English really well!"

"What is it like to be from a family of poor farmworkers?"

I didn't hear these stories often, but when I did, I knew they badly punctured the recipient's confidence. Some of these questions and comments were naïve, and I'd like to think, not meant to hurt. Some were downright ignorant or callous and deeply offensive. Whether done intentionally or not, they still caused damage.

Despite knowing that the university's commitment to increasing the ethnic and racial diversity among undergraduates was working, I didn't realize, at the time, the depth of harm caused by these episodes of what we now call "racial microaggressions." They were part of larger issues simmering just below the surface for many students of color—issues that I would eventually strive to solve.

———

How do you juggle multiple responsibilities at work and home? Determining what matters most in your life and setting your priorities so those things don't get overlooked sure helps. That's why, after securing tenure at Stanford and starting a family with Susan, I set my sights on three broad priorities.

First and foremost, I wanted to be the best father I could be to our children. My dad loved us and provided for us, but he never played with us and was distant in most respects. I wanted to be the opposite kind of dad for our children.

Next, my goals as historian and educator simply sharpened once my career at Stanford was secure. I sought to advance and expand the field of Mexican American history, Chicano studies, and ethnic studies at Stanford—and beyond, if possible. Finally, I wanted to open as many doors of opportunity as I could for young people.

The guideposts for me as an emerging educational leader were clear. I benefited from a growing understanding of how social and institutional change happens, and learned more every year about how a university functions. That helped broadly in being ready to launch a new research center at Stanford that I hoped would make a difference in promoting Chicano studies.

Yet I was naïve in 1980 about many aspects of directing the new Stanford Center for Chicano Research (SCCR). As a young professor, I had no experience hiring staff nor working with human resource experts. A budget spreadsheet was foreign to me. And I had never written an annual report for an academic unit, besides knowing squat about fundraising.

Learning how to raise money was a huge part of my learning curve, and my expanding cultural experiences as a scholar. Although the university provided funds for staff positions and the center's basic operations, I had to raise funds to support SCCR's research and other programs.

I spent much of my first year making hires for an associate director and other administrative staff and developing plans for programming. The second year, a staff member at Stanford's Office of Development gave me a hit list of possible private and corporate foundations to target for fundraising. Most were in the Big Apple, so I scheduled my first visit to the metropolis.

As suggested, I initially sent a letter of introduction to foundation program officers and, in some cases, to the CEOs of corporations. A Stanford affiliation, I learned quickly, can get you in the door to share a synopsis that would help make my case for funding Chicano-related research projects. But my initial excitement was often dashed after in-person meetings.

"What is a Chi-cay-no, anyway?" the CEO of Revlon, the cosmetics company, asked me immediately after I sat down in his office. He had apparently never heard the word. Even after explaining it, I could plainly see during the very brief meeting that any follow-up request for funding was futile. I still wonder how Revlon was included on my target list.

I walked a good portion of Manhattan over two days visiting various foundation offices, as I was becoming more familiar with this city of towering skyscrapers, concrete, steel, and asphalt. The program officers at the Rockefeller Foundation and the Carnegie Corporation were also only mildly interested, despite Stanford ties to the presidents of both. I was striking out, with one exception—the Ford Foundation (even though the company's founder, Henry Ford, was well known for his racist, anti-Semitic views).

The independent foundation founded by Henry and his son Edsel became one of the world's largest upon the death of both co-founders in the late 1940s and allocation of their bequests to the organization. The Ford Foundation's mission was to support "scientific, education, and charitable purposes, all for public welfare." It had become one of the most progressive philanthropic organizations in the nation and globally and was among the first in the 1960s to fund a variety of organizations and projects related to communities of color.

After I became a recipient of its new programs in support of Mexican American graduate student education in the early 1970s, I had happily agreed to serve on the program's fellowship selection committee in 1978. It was the only foundation in New York City to which I had a direct tie.

The Ford Foundation was also a rare private foundation that supported civil rights efforts and other projects aimed at Mexican Americans in the Southwest. The foundation funded the Mexican American Legal Defense and Education Fund in 1968, the nation's first legal advocacy group for Chicanos. In the early 1970s, it also provided funds to launch the Southwest Council of La Raza (most recently renamed UnidosUS), a leading advocacy organization that represents Latino community groups nationally. Additionally, it funded the Southwest Voter Registration and Education Project, which promoted voting rights among Mexican Americans in Texas.

"Aha," I thought to myself, "if I have any chance whatsoever of getting a foot inside the door of a foundation, the Ford Foundation is my best bet."

Ford was also the last of many foundation visits during this foray in New York City.

As a historian of urban America, I had read several books about the city's fascinating past. I had taught Stanford students about New York's central role as the port of entry for European immigrants and about the formation of African American and Puerto Rican neighborhoods in Harlem. It was exciting to visit many of these historic neighborhoods for the first time.

Meeting a program officer at the Ford Foundation took me to the city's Midtown section on the eastside. I easily spotted the building and entered through the large doors to gaze upward at the gleaming glass offices that all front a huge central atrium filled with greenery. Enjoying the beautiful architecture masked my nervousness, at least for a moment. I didn't want to be rejected again by another foundation.

"Hello, my name is *Dr.* Albert Camarillo, of Stanford University," I said to the receptionist, hoping to appear more important than I actually felt. "And I am here to meet with Mr. Diaz."

The ground floor receptionist, a woman probably in her sixties, looked up at me, seemingly unimpressed. "Please sign the visitor register and take a seat over there," she replied, and pointed to a couch in the nearby waiting area, "and I'll call *Dr.* Diaz's assistant." A minute later she called out to me with an added snub, "Okay, *Dr.* Camarillo, take the elevator to the fourth floor."

As the elevator doors opened on four, I was met by Diaz's smiling assistant. I followed her down the hallway to his office. "It is a pleasure to meet you, Dr. Diaz," I said to him upon entering, sure to include his title.

"Please call me Bill," he immediately replied, putting me at ease right away. We had a long conversation, with questions about the Stanford Center for Chicano Research and my background. He shared some of his own background as well. He was a Nuyorican, a Puerto Rican born and raised in New York. He'd earned his undergraduate and graduate degrees locally from Fordham University. But best of all, his academic work and public-related research had centered on Latinos, before being recently hired by the Ford Foundation. We also were almost the same age—and even wore similar mustaches. Talk about perfect timing for a request!

Bill was charged with developing what became the second major phase of the foundation's "Hispanic Initiative" programs, and he had some guidance on what might land best there.

"I like your plans for policy research at SCCR," Bill said straight up, "but the foundation is looking to fund projects that address issues beyond a single Hispanic subgroup." He suggested diversifying the research projects I described to him, and asked if I knew Frank Bonilla, who directed the Center for Puerto Rican Studies at CUNY (City University of New York). When I noted I'd heard of but never met him, he replied, "I suggest you speak with him." The Ford Foundation was clearly poised to entertain funding requests for policy-related research projects and programs, *if* they applied to Latinos in general.

I followed his advice and reached out to Frank Bonilla, who had been on the Stanford faculty for a few years before joining CUNY in 1973 as founding director of the Center for Puerto Rican Studies. He agreed to meet with me. But before returning to New York, I reached out for advice to Juan Gómez-Quiñones, my longtime mentor at UCLA, who was the director of their Chicano Studies Research Center. Juan suggested I contact colleagues at the Center for Mexican American Studies at the University of Texas, Austin, as well, to see if they too were interested in being part of this collaboration with Puerto Rican scholars.

Traveling outside of California was becoming routine, so I decided to bring Susan and the boys with me whenever possible. They accompanied me on the return trip to New York. I didn't want to miss out on experiences with the kids, and since Susan was able to reduce her school social work position to half-time before Greg was born, it made travel easier as a family. As my work at Stanford increased both in scope and in time commitments, I would not give up any precious time I could get with my growing family.

Meeting with Frank Bonilla and colleagues at his center involved many firsts. I may have been the first Chicano the staff at the Center for Puerto Rican Studies, mostly young graduate students, had ever encountered. They all were certainly the first Puerto Ricans I'd ever met. Frank was cordial and open to my invitation to collaborate, though, with his experience at Stanford providing some common ground. It didn't take much to convince him about the value of comparative research for Latinos across national origins.

Frank agreed to support my initial request for a planning grant from the Ford Foundation that would allow us to meet with the directors of the centers at UCLA and in Texas to discuss formal affiliations in support of Latino research. Judging by the graduate students' very serious demeanor and stern-looking gazes, however, they were far less sure about trusting this Chicano from an elite California university.

As I prepared to leave the meeting, Frank addressed this by asking the students, "Go fetch some glasses." While two quickly went into a nearby kitchen, he reached into a lower drawer on his desk and pulled out a bottle of rum (which I hate the taste of). Puerto Rican rum. A World War II veteran and one of the founders of Puerto Rican studies, Frank was almost twenty-five years my senior, and commanded respect. He knew about ways to build camaraderie, pouring a good amount of rum into all the glasses the students had neatly lined up on his desk.

"Salud," Frank said, raising his glass, "y a la cooperación entre Chicanos y Puertorriqueños" (Cheers, and to cooperation between Chicanos and Puerto Ricans).

I understood this group drink for Puerto Ricans was like a *tequilaso* among Chicanos. So I downed my glass of rum in one shot like the others, holding back any sign of gagging to not offend newfound colleagues. I chased the taste down with the only post-toast response I could muster. "Salud, that sure is good rum!" Sometimes *una mentira pequeña* (a little lie) is needed.

As I stood up to head back to my hotel and family, one of the graduate students came up behind me. "Hey *camarada*" (comrade), he said while pointing to the back pocket of my slacks, "if you walk around New York with your wallet halfway out of your pocket, you won't have it long." The other students laughed out loud. "Thanks, man," I said quickly, as I pushed it back into place. "There's not much money in there but without my driver's license, my family and I will be staying at Frank's place this weekend." Any tensions were slipping away amidst the jesting and sharing of several other good tips from my new friends in the Big Apple, who helped me navigate the metropolis and begin to build a community of Latino academics.

After that meeting, I called for a planning meeting at Stanford so the UCLA and University of Texas directors of the Chicano studies centers could meet with Frank and me to discuss our plans for the Inter-University

Program for Latino Research (IUPLR). With the grant proposal I then drafted, we soon received Ford Foundation funding to bring together, for the first time in higher education, diverse Latino scholars from four universities to plan collaborative, interdisciplinary research projects.

I served as the founding executive director of the program from 1984 to 1988, and my colleagues at the three other university centers served as co-directors. I continued to direct the Stanford Center for Chicano Research during those four years but stepped down as my duties with the IUPLR expanded. I also continued to teach three courses a year. My workload had increased significantly still, but it was okay because I knew of the payoffs we were getting for Chicano studies and Latino studies as a result of Ford Foundation recognition and support. Success builds on success, I quickly learned. Securing funding from a leading foundation like Ford opened other doors, with the Carnegie Corporation and Tinker Foundation soon providing their own grants to get the IUPLR started.

The program's first gathering of about forty Latino/a faculty and advanced graduate students from the four universities met at Stanford in 1984. We formed the first of several research working groups, and each worked on developing a research project proposal about an important Latino issue.

Now, alongside gratitude that I felt in general, ten years into my career, I was grateful to be in a position to help create such opportunities for others, thanks to the commitment of the Ford Foundation and other funding sources. I also am grateful for my longtime, deep friendship with Frank Bonilla, who helped me to see how the history of his people so closely connected to the history of my own. Using the term "Latino" to describe pan-Hispanic experiences took on new meaning for me as a result.

Over the next six years, the Ford Foundation invested millions in the IUPLR. Bill Diaz and the foundation supported our research working groups and, together with funding from the Social Science Research Council, led to grants to promote research on Latino-related public policy issues. We also sponsored Latino graduate student summer institutes at Stanford and developed leadership training programs for undergraduates at the four IUPLR member universities.

I couldn't have known in 1980, when I first assumed a leadership position at Stanford, where it might lead. Building coalitions among faculty and students at a university research center, and among several universities, was really hard work. I learned that it required a vision, a plan to put that vision in motion, and a way to orchestrate cooperation among varied people. You must also be proactive, patient, and willing to absorb failure without quitting, as well as to take on responsibility, if and when opportunity avails itself.

In effect, being an academic leader was not unlike leading by example when building up a family. Partnerships with colleagues must revolve around trust, respect, confidence, and mutually shared goals. You must nurture relationships with good will, understanding, and communication. I learned how important it is to work with institutional partners who share your vision. Working with Bill Diaz and other Ford Foundation staff on its Hispanic initiative allowed me to gain a broader perspective, too, on how new opportunities can advance the footprint for Latinos in higher education.

When I stepped down from leading IUPLR in 1988, I felt a sense of pride and accomplishment. Two decades after racial justice movements had opened new doors of educational opportunity for fortunate students like me, some of us had attained positions to promote ethnic studies and ethnic/racial diversity in higher ed to the next level.

A new chapter began as I returned to full-time teaching duties at Stanford; my courses attracted more undergraduates than ever before, and I was mentoring a growing number of graduate students, the next generation of Latino/a faculty. As I walked through the Quad and across campus each day to reach classes, I could see the unprecedented level of ethnic and racial diversity Stanford had achieved in its student body. So much had changed in the thirteen years since I'd first stepped foot on the Farm. It was cause for celebration. And for concern.

With diversification of the Stanford family came serious growing pains and dysfunction in the 1980s. In spring 1987, a coalition of student of color organizations mobilized to form a "Rainbow Agenda" and presented the university administration with a list of demands to express their discontent with microaggressions and more. I was at the center of these troubling times at Stanford after the university's president, Don Kennedy, and the provost, Jim Rosse, asked me to chair a committee to assess and to help chart a better way forward for our increasingly diverse community.

PART III

Circling Back to My Origins

SEVENTEEN

Challenges to Equality

Personal security, stability, and happiness are wonderful for bringing a sense of satisfaction, joy, and comfort. I felt that at forty, when I was a dozen years into my career at Stanford, while helping build the field of Chicano/a and Latino/a studies, teaching talented undergraduate students, and mentoring a growing number of grad students in U.S. history who'd become future Chicano/a historians. Susan and I were in the thick of raising our two little guys and were comfortable enough to consider a third child as well.

Many developments—on campus, in my hometown, and in society—took me out of my comfort zone by the mid-1980s and forced a recommitment to racial equity and social justice advocacy. As an experienced faculty member at an influential university, and a privileged citizen of color, I felt compelled to do more. I had to do more—especially when universities like Stanford faced an intensifying backlash against many state and federal policies it had implemented that promoted racial equality.

Racial incidents on American college campuses had become alarmingly frequent into the late 1980s. Dozens of universities each year faced toxic racial environments spurred by hate speech and various deeds of racial animus. Yet I badly wanted to believe that colleges and universities could become models for how institutions that committed to ethnic and racial diversity could succeed. I also wanted to believe that race relations in American society had been improved by our efforts in the civil rights era. But the question remained: Could college-educated, younger citizens of our nation discard the caustic racial attitudes and intolerant behavior of so many of their elders? Could we inch society closer to becoming a more socially/racially equitable nation?

I was gratified to have an employer that'd made earnest diversity efforts and to see diverse Stanford students building bonds of friendship, and I found their respect and appreciation for each other's differences comforting. From my experiences as a young man in Compton, I knew that it was possible, albeit really difficult, for people from different ethnic, racial, cultural, and religious backgrounds to successfully bridge historic divides.

But the growing contentiousness nationally over race-related issues troubled me. I worried because the newfound pillars in support of racial justice and equity were being assaulted and eroded on many fronts.

Most of all, I feared that some students at Stanford would absorb comments from a growing chorus of conservative pundits that affirmative action was about policies of "mediocrity," or worse yet, "reverse discrimination" against Whites. Many students of color already anticipated being viewed as outsiders and imposters on campus, despite their growing presence.

What became known as the culture wars, political and ideological skirmishes that pitted conservative-traditionalists against liberal-progressives, have long existed in U.S. society and politics. These ongoing wars morphed after the 1960s and reached a crescendo during the Reagan years in the 1980s. Abortion rights, gay rights, gun rights, separation of church and state, shifting gender roles, mass immigration, race-based policies, and other issues intensified longstanding cultural divides.

In the waning years of the Cold War, the rising voices of White evangelical Christians helped turn conservatives' attention away from the threat of communism to the internal threat of what they viewed as the moral, religious, and cultural decay of America. The society they preferred was changing, and ideological battle lines were being sharply drawn. The escalating culture wars reached college campuses at a time when their racial demographics had changed dramatically. I suspected, correctly, that these battles would soon reach Stanford.

The first skirmish at many universities in the late 80s centered on a debate over the freshman Western culture curriculum. The required, year-long curriculum that applied to all first-year students at Stanford was a sacred cow. That's because, for generations, having a solid liberal arts education in the United States was predicated on being introduced to the humanities through the writings of great Western thinkers. For instance, as a history major a UCLA, I had to enroll in three courses on Western civilization.

In 1987, hundreds of Stanford students and some faculty questioned why the required curriculum excluded non-Western authors and a discussion of other world cultures. Students questioned why only books by "dead White men," as they sometimes called the classics, were the course's reference point. "Where were the voices of women?" they asked, "The authors of color, the great literature from other parts of the world?"

At a basic level, they were questioning the same things we'd asked about twenty years earlier in advocating for ethnic studies. Like us, they'd failed to see themselves or their communities reflected in the required humanities coursework, adding to their sensitivities about being excluded, about not belonging. Marcos, an undergraduate Chicano student whom I knew well, shared this with the student newspaper: "Imagine the alienation, the pain that many of us felt when we came to this great institution of learning and discovered that all that our parents had stood for doesn't matter."

Stanford's Faculty Senate, composed of elected professors, oversaw decisions about curriculum and degree-granting requirements. After considerable debate, the longstanding Western culture-centered core curriculum was modified.

That didn't settle things, though. Nationally, President Reagan's secretary of education, William Bennett, claimed that Stanford was "trashing Western culture" to have made this change. And, without my realizing it initially, the alienation and exclusion experienced by some students of color increased after the Western culture curriculum debates.

The heightened racial tension on campus prompted campus organizations that represented students who were Black, Asian American, Native

American, and Chicano/a to unite for the first time that I'd seen. They formed a Rainbow Agenda to confront racism on campus and to request that the university's administration assess the problem.

My naïveté about the problem's depth ended on a bright spring day in early May, when I walked out of my office. A group of mostly students of color had gathered in front of the president's office on the Main Quad. Stopping by, I learned about the new student groups' five demands. They called on President Donald Kennedy and Provost James Rosse to form a commission to assess the quality of minority student life; asked for expanded ethnic studies courses; wanted a new high-level administrative position on minority affairs; asked for the establishment of a multicultural student center; and demanded increased minority student admissions. The students followed up a few days later with an added list for the provost.

The university's leadership replied that their concerns would take time to consider. The president wanted to appoint a small working group of staff to direct the Rainbow Agenda demands to appropriate campus offices, which the students viewed as a positive sign; but they grew impatient.

About two weeks after the coalition's first demands, several Rainbow Agenda members peacefully occupied the president's office for five hours. A quickly called meeting between the twenty-one students and the Kennedy-appointed committee led to an agreement that the university would sponsor a forum on campus racism, ending the occupation. It comforted me to learn that mutual respect was shown by both sides.

The large auditorium assigned for the forum was packed with a diverse audience of students, sprinkled with some administrators and faculty like me. An African American woman who served as a student services administrator moderated a panel of students from the Rainbow Agenda, who shared personal experiences of racism and harassment—many of which I'd heard before.

"We are being told every day that we do not belong here," a female member of the Asian American Student Association declared, citing as an example a time when a White male student, whom she didn't know, told her, "Hey, what's the matter with you? Don't you speak English?" I immediately recalled a similar encounter by one of my students, a leader of the Black Student Union, who had publicly favored changing the Western culture curriculum earlier in the year. After an event where Amanda stated she wanted to study African American history, a White male student said, "Go back to Africa."

A Native student at the race forum recounted hearing his people called "savages." "Very few people realize what is being said," he claimed, lamenting the fact that most Stanford students lack any appreciation of the cultures of Indigenous people. I was also taken aback by the story of an African American male student who headed the Black Student Union. The student sought out his chemistry professor for help in understanding a graph presented in class. The reply? "Your people don't always have an aptitude for this." Could it be that a colleague would say something so inherently racist?

Such words undermine confidence. They can reinforce alienation. They can instill bitterness. And, expressed publicly, these hurtful words can inflame racial tensions. Take, for example, this statement by a White freshman around this time in the *Stanford Daily*: "I will admit the university is far from egalitarian in its treatment of students. In truth," he declared, "the university caters to minorities. It makes it easier for them to get in, and it goes outside and actively recruits them." Talk about throwing kerosene on a smoldering fire.

Perhaps the most troubling comments that night at the forum were by my friend Cecilia Burciaga, an associate dean of graduate studies and the resident fellow in Casa Zapata. She mentioned keeping a log of race-related incidents and reported hearing a group of students shouting outside their Chicano theme dorm, "Up with racism! Up with fascism! Down with Zapata!" which made the audience gasp. Individual microaggressions or hurtful words were one thing, but this type of brazen, collective racist behavior at Stanford took my concerns to another level.

I left the forum that evening heavyhearted. It pained me to hear that so many students of color experienced such intolerance. I now began to question the belief I'd held in my bones that the university had made real progress as a supportive multiracial place. After that forum, I realized another race-related incident could blow the lid off the already tense campus environment. To my relief, that academic year ended without added incidents and with hopes that the long summer break before the 1987–88 academic year would reduce the campus's racially charged temperature.

In early September, Stanford's autumn quarter was just a few weeks away. Weekday mornings for Susan and I had fallen into a routine of alternately dropping off our two little guys at school. Jeff was in the third grade and Greg, in kindergarten. After leaving the boys at school one day, I stopped to pick up some coffee before the short drive to campus and walk to my office.

While at my desk, enjoying the early morning quiet to prepare some lecture materials, the telephone rang.

"Damn, who is bothering me this early in the morning?" I said out loud.

"Good morning, Professor Camarillo," a pleasant voice responded, noting she was from President Kennedy's office. It turned out he and Provost Rosse wanted a meeting with me.

Good thing I didn't share my next thoughts: "Oh, shit, what the hell do the president and provost want with me? And why the ASAP?" I had never met with them together either.

After a polite yes, I added "Can you please tell me what the president and provost wish to discuss?" "They will explain when you meet," she responded quickly.

I was nervous and intrigued, given that Don Kennedy and I had developed an excellent rapport during his year as provost before being selected president in 1980. I didn't know well, but also trusted and deeply respected, Jim Rosse, an economist and former chair of his department and associate dean. He'd become provost in 1984 and already proven himself an astute, fair-minded, no-nonsense type of CEO of academic affairs who put the university's best interests first.

We met in Don's office, where they sat at a large table. Always cordial and friendly, Don rose, slapping me on the back and thanking me for meeting on short notice before getting to the point.

Don explained that they had decided, after meeting some staff advisors over the summer, to convene a large committee to tackle the issues raised by the Rainbow Agenda in the spring. Jim noted the importance of expanding this committee's focus: setting the university's future course as a model of how an ethnically and racially diverse campus can function cooperatively and thrive.

"That's a tall order, but an important and admirable one," I said, assuming that they'd ask me, an associate professor, to serve on this committee.

They wanted me to chair it instead.

I tried not to act surprised, as I was hoping to be promoted to full professor in the next few years. This final formal review required many more publications beyond the earlier tenure step. I was not quite forty, with two small children at home. And, I was wrapping up seven years of major administrative roles, with the past three as executive director of the Inter-University Program for Latino Research. Because that and the Chicano research center I'd previously established were flourishing, I was set to take a sabbatical the following year to devote myself to full-time research on my next book.

When they shared plans for forming a very large committee, including a few non-Stanford members, I almost said loud out, "Are you kidding me?" I responded instead with something like, "That sure is big!"

I'd never tackled a major, university-wide assignment of this scope, and this committee would not only be high profile, but it would dig into really sensitive and extremely difficult issues about race and ethnic relations. The good news was the president and provost didn't expect a report for at least a year.

They shared their faith in me, with Jim adding, "You will report directly to me, and I will make every resource available to you and the committee to get the work done."

After thanking them and shaking hands before I departed, I shared that I'd discuss the offer with my wife, and my department chair (with whom, it turned out, Jim had already cleared this).

But no sooner had I left the meeting than I knew the answer. This committee was just too damn important for the well-being of the university's increasingly diverse community of students, staff, and faculty. And the committee's work, done properly, could make Stanford a more equitable institution, while I could perhaps strengthen ethnic studies on campus along the way. A bigger motivator lurked in the back of mind: that the eyes of higher education would be on the Farm, again, but this time as it dealt with sensitive race-related issues.

Although I'd expected this committee work to be time-consuming, I hadn't bargained for how big and difficult it would be. The timing unexpectedly coincided with Susan expecting our third child, too.

Called the University Committee on Minority Issues (UCMI), we first met in October 1987. It was a huge, diverse committee of students, faculty, staff, alumni, and people from outside the university.

The twenty members had one year to address the goal spelled out in the president and provost's charge: "To promote a University environment in which all members have equal opportunity to develop full human potential—an environment in which respect, mutual regard for cultural differences and full participation and partnership are the norm."

Given our marching orders and the committee's broad composition, we would tackle issues beyond those brought by minority undergraduate students. We focused on assessing racial climate issues for *all* students, staff, and faculty, while examining issues and proposing recommendations to improve the entire campus community. Nothing like it had ever been done at Stanford or, to our knowledge, at any other university.

Our list of questions expanded after every meeting: How and in which ways were minority and majority students interacting? Were race and ethnic tensions on campus fueled by acts of overt racism or was insensitivity and ignorance more at play? Did the university's undergraduate curriculum help students better understand and appreciate ethnic and racial differences? Did faculty and staff of color perceive their workplace environments as supportive? "What did I get myself into?" I often thought after meetings, as we dug deep into questions and issues, and generated tons of new survey data and interviewed hundreds of students.

By April 1988, we knew we couldn't complete the committee's work by that fall quarter. So we decided to issue an interim report in May and make the final report available in January 1989. The president and provost agreed. However, I hadn't counted on this being an unbelievably time-consuming fifteen-month assignment.

Besides the committee and several subcommittee meetings that were bimonthly, and meetings with staff, I was managing a growing list of committee affairs, overseeing the research projects, and putting out fires from student members wanting more action than research from UCMI. I "ate, slept, and breathed" UCMI at the time. Meanwhile, I still taught several courses and advised dozens of undergraduate students and history PhD program advisees.

And I needed to prioritize my family, including co-coaching Jeff's

AYSO (American Youth Soccer Organization) team in the autumn and a Little League baseball team in the spring that both sons played on together. Susan and I were also excited to soon be welcoming a baby girl to the family in May. Come hell or high water, I was going to shift attention to family after the baby was born. As a result, I told committee members that we had to write UCMI's interim report before the mid-May birth (there was no paternal leave policy in 1988).

While I edited the final draft of the interim report on the last day of April, two weeks before Lauren's due date, Susan shared that, "I think the baby may be on her way."

"Oh my," I said, "How am I going to finish this report? Do you think there is any way to hold off through the weekend so I can finish the interim report?" To this utterly insensitive, disgraceful ask, she understandably looked at me with astonishment. Yet somehow, full labor didn't commence until Monday morning. Lauren was born Monday afternoon—the same day I forwarded the report to the president and provost.

In September, Susan returned to her school social work position, and the expanded Camarillo family settled into a routine that included campus day care for sweet baby Lauren. As students returned, I was glad the end of my UCMI-related work was near.

A week after classes started, the campus energy shifted when a flyer advertising auditions for the Stanford Symphony Orchestra was defaced. It featured the face of Ludwig van Beethoven and was captioned "Uncle Ludwig Wants You!"—a takeoff on the Uncle Sam "I Want You for the U.S. Army" image of decades past. The poster was on a bulletin board outside the room of an African American resident in Ujamaa, the Black theme dormitory. The famous composer's mug shot, though, had been turned into a caricature with black skin and a large Afro hairstyle. Ujamaa staff informed the Office of Residential Education about this, while trying unsuccessfully to keep the incident from dorm residents.

A week later someone scrawled the N-word on a poster in the dorm announcing a Black fraternity event. Outrage understandably grew.

An investigation found that two White male freshmen in a Lagunita dorm, adjacent to Ujamaa, had defaced the orchestra poster. At a special meeting for residents, the two culprits confessed and apologized publicly. Black residents considered their apology "arrogant, condescending, and patronizing." The meeting spiraled into anger, tears, and, as described by Ujamaa's resident fellow, "mass chaos."

A few days later, someone stapled a bumper sticker to a Lagunita dorm bulletin board: "Avenge Ujamaa/Smash the Honkie Oppressors." A flyer was also found that announced payback time for the two freshman confessors, who were removed from the dorm. Provost Rosse also initiated a university investigation into the incidents.

The spark I'd worried about the previous spring was primed to ignite. Local and national media jumped all over the reporting of racism at Stanford. The campus was tense. I was tense. Would violence occur?

This all added pressure to UCMI, especially after a new group, Students of Color Coalition, formed in anticipation of our report's release. I was feeling the heat, especially after I'd announced the delay in publishing for a few more months.

UCMI's final report, *Building a Multiracial, Multicultural University Community*, was book length at 250 pages. The most comprehensive study at a U.S. university of its kind to date about the state of ethnic and racial diversity, it outlined over a hundred recommendations the committee deemed critical for Stanford to implement. The report proposed a new vision and called for a renewed commitment to making ethnic and racial diversity work at Stanford.

Although the committee applauded the university for its remarkable success over twenty years in achieving numerical diversity among undergraduates (nearly 40 percent of the 1988 class were students of color), we minced no words about meager progress on faculty and graduate student diversity. We emphasized, in addition, that the curriculum was woefully inadequate for students to grasp the complexities of race relations. We noted, as well, the inadequate institutional programs for students of color and the need to redouble efforts to create an amicable, positive campus environment for all students.

The report was part vision statement and part blueprint for creating what we called "interactive pluralism." It sought to answer how a university of diverse members could build a community that interacts well across ethnic, racial, and cultural divides. Not many college campuses had similar efforts, amidst a society still badly fractured along racial fault lines.

I believed in my gut that the process outlined for creating a truly interactive, multicultural/multiracial campus community was not a pipe dream. I had devoted a year and a half of my life—and eight months that'd been slated for my sabbatical—to UCMI work. As is common, Kennedy and Rosse appointed a committee to assess the final report and its extensive recommendations. They also agreed to appoint a team of outside reviewers who would annually assess progress on implementation of UCMI's recommendations.

The first review found, to my great satisfaction, that 75 percent of the 100-plus recommendations had been or were being implemented. But the Students of Color Coalition wanted more direct responses to the UCMI report and its recommendations and grew frustrated. Joined by a group of progressive White students, some from student government leadership, they formed an Agenda for Action Coalition.

A few weeks before the academic year ended, fifty-three coalition students—including several of my advisees—staged a takeover of the president's office. When they refused to leave after police warnings, they were arrested on charges of unlawful trespassing. I fully understood the students' frustrations and admired their commitment to protest, though I feared some might be brought up on serious charges. In the end, they eventually pled guilty to misdemeanor charges.

For me, the exhausting academic year ended, and my family and I headed to the Sierra Nevada Mountains and Lake Tahoe for several weeks, a summer tradition while the kids were growing up. In part, I needed emotional and physical distance from the campus.

Fall returned, and with my batteries recharged, I relished the normalcy of dodging a throng of students walking and biking to class. As I walked to my History Department office one early October morning, I picked up the *Stanford Daily* newspaper from a pile just outside the building. I was feeling particularly fortunate that sun-drenched day because the provost had kindly agreed to restore six months of my sabbatical leave. With this time off from teaching, I planned a deep dive into research about the African American urban experience for a book-in-progress.

Once at my desk, the lead story in the *Daily* caught my attention: "53 Protesters Sentenced, Lectured." Relief came that all but one student who'd participated in the May takeover of Kennedy's office had received a slap on the wrist. The Santa Clara County judge ordered six-months of community service.

At the end of the *Daily* article, the newspaper published two accompanying statements that were read in court. One was a lecture by the judge to the students. The other was a statement, read before the judge, by a representative of the Agenda for Action Coalition students. Besides stating acceptance of their sentencing, the students explained the reasons for their spring protest:

> As members of the Stanford community, . . . we are committed to the betterment of our University and the realization of its vision of democratic education. It is out of this commitment . . . that each of us became involved in contributing to the multicultural advancement of the University. On May 15, we acted out of our deepest belief in the fundamental ideals of Stanford, and more broadly, of this country—that all people are equal, and that our institution and education should reflect that equality.

What an honest, inspiring statement! It reminded me of why I chose a career in higher education and felt compelled to chair a committee that could advance multicultural education and promote a more racially democratic institution. It was a declaration about a noble idea, a goal, a vision. I couldn't hold back the tears.

A renewed sense of hope washed over me. Their words also provoked me to remember the bigger picture after being so deep into the research and the weeds of the UCMI work for the previous two years. My vantage point as a historian also kicked in quickly. I thought about how my multiracial experiences in Compton had molded my personal development, and how previous generations of good people had fought and struggled for the opportunities that made a career at a place like Stanford possible. My racial equity commitment as a historian and educator was renewed by their words, just as opportunities arose for me to use my skills to make a difference outside the university.

Not long after I completed writing the UCMI report, a call came from the lead attorney of the Civil Rights Division of the U.S. Department of Justice. He wanted me as an expert witness in a Voting Rights Act–related lawsuit involving Mexican American plaintiffs. They claimed that political gerrymandering by an all-White group of politicians had kept them from electing a candidate of their choice. Their lawsuit was against the Los Angeles County Board of Supervisors—the county of my origins.

I knew a great deal about the landmark Voting Rights Act, the companion piece of federal legislation passed into law a year after the monumental Civil Rights Act of 1964. The Voting Rights Act took aim at the many barriers erected in the name of White supremacy to keep Blacks from exercising their constitutional right to vote. The legislation barred localities and states from using methods to prevent Blacks in the South from casting their ballots. The Voting Rights Act (VRA) had teeth and, over time, had had enormous consequences in unlocking the ballot box for African Americans. In 1975, the law was extended to protect Latinos and other "language minorities."

With the extension, the U.S. Senate Judiciary Committee included what became known as "Senate Factors" for determining violations of the law. That is where my value as a historian came into play. One of the seven additional factors to qualify as a violation was demonstrating a history of official discrimination and how that affected a group's ability to participate in the political process. Discrimination in other areas—including education, housing, employment—was also relevant.

The DOJ and the ACLU joined with the Mexican American Legal Defense and Education Fund (MALDEF) in its lawsuit, *Garza v. Los Angeles County*. I was one of two historians who submitted reports and testified before the court, while getting my first taste of aggressive attorneys for the opposite side. While giving sworn testimony before a judge, these attack-dog-style attorneys contested every key report conclusion and tried to undermine my testimony. I held my ground as best as possible, knowing in my heart they couldn't refute the truth that historical scholarship had unearthed about the discrimination Mexican Americans had endured in Los Angeles County for 150 years.

I learned a lot on the way to the plaintiffs' victory. In 1990, David V. Kenyon of the U.S. District Court in Los Angeles, the judge who presided over the *Garza* case, found the LA Board of Supervisors had engaged in gerrymandering of Hispanic majority districts to preserve the powerful, all-White board. The five-member board, representing 10 million voters in the county, had to redraw electoral boundaries and establish the first Latino-majority district. With pride, I can say that my report and testimony helped the judge feel compelled to rule in the plaintiffs' favor. The consequences for Latino/a voters were huge. After supervisorial districts were redrawn, Gloria Molina—the first Latina elected to the California State Legislature in 1982 and, later, to the LA City Council in 1986—joined the LA County Board of Supervisors in 1991. She was the first Latino/a on the board in almost a century.

The *Garza* case was the first of many expert witness testimonies—some successful, some not—over the next thirty years. Other than a college admissions affirmative action–related case, *Gratz v. Bollinger* (2000), all others were VRA cases brought by MALDEF in support of Latino/a voters. My involvement in them all proved why knowing history matters.

My newfound role as a "public historian" in Voting Rights Act cases coincided with a decision to refocus my academic lens on the place of my origins. Compton had been on the public's radar for the wrong reasons for nearly two decades, and by the late 1990s had emerged as the focus of my historical research and community-based, service-learning teaching.

EIGHTEEN

Compton on My Mind

"Hey Bones," my brother Art opened his phone call. "Did you hear about Compton as the new murder capital? I could see it coming by the time I retired, man," he said.

Art had retired nine years earlier as a Compton cop, back in 1980. Since then, Compton had surpassed Los Angeles and Washington, DC, as the most dangerous city based on homicides. Our town, becoming famous for all the wrong reasons, was on my mind.

After occasionally reading articles about Compton in the *Los Angeles Times* in the 1980s, I began to follow reports on it more closely in the early 1990s. The newspaper coverage read like an unfolding dystopian novel, full of frightening depictions of gang violence, political corruption and scandals, poverty, school failure, and Black versus Latino conflicts. Could these national media depictions of the city and its residents be true?

Regardless, the growing infamy of Compton seeped into popular culture—and into the Camarillo household through a subgenre of hip-hop music called "gangsta" rap. Unbeknownst to Susan and me, our eldest son Jeff, at the tender age of ten, was listening to this subgenre with its origins in Compton.

"What are you listening to?" I heard Susan shout after she walked into Jeff's bedroom one summer afternoon. He was busy gyrating to music blasting in his headset, and she stood in shock in his doorway hearing cuss word after cuss word flow from our young son's mouth.

Jeff quickly shut off his yellow-and-black Sony Walkman cassette recorder when he saw the stunned look in his mama's eyes.

Susan's even-tempered, kind, understanding disposition flashed from horror to anger. Grabbing the recorder and yanking out the cassette tape of Eazy-E's hit album *Easy-Duz-It,* she asked, "Where did you get this?" She pulled the recording strip from the cassette while waiting for a response, crumpling it in her hands and tossing the whole thing into a nearby wastebasket.

Jeff confessed to hearing some teens listening to Eazy-E at a basketball summer camp. Curious, he'd tricked his Grandma Rose (my mother) into buying him the tape during a recent visit. "There is a wonderful singer who grew up in Compton," Jeff had shared, "and I really want to buy his album." "That's wonderful!" she told her little grandson, about the Compton connection, before pulling out $5 from her purse to unknowingly feed her grandson's growing appetite for rap.

Although Eazy-E's music was banned at home for a while, Jeff was part of a generation of young people across the United States drawn to rap and hip-hop music in general. For instance, Jeff fessed up that he and two best friends in middle school—the only two African Americans in his grade of the predominantly White student body—were secretly listening to other rap artists from Compton, especially N.W.A., which Eazy-E helped found. N.W.A. had furthered Compton's image and put it on the national cultural map with its popular, controversial debut album in 1988, *Straight Outta Compton.* The lyrics referenced police brutality, violence, and drugs. Mixed in throughout were sexist language and profanities, drawing lots of media attention and criticism.

In N.W.A.'s own words, their music was "reality rap." It included a political message about the lives of many Black youth in Compton. So, too, did the film that introduced Compton to hundreds of thousands of moviegoers a few years later. The 1991 critically acclaimed motion picture *Boyz n the Hood* portrayed Black youth in a South Central Los Angeles neighborhood surrounded by the specter of gang violence, police harassment, and perilous futures.

In one brief scene in the debut film of John Singleton, Jason "Furious" Styles (played by Laurence Fishburne) is the father of the one of the young male protagonists. Styles drives his son Tre and best friend Ricky to visit nearby Compton on a bright, sunny day. Furious planned the outing as a sobering message about racism and violence in the hood for the coming-of-age young men.

"What the fuck are we doin' walkin' around Compton," Ricky says to Tre, as they step away from the car with a police siren blaring in the background. They both gaze, with trepidation, at some young Blacks drinking and hanging out on the steps of a house across the street. Ricky and Tre obviously knew that Compton held even greater danger than their neighborhood.

Director Singleton, a product of South Central LA, used this scene to impart a powerful message about inequality and racism in Black communities. Yet he also reinforced the stereotype of Compton as a violent place where rudderless young Black men, with easy access to guns and booze, kill each other.

By the time I had a chance to start returning to the city of my youth regularly in 2000, this stereotype was clearly etched into the American psyche. Compton had become the poster child for all that was wrong with the "Black ghetto."

Compton was, still, on my mind, though not often in ways I wanted it to be.

"Oh, you are from Compton!?" people sometimes asked after learning my place of origin. Surprise and curiosity came with the question, and sometimes a judgmental edge. I could predict the next question almost verbatim: "What was it like to live there?"

"It was a different time," I typically replied, seeking to end most conversations. Occasionally, depending on the person's open-minded demeanor and such, I gave a fuller explanation.

When the questions came from people who had passing knowledge about Los Angeles, I instinctively knew what they were really asking, in a loaded, coded way: "How did this nice, middle-class, all-White community become a violent, gang-ridden Black city plagued with so many problems?"

That was misguided. Yes, Compton had once been a predominantly White community, but by the 1940s it was racially mixed. In addition, the city was always mostly working class. Compton, in fact, remains a working-class suburb, though White folks in 2020 made up less than 1 percent of residents. It is a "city of color," a term I use to describe formerly White suburbs where minorities have become the majorities.

With a historical lens, I did get why people viewed Compton as what they thought a ghetto would be like. A starkly negative image of inner-city Black neighborhoods began to emerge in public consciousness by the 1950s. Television and print media coverage of the urban "ghetto riots" of the late 1960s, beginning with the Watts Rebellion, had furthered the collective assumption that urban African American neighborhoods are destitute, crime-infested places.

Conservative commentators embellished that ghetto image from afar. It was not too much of a stretch for uninvolved Americans to think "the ghettos" were also populated by nothing other than dysfunctional single female-headed households, violent unemployed Black men, and cheating "welfare queens."

I had taught Stanford students about the history of U.S. cities for decades, covering how, over time, Americans began collectively viewing "the city" in negative ways. By the 1980s, stories about urban decline were superimposed upon stories about the inner-city poor, particularly African Americans. To combat this, I cautioned students to critically examine broad assumptions and stereotypes while determining why such views gained widespread acceptance. There was everything from truths to utter falsehoods about Black "ghetto life" in general, and about Compton.

Yet in the early 1990s, I began questioning what I really knew of Compton. For over three decades, after all, I'd lived in a White suburb in the San Francisco Bay Area, next door to an elite university. How could I determine if what I read about Compton was truth, exaggeration, or both and more?

Less than a year after the release of *Boyz n the Hood,* racial violence and destruction on a scale not seen since the Watts Riots erupted in South Central LA neighborhoods. People, including me, stayed glued to televisions while protests and violence unfolded in real time in response to Rodney

King's beating. But what most people didn't know—including me initially—was that Compton got swept up in the chaos of spring 1992.

The kindling for the April fires were lit the previous year when motorist King and two friends were seen by California Highway Patrol officers driving faster than the speed limit on an LA freeway in the early morning hours. King didn't pull over after seeing the CHP's flashing lights. A high-speed chase began in which Los Angeles PD cruisers joined the helicopters, which hovered above, directing bright spotlights.

When King finally stopped his car, LAPD cops ordered the three men to exit and lie on the ground to be handcuffed and arrested. Four officers swarmed King, and while subduing him for what they considered resisting arrest, he was battered repeatedly and mercilessly with baton strikes and kicks.

This routine arrest of a suspected drunken motorist turned into a spectacle because a nearby resident captured it all on videotape. The video went viral soon after.

I certainly understood the long, troubling history of beatings of Black and Brown folks by LA cops. But watching the video of King's bludgeoning into bloodied submission on TV, time after sickening time, brought rage and expletives from my mouth and disturbed millions of other viewers globally, sparking an outcry.

An investigation by the Los Angeles County district attorney resulted in a trial of the four policemen for assault and excessive force. Because of the high visibility case, the trial had been moved forty miles away to adjacent Ventura County in a courthouse in Simi Valley, in an overwhelmingly White city with a deep politically conservative bent. My concerns for the trial's outcome became full-on anxiety when a mostly White jury was selected. Given the unfairness of the venue, I was appalled, but not shocked, when those cops were found not guilty of excessive force. How could this be? Is there no justice? "Oh man, the shit is going to hit the fan," I said to Susan as the verdict splashed across our TV screen.

It didn't take a historian or a rocket scientist to predict what might happen next. Within hours of the news, protests and violence occurred on a massive scale. Neighborhoods and businesses in South Central LA bore the

brunt of the arson fires and looting. Violence and property damage extended
to nearby Korea Town, a place where tensions between African Americans
and Korean American store owners were already at a boiling point. Over six
nightmarish days and nights, the rebellion resulted in 63 deaths, more than
2,000 injuries, about 7,000 fires, 3,000 damaged businesses, and the arrest
of thousands of Black and Latino people.

The rebellion was only quelled after an army of California National
Guard troops joined the LAPD and other local law enforcement agencies
who patrolled streets and enforced curfews. The toll of property damage was
staggering, estimated at $1 billion.

About a week later, I learned Compton had also suffered major property
damage from fires and looting. An *LA Times* article that listed the many
affected businesses made me wonder, "How in the hell can the city and its
people deal with more trauma?"

It was time for me to return home to the city of my birth, but not as a
detached academic who'd study the place and its people without a sense of
context. I also didn't want to return to Compton to conduct spotty one-visit
research, where I'd speak to a few residents and join the growing list of jour-
nalists who'd focused mostly on the problems of gangs, violence, and political corruption. Call me biased, but I had long considered the *LA Times*'s
reporting about Compton to be skewed. Especially after the destruction in
the spring 1992 rebellion, I thought Compton needed coverage by a trained
historian. That came initially in 1994, but not from me.

The September issue of *The Nation*, a venerable progressive magazine
with a national audience, included a cover with the bold-faced title "The
Compton Blues" and the eye-popping subtitle: "The violence of everyday life
claims Latinos, blacks, anyone on the edge in this notorious city, where the
kids are beaten and the pols are crooks."

Inside was the lead essay, "The Sky Falls On Compton," penned by
fellow urban historian and social commentator Mike Davis. Despite its title,
I'd hoped Davis's piece would offer a more balanced view of the city and its
people. But Davis offered a stark, almost horrifying critique of Compton.

"Could this really be the Compton I once knew?" I kept saying, while
reading the depressing piece. Davis had visited there in 1993 and had spoken
to several residents before writing his essay. I wondered if he'd fallen prey to

sensationalized media hype about the city. I had read Davis's two previous books on Los Angeles history and respected his brutally honest critique of that city, its institutions, and people. So, my head was spinning after reading his exposé of my hometown.

He peeled back layer after layer of problems with graphic examples. With the keen eye of an academic and the biting analysis of a social critic, he laid bare the mountain of crises under which Compton was buried. The references he made to city streets and buildings I knew so well—Compton Boulevard, city hall, the police department where my brother worked for nineteen years, and the *panadería* (bakery) across the street from my childhood elementary school—rekindled vivid memories of my youth.

Davis's descriptions also put a lump in my throat. His takeaways were crystal clear. The sky had not only fallen on Compton, but the city was descending into a hellish pit of no return. Violence between two main gangs, the Crips and Bloods, often erupted in bloodshed and death. By the Compton Police Department's count, almost all African American, Latino, and Samoan young men were gang members. The iron fist of the Compton police was everywhere, with their brutality toward youth sometimes chronicled. In the summer of 1993, for instance, a scandal had erupted after a video of a Black cop brutally beating a skinny Latino teenager was aired by a local TV station, causing some Latinos to join forces with African American residents to protest local law enforcement violence.

Davis's story added to the reputation of Compton as a violent place. Compton, it seemed, was now the modern-day version of a "shoot-em-up" city of the Old West, with gangbangers being the new outlaws.

Davis's mind-boggling findings included what he claimed was "something akin to a complete meltdown of its governing institutions" amid political scandals. Charges of fraud, bribery, mismanagement, and theft of public funds by elected and appointed African American leaders were considered serious enough to bring federal and state investigators to town. Scandals tainted the offices of the mayor, the president of Compton Community College, the police chief, and city council and school district officials. Some former municipal leaders were indicted; others were under investigation. A few, including a former mayor, eventually went to prison.

Mike Davis's essay spurred me to dive deeper into the city's past and present than I'd done in the early 70s. Much of what I read in this second soul-searching study—from newspaper accounts to FBI crime statistics to other media coverage—confirmed his observations.

At the time, my research in Mexican American urbanization had already expanded to include comparisons with European and Asian immigrants and Blacks in U.S. cities. But the time frame of that comparative research didn't go much past the 1960s. I refocused my research into the 1970s and 80s to understand what was happening in Compton in the 1990s. I also had to widen the lens, as I'd learned that what Compton experienced in the last third of the twentieth century was tied directly to regional, state, and national developments. Compton's story, I soon learned, mirrored realities of many other suburbs in Los Angeles and across metropolitan America—including East Palo Alto near my home.

The story of Compton after the 1960s is complex, but the gist of what I'd learned as a graduate student still provides a good handle on the city's past. White exodus was lightning fast in Compton in the wake of the 1965 Watts Riots (with the same happening elsewhere in LA and nationally, as formerly race-restricted suburban neighborhoods opened up due to new state and federal anti-discrimination housing laws).

By the time Douglas Dollarhide, Compton's first Black mayor, took office in 1969, municipal finances were teetering on insolvency from bad leadership decisions over decades: to not annex substantial industrial or manufacturing zones nearby to bolster city revenues; to fund schools mostly through high residential property taxes, after (predominantly White) downtown businesses closed; and to use tax bonds to rebuild schools and other public buildings after a 1933 quake. School funding issues worsened after World War II, when the goal became building new schools to separate White students from the growing numbers of Black students arriving in the 60s (since 1940, the city's population spiked about five-fold, to 72,000 in 1960).

The belt squeezing strained law enforcement capacity and city schools; they were overcrowded, and educational quality declined further, as debts kept mounting. Middle-class and stable working-class Black and Latino families that could afford to often moved elsewhere.

Some Black and Latino families also moved out to keep the good-paying jobs in the aerospace and other industries that had relocated to distant suburbs in LA and nearby counties. Others had lost manufacturing-related jobs as part of a national deindustrialization trend in California and other states.

By the mid-1970s, after my earlier survey, even more downtown stores on Compton Boulevard had shuttered. The once-thriving auto dealerships that dotted Long Beach Boulevard also became vacant. City tax revenue shrank despite excessive property tax rates locally. State test scores of Compton school district students, more of whom were poor, were at or near the bottom, and school dropout rates, double the county average, were rising.

Impoverishment thus had a stranglehold on the city in the post–civil rights years. Over time, middle-class families had been replaced by poorer African American residents and Latino immigrant families who rented homes and apartments. The percentage of unemployed Compton residents rose dramatically in the 1970s and 80s, as well as those on public assistance and those who lived in poverty (about double the rate for most LA County communities). Municipal institutions began to collapse under the weight of limited resources as the dream for a better future and more opportunities became out of reach for so many residents of color. The federal anti-discrimination laws that Dr. King and thousands of civil rights warriors fought to attain had been achieved by the mid-1960s, but the challenge remained of overcoming generations of economic subordination for Blacks and other poor people of color.

Yes, greater freedoms had been won and new opportunities were created back then for Americans like me who were fortunate to grow up in the right place at the right time. But millions of others floundered, including thousands of Compton kids who had limited support to overcome neighborhood and family circumstances. As the city's schools deteriorated, their chances of accessing opportunities became especially slim.

The condition of schools in the Compton Unified School District by the 1990s was emblematic of the city's plight. As covered in an excellent book about Compton's history of public education, *Death of a Suburban Dream* by Emily E. Straus, Black political and educational leaders inherited an inefficient and costly educational system with five independent school districts. In 1969, Comptonites voted to incorporate the various districts under one unified administrative roof. Although a smart managerial move, creating the Compton Unified School District couldn't correct the schools' growing financial shortfall. Compton's anemic budget, due to dwindling property and business taxes, meant little money for repair and upkeep of buildings, teacher's salaries, and more. Even worse, public confidence waned with revelations about some shady and expensive "sweetheart" contracts to repair worn-out school facilities. Corruption and fraud by a few employees later surfaced.

By 1992–93, the Compton Unified School District went bankrupt. The $10 million of debt led district officials to plead for emergency state aid. To avoid a shutdown of the fourth largest district in LA County, with over 40,000 enrolled students and about 3,000 employees, the state legislature agreed. The bailout came with an unprecedented requirement, though: an administrator was appointed to oversee operations of the sinking district. The administrator reported needing $10 million more just to stay open the next academic year.

The heart of the city's problems was far beyond the state's capacity to address with the district takeover. Poverty, joblessness, and crime overwhelmed Compton's municipal government and its families, left in ruins after White flight. Despair and hopelessness were byproducts. It's likely the children suffered the most.

What happens to young people when hope fades? When students step into classrooms crumbling from neglect? What happens when parents are employed below livable wages, or worse yet, can't get any work at all? When family units dissolve under the strain of poverty and hopelessness and grow dependent on public assistance? What happens when you watch what television commercials advertise but can't afford? When, basically, the life you would like to lead isn't remotely attainable?

For kids of any color in poor communities, turning to crime becomes one of few ways to attain possessions and money. Crimes against property soared throughout the United States in the 1970s and 80s, bringing up crimes against people and violent crimes along with them.

As is so often the case, the media ignored the underlying problems that bankrupted Compton's schools and covered crime and gangs instead. An early example was written by Bruce Henderson, a young newspaper reporter. Henderson convinced Thomas Cochee, the city's new and first Black police chief, to permit a "ride along" with cops on patrol. Bad decision. To read Henderson's 1974 book, *Ghetto Cops: On the Streets of the Most Dangerous City in America*, brings a sense of out-of-control crime in a city unable to cope. Characterizing the city as "ghetto" and as "most dangerous" framed Henderson's view. Compton, to Henderson, was a run-away crime train.

Compton's reputation was further sealed when the FBI's annual Crime Index revealed the city's startling murder rate. Gang activity was the reason for this upswing in violence. The Crips, from nearby South Central LA neighborhoods, came to the city sometime in the 1970s with their red clothing. Compton's Westside Crips, as they labeled themselves, began to move into other neighborhoods, causing rivalries with various other Crips "sets," while other groups of young Black men banded together to keep Crips out of their hoods.

One such group, the Piru Street Boys, or Pirus, soon emerged as the Bloods. They donned blue, and those who wore a blue bandana risked their lives if they entered a Crip neighborhood, and vice versa.

Former Compton Mayor Omar Bradley, in his memoir *The King of Compton!*, claimed that as a senior at Centennial High School in 1975 (a school where Crips predominated), "the streets of Compton were running red with blood." He noted that many guys from his neighborhood "had already been stabbed or shot to death by young men who lived a stone's throw away." By then, he added, "the gang wars had become so inflamed that just crossing the street going to school had become a challenge."

Sergeant John "Rick" Baker, a Compton cop, had also grown up there. "The rise of the gangs," Baker wrote in his tell-all book (*Vice*), "represented yet another dividing line in Compton. Kids who had grown up in the same neighborhoods, who had gone to school and played sports together, who dated one another's sisters, and danced at the sock hops in Cressey Park [Gonzáles Park], were taking sides across a barrier that separated criminality and the law."

Beyond violence, gangs brought other criminal behavior, especially illicit moneymaking activities. Selling stolen goods, pot, cocaine, and other drugs on the streets brought in cash. "By the time Tim [Brennan] and Bob [Robert Ladd] joined the Compton Police Department—one in 1982, the other in 1983," wrote Lolita Files, the author who helped Brennan and Ladd pcn *Once Upon a Time in Compton*, "there were over fifty gangs operating in Compton."

Gangs protected their turf, with violence between the dominant Crips and Blood sets intensifying when they organized around drug distribution and sales of crack cocaine in the 1980s. Several Latino gangs in and around the old barrio joined the fray, and the bloody violence worsened as gangs equipped themselves with weapons of war.

Gangs relied on drawing in young men, especially marginalized boys who lacked a sense of belonging and wanted protection and dollars in their pockets. As Files correctly stated: "Young people who felt alienated, put-upon, and misunderstood could be easily shaped. Those who'd never had any money to speak of could, after just a short time, buy fresh gear, nice kicks, video games, new bikes, even cars, expensive cars, and houses of their own, depending on how high they rose up the criminal food chain."

Innocent bystanders and other citizens were among the causalities from stray bullets and more. If racist cops in Compton thought you might be a gangbanger, you were targeted. Ditto if gangbangers thought you were from a rival gang.

The depressing print and broadcast media research I'd conducted from afar suggested my hometown had descended into utter despair. But, as a historian, something told me there was more to the story. In 1995, I made plans to return to Compton to find out for myself.

For every tale of sadness and loss, I would eventually return and discover stories of perseverance and hope that could fill volumes. For every story about Compton school failures, I'd hear from teachers and community members committed to opening doors of opportunity for youth. I met hard-working people who were making life livable for themselves and their children.

NINETEEN

Detour to Homecoming

My plan was to use a sabbatical leave in 1995–96 to reacquaint myself with Compton and its residents, and I was eager to get going. I had hoped to return years earlier but there were several unavoidable delays.

The initial glitch came a few years earlier while I served as the associate dean of undergraduate studies in Stanford's largest school, the School of Humanities and Sciences (H&S). I'd only stepped into central university administration because Ewart Thomas, the school's dean then, asked me to join his staff. In part, accepting Ewart's offer would allow me to tackle some unfinished work on my bucket list tied to recommendations of the University Committee on Minority Issues. Despite dozens of other recommendations from the UCMI final report being adopted by the early 1990s, the university hadn't added ethnic studies to the undergraduate curriculum. Ewart had made significant progress in encouraging departments to hire more faculty of color, many of whom specialized in race and ethnic studies. The campus was primed for an ethnic studies curriculum as a result, and serving as associate dean with Ewart at the helm would allow pushing for this.

The historical moment for Stanford was important. Ewart Thomas had been one of the first Blacks appointed to the faculty in 1972, and later the first Black chairperson of the Psychology Department, and Dean of H&S. I was the first Chicano professor to become an associate dean.

Among my many duties related to undergraduate studies, I had direct oversight for most interdepartmental, degree-granting teaching programs in the school. That included the programs in African and African American Studies (AAAS), in American studies, and the Chicano Fellows Program (a non-degree program in Chicano studies). These three programs were the only ethnic studies curriculum in 1991, putting Stanford far behind most comparable universities. Ewart gave me carte blanche to explore ways to boost ethnic studies on the Farm.

After speaking with many colleagues in the small cadre of departmental faculty who taught courses that foregrounded race and ethnicity, I consulted with my close colleague in the History Department, George Fredrickson. At the request of the former dean of undergraduate studies, and in the spirit of UCMI recommendations, George and I had already developed a core course in 1990 on comparative studies in race and ethnicity to enhance the curricular offerings in the American Studies Program and in the History Department.

George's pioneering scholarship, such as his influential book, *White Supremacy: A Comparative Study in American and South African History*, had already greatly influenced me. My research had also become comparative in scope by the time we launched our course as part of advancing comparative studies in race and ethnicity. We understood how valuable these scholarly frameworks were on many fronts.

The course allowed us to grasp the growing disciplinary and interdisciplinary literature about ethnic and racial group experiences, in the United States and beyond. It allowed our students to compare different groups' experiences over time, opening their eyes to new and different ways to understand how racial ideologies influenced inequalities of many shades. Along the way, they would better understand how societal institutions across time and place were structured to maintain and reinforce racial inequality. Comparative perspectives, in addition, equipped students to examine how social movements by various groups to advance specific racial justice goals had common historical threads.

Luckily, George and I had no problem getting colleagues to give guest lectures in our course, and it drew high student interest. We were clearly onto something special.

With Ewart's encouragement, George and I also proposed an interdisciplinary faculty seminar in comparative race and ethnicity—which the university endorsed—to be funded by the Andrew W. Mellon Foundation. The foundation accepted our proposal.

The seminar ran for two years. Starting in 1992, a richly diverse group of faculty—women and men, Black, White, Chicano, Native American, Jewish, and Asian American—came together at Stanford to discuss readings and present their own race studies–related research. The seminar covered the United States and race and ethnic relations in eastern Europe, Africa, Asia, and Latin America, while drawing in not only humanities faculty, but social scientists and law and education professors.

The galvanizing seminar forged new contacts, while showing that comparative studies in race and ethnicity can provide an intellectual glue for faculty across disciplines and for the study of various groups across time and national boundaries. Equally important, because such seminars lack the scope to drive permanent institutional change, the successful seminar helped establish a pillar on which to build a community of scholars with similar interests.

The timing was prescient, for when our seminar ended in spring 1994, a student-initiated protest began that provoked campus interest in advancing ethnic studies. Those changes had enormous consequences for me professionally and personally, while putting Compton travel plans on hold again.

On a seemingly routine morning in early May 1994, I dropped Lauren off at her elementary school and headed to my office in the History Department for some course preparation. Then I took the typical short walk to my dean's office in the H&S building.

A group of students was assembled in the center of the Quad, yelling chants of protest. Though I couldn't clearly hear the words while approaching, I soon realized that they were mostly Chicano/a students. I knew many, and quickly realized this was no casual, spontaneous student protest. My line of sight shifted quickly to four Chicana students seated next to two tents and flanked by a growing number of students. It sure looked to me like a strike. It was the start of a hunger strike.

A male student on the opposite end of the Quad, with a bullhorn in hand, shouted toward students marching nearby: "What do we say?" The students replied, "Strike! Chicano Studies Now!" When the leader asked their demands be articulated, they shouted back, "Stop Immigrant Bashing Now!" at the top of their lungs. The group of marching students, holding banners, came to a stop next to the hunger strikers.

The crowd of students grew quickly. I asked one what was going on. "We are protesting many things," she explained, "and we are committed to the hunger strike until our list of demands to the president and provost are met."

I wasn't surprised by the Chicana student protest. The hunger strike? That was a shocker. Several months earlier, Provost Condoleezza Rice had announced across the board budget cuts at the university because of the lingering effects of a national recession in California. The budget reductions resulted in staff layoffs, which had included Cecilia Burciaga the previous month. As Chicano/a faculty had predicted, this created a huge stir.

Cecilia had been at Stanford for twenty years, most recently as associate dean of graduate studies. Undergraduate Chicano/a students also knew her and husband Antonio "Tony" Burciaga, a well-known artist and author, as the live-in resident fellow family for many years at Casa Zapata. They were fixtures in the local community too, and Cecilia—a beloved role model for Chicana and other students—was the highest-ranking Latina administrator on campus.

Unbeknownst to us Chicano faculty, dozens of Chicano/a students had previously mobilized behind the scenes to contest Cecilia's dismissal. Various university administrators had replied that Cecilia's termination was a *fait accompli*. So, a group of Chicana members of MEChA (Movimiento Estudiantil Chicano de Aztlán) took a page from the protest playbook of the United Farmworkers Union in staging the hunger strike. I learned that they were ready to camp out in the Quad until their demands were met, including Cecilia's reinstatement.

The four Chicana hunger strikers were soon joined by a male peer, despite the fact that surviving on liquids alone for several days was physically hazardous. News of the strike spread, and a rainbow of students numbering in the hundreds gathered to support the cause.

The president and provost of the university agreed to meet with students to discuss four core demands: a ban on table grapes served in student cafeterias, establishing a center in East Palo Alto's Chicano community, creating a Chicano studies program, and providing a high-level position for Cecilia Burciaga. When the campus leaders agreed to channel all but the Burciaga demand to university committees for discussion, the strike began.

By day two, over a hundred students had joined the fast. Out of concern and support, the Chicano/a faculty drafted a letter to the president, a copy of which was published in the student newspaper. On the third day, some of the students asked a few of us to meet with them in a closed-door meeting with the president and provost, hoping to settle the strike. Though they dropped the Cecilia reappointment demand, they asked President Casper and Provost Rice to meet with them publicly in the Quad to sign a mutual agreement. The next day the strike ended, just as some of the hunger strikers were scaring me with the early signs of physical distress.

After many months, three committees were assembled. The one actionable plan that surfaced? Formation of a formal, degree-granting Chicano studies program. The committee of students and faculty appointed to consider this request decided to recommend, instead, the formation of a broader, interdepartmental undergraduate degree: the Program in Comparative Studies in Race and Ethnicity. Students in this program could declare a major in Chicano studies, Asian American studies, Native American studies, Jewish studies, or Comparative studies, all under one roof. The Program in African and African American Studies would be affiliated, but its autonomy maintained.

How much this would change my life soon became clear when John Shoven, who'd succeeded Ewart Thomas as H&S dean, called with an ask for my help with the new program. (I had remained an associate dean under John's leadership.)

I wasn't surprised by his request that I direct the new undergraduate degree program. But I wanted to do what was best in the bigger picture of things, and I consulted with fellow colleagues first. I ended up agreeing to direct the new program with several conditions: it would became part of a larger university center that would build collaboration among faculty across the university; it would promote multidisciplinary research in general; it would engage in public policy analyses; and it would enhance graduate student professional development.

John agreed to what would be the only center of its kind at a private university in the nation. After I chaired a committee charged with writing the new center's proposal, the Center for Comparative Studies in Race and Ethnicity (CCSRE) opened in 1996. For six years, I directed the center and its undergraduate teaching program (CSRE), and I chaired the major in Comparative studies, which quickly became the most popular degree option for program students. George Fredrickson and Claude Steele, giants in their respective academic fields, co-directed the CCSRE's affiliated Research Institute. Dorothy Steele, a specialist in early education, later joined the team as executive director.

Together, and with many other colleagues, we built the foundation for this unprecedented center and its all-star cast of faculty. We enthusiastically launched what I now call "Ethnic studies 2.0" and what many other universities now refer to as the "Stanford model."

Our program differed from other ethnic studies programs in higher ed for being based on a comparative studies framework. Our approach was interdisciplinary and multidisciplinary in orientation, national and international in scope, and involved a variety of undergraduate degree programs. It was a new venture for Stanford too, in combining a research institute with a teaching program for faculty and graduate student research and intellectual exchange. It was also the organizational umbrella for majors in Asian American studies, Chicano/a (later Chicanx/Latinx) studies, Native American studies, Jewish studies, and Comparative Studies in Race and Ethnicity, with a close affiliation with the program in African and African American studies.

Comparative Studies in Race and Ethnicity (CSRE) immediately attracted undergrad students' attention. Fifteen students initially declared one of the ethnic-specific majors or Comparative Studies. Within five years, that number surpassed 100, the fastest-growing undergraduate degree on campus at the time.

Helping to build the center and advise hundreds of students was officially a half-time appointment. I worked my tail off during those years, though, while still teaching two courses a year and mentoring many doctoral students. But it was a labor of love, to see this innovative, new platform for ethnic studies prosper.

For this bigger cause, I'd put my interest in returning to Compton on hold. After all, it would require hundreds of hours in the city to truly ground myself in its current realities and to apply skills that I'd gained over decades as a historian. Yet I knew I had to make it there to bring my unique position as a native son and seasoned scholar activist to bear on more deeply understanding Compton's past and present. I also wanted to explore how I could help Compton youth. But with my incredibly busy schedule, it took the growing interest in Compton of my eldest son, now a college student, for me to make a return.

Despite his parents' early reprimand, Jeff's interest in rap music increased over time. With it came interest in Compton as a hub of rap music and culture. When he learned from me that Compton, despite its all-Black image, had as many Latino people, he shared that it reminded him of his racially diverse high school friends, and the racial divide between our overwhelmingly White westside of Menlo Park and the Belle Haven community (in east Menlo Park) and the city of East Palo Alto. Most of his friends of color lived in these two neighborhoods located across Highway 101.

In addition, unlike middle school, Jeff's public high school was multiracial. His basketball teammates were White, Black, Latino, and Pacific Islanders; his girlfriend and closest buddies, Black. From his Menlo-Atherton High School experiences and his role as a student body leader, he saw for the first time how different groups of students were divided residentially, socially, and academically along racial, ethnic, and class lines.

But it was Jeff's University of Pennsylvania experience that ignited the intellectual and educational/social justice passions that took him—and me—to Compton. Soon after his freshman year began in 1997, Jeff took a sociology course on race in American cities and then decided to apply for a summer internship opportunity created by a close colleague, Ira Harkavy. Ira, a UPenn historian, and I became instant friends a decade earlier during a faculty summer institute sponsored by Stanford's Haas Center for Public Service to promote service-learning curriculum, or what is today often referred to as community-engaged education.

Jeff became an intern and spent the summer working with African American students at a West Philadelphia middle school. Along with Samy Alim (who later joined the Stanford faculty), he developed a successful hip-hop–themed literacy project for Turner Middle School students. While shepherding the project for three years, he became hooked on the idea of teaching at a school with kids like those he'd worked with at Turner.

Although that middle school was only about twenty blocks from the UPenn campus, Jeff shared that "it was a world away" economically and otherwise. "West Philly and Turner School," he added, "taught me more about race and inequality than any one experience I had in the elite Ivy League bubble of UPenn."

His "world away" comment hit home immediately, from my early days of experiencing UCLA after leaving Compton. And I knew that Jeff's future teaching experiences might also deeply influence his worldviews about race and ethnic relations.

Jeff's academic and racial justice interests began to gel around issues of urban education and racial inequality. And he decided to write a senior honors thesis about Compton, following in my footsteps in many ways.

That became true, literally, when I traveled with Jeff to informally introduce him to Compton on a comfortably warm, sunny day in July 2000. It was, in many ways, a homecoming for my family in general. Although many of my relatives had lived in Compton into the 1980s, like many other families around then, they'd become part of the movement of White, Mexican American, and African American families out of Compton during its years of economic decline.

The city had gone through a transformation since I'd initially left for college in 1966, and so had I. Back then, I'd been an uninformed, naïve eighteen-year-old. I returned at fifty-two with a wealth of knowledge about racial and ethnic groups in American cities.

When I came of age in Compton, the city's demographics were undergoing sweeping changes along a White–Black color line, with tensions defining race relations. Three decades later in the late twentieth century, tensions were spiking again, but between different groups, which no one could've forecasted.

The racially segregated Compton into which I was born in the mid-twentieth century was over 90 percent White. But by 1970, Black folks represented 71 percent, and Latinos, about 13 percent, of city residents.

Now I was introducing my eldest son to a Compton that some had begun referring to as a "minority-majority" town—a city of color. And the city had undergone a second demographic shift, becoming decidedly more Latino. Mostly Mexican residents predominated now, primarily on the city's eastside. The 2000 U.S. Census reported a Hispanic population of 57 percent, but they probably represented closer to two-thirds of the 93,000 Comptonites. African Americans had become the minority at roughly 40 percent.

Compton's changing population reflected what some commentators call a general "browning" of Los Angeles and Southern California. Massive immigration from Mexico since the 1970s, and to a lesser extent from Central American nations, changed the face of California, especially down south. Nearly half the 10 million people in Los Angeles County in 2000 were Latino.

I had prepped Jeff about the city's demographics before we visited Compton in summer 2000. We began a driving tour of city neighborhoods soon after exiting the Long Beach Freeway on Alondra Avenue and entering East Compton (which had been the non-Black half of the city into the mid-1960s). Dominguez High School, the White high school I'd resisted transferring to in 1963, was located at the outskirts of eastside Compton.

"Hey, look, Dale's Donuts is still here!" I said, pointing out the Compton landmark, famous for its drive-up window and the huge plaster donut perched on its roof. "I worked part-time during high school at the Atlantic Richfield [ARCO] gas station across the street," I added, though Jeff seemed more interested in a local map.

"This isn't Compton," he said with a look up from the street map on his lap. "This area is called East Rancho Dominguez." "Oh, yeah, that's right," I replied, explaining how we'd all known this area along Atlantic Boulevard that bordered the Los Angeles River and the Long Beach Freeway as East Compton. What few knew then was that this area was officially an unincorporated area of Los Angeles County, surrounded by Compton's city limits.

Sometime in the 1980s, business owners and residents here had opted to call themselves East Rancho Dominguez. They didn't want an association with Compton's bad reputation and staved off attempts by the city to annex the area, as did a similar area on the city's westside (West Rancho Dominguez). Neighboring cities—Paramount to the east and Lawndale, Hawthorn, and Gardena to the west—mirrored that approach, even discarding the name of Compton Boulevard, a main thoroughfare coursing through them.

I recognized other buildings along E. Alondra Avenue and saw that they desperately needed paint or repairs. Most had iron grates on windows and doors, while some were shuttered. I found myself repeating to Jeff: "See that place selling *llantas* (tires)? It used to be . . . See that *taquería*? It used to be . . . See that *tiendita* (little store)? It used to be . . ."

We turned on to S. Long Beach Boulevard, which was the main business avenue of East Compton. The boulevard had once been home to no fewer than twenty-five new and used car dealerships. The so-called Hub City could've also rightly claimed to be "Hubcap City" years ago. "They're all gone," I blurted out, as I drove the short distance to Compton Boulevard, while sharing where Chevy, Chrysler, and Ford dealerships had once been. Jerry's BBQ Pit, a 1950s- style carhop restaurant and hangout, was also gone. The strip I'd once cruised in my cool 58 Chevy Impala was no more.

The landscape of Compton's eastside had changed remarkably. Many businesses there bore Latino names, and pedestrians were almost exclusively Latinos/as. I didn't spot one White person as we drove through the eastside.

Our first stop was the historic barrio, where my earliest memories had been shaped. We parked next to Alatorre Market, the former Gonzáles Market of my youth. I shared how my father and grandfather had built the building about seventy years earlier. "The original sandstone bricks are plastered over," I muttered, "but it is the same old tienda."

As we exited the car, Jeff asked if the barrio looked a lot different. "It really hasn't changed much," I replied after glancing around. As we walked to the front of the old store, I stood for a moment, gazing at the building's interior while memories flooded in. The meat counter was still on the store's left side. I could imagine the five-gallon jar of pickled pig's feet on the counter. I'd loved those pickled things.

In a rush, I was eight again, heading into the store of Padrino Ramón Gonzáles, to redeem a few Coke bottles for candy. Then I was sitting on the Willowbrook Avenue curb outside the store sipping sodas across from the streetcar tracks, with buddies Luli, Beegie, and Popito. For a moment, I was home in the barrio, in my roots.

We entered the little market for our scheduled interview with the owner, Arnold Alatorre. Two women shoppers talked in Spanish as we passed through the open doors. Though the interior looked only slightly different from childhood, it felt different. Now in the mindset of an older man, I felt at home, but as a visitor.

An employee at the check-out counter directed us to Alatorre's little office at the back of the building. A man of about forty years, he greeted us and immediately turned to two older men seated next to him. "I hope you don't mind," he said with a smile, "I asked Jesse and Larry to join us today because they remember you as a kid."

Jesse Madrigal and Larry Gonzáles, both in their mid-seventies, were born and raised in Compton's barrio and knew my uncles and aunts. I vaguely remembered them living within a block of this market. Larry's home was literally across the alley from ours. He and Jesse were among the few of their generation who never left the barrio, or their childhood homes. As I later learned from Uncle John, one of my mother's brothers, Jesse had been his close teenage friend during the 1930s and early 40s before they were shipped off to fight in Europe during World War II.

I learned from Alatorre that his father, who immigrated from Mexico to Compton in 1953, purchased Gonzáles Market sometime in the early 1970s. My conversation with Arnold, Jesse, and Larry revealed much about how the barrio had changed and, yet, how it was much the same. The residents, mostly Mexicans, who lived in the area had primarily moved there since the 1970s. The White families once in homes scattered along the barrio boundaries had long departed. More and more immigrants from Mexico replaced them, expanding the barrio's area. According to my interviewees, very few African Americans had ever settled in the area.

To continue the tour of my old stomping grounds, we drove a short distance to the Compton Town Center for some coffee before the next scheduled meeting. The two-block downtown business district of Compton of my youth had been demolished in the 1970s. In its place, on both sides of Compton Boulevard, sits a glorified strip mall with parking lots ringed by small businesses, a grocery store, a chain pharmacy, and a few fast-food restaurants. We stopped at the only full-service restaurant in this central part of Compton, IHOP.

Once upon a time, I'd shopped for clothes at King's Store for Men where Jeff and I were now sipping coffee and dining on pancakes. When we exited the restaurant, a quick scan showed no remnants of the classic "Main Street U.S.A." downtown of the past.

We walked a short distance to the Compton Police Department, approaching the only building still standing from the days of my youth, the Compton Post Office. Across from the LA Metro Blue train tracks (where the old Red Cars once clanked) was this little post office, built after the 1933 quake. The Spanish mission–style building of the Great Depression era was still open, and looked unchanged, except for an added ADA ramp entrance. Iron grates, a now familiar sight in the city, also framed its windows.

Best of all, we could peek inside at the colorful mural, depicting Native Americans, Spanish, and Mexicans in early California. I always wondered who'd had painted the cool mural I admired when I accompanied my mama to buy stamps at the post office. (Much later, I learned the Compton Post Office mural was part of a New Deal WPA-sponsored cultural arts initiative to put unemployed artists to work during the 1930s. James Redmond was commissioned by the U.S. Treasury Department's Relief Art Project to paint it in 1936.)

The post office now sits in the shadow of the thirteen-story Los Angeles County Superior Courthouse. This tall, ominous-looking white courthouse dwarfed all other city structures, including the nearby LA County Branch Library, City Hall, and the Compton Police Department, all rebuilt in the 1980s. Tensions between residents and law enforcement in the late 1980s were reflected, in part, in the courthouse's nickname, "Fort Compton." The courthouse would occasionally became target practice when someone would shoot at the windows and pepper the exterior walls with bullets, yet another example of these tensions.

Next to the post office and courthouse sat the new police department, where Jeff and I met with Lt. Reggie Wright. A colleague of Art's back in the day, Wright headed the department's Gang Enforcement Unit. He gave us a personal, detailed professional assessment of gang activity in the city, past and present. Reggie grew up in the Imperial Courts housing projects of nearby Watts, but he'd attended Compton schools and knew Compton deeply from twenty-four years on the force. As we departed, Reggie advised us to avoid certain hot spots in the city, neighborhoods where gang violence had recently spiked.

To get back to the Town Center parking lot, we crossed the LA Metro railway tracks in front of the post office, while other memories washed over me. "It's gone, too!" I said to Jeff, pointing out the restaurant on the corner where the Red Car passenger waiting station and its diner had been located. A warehouse with a loading ramp had once stood next to the Pacific Electric Railway station, too; it was replaced by the Compton Transit Center for the LA Metro railway service. As Jeff and I continued touring, I wondered if West Compton neighborhoods I'd roamed in the early 1960s would also be unrecognizable.

"Farms in Compton?!" Jeff replied with a curious giggle, as I blurted out the next stop. "Yeah, man, there were farms in Compton—Richland Farms," I said laughing, because no one Jeff's age could imagine the city with farms and farm animals. We'd moved to Richland Farms in 1956, after the church bought our barrio property.

We stopped in front of my old home that his grandfather had built on the corner of Oleander and Greenleaf Streets. Though the house was now a puke-green color, it felt very familiar—but not so the view from the southern side of the home. Where dozens of farms had once spread over thousands of acres, we saw one of the largest light industrial districts in Southern California.

"Close your eyes, Jeff," I instructed after pointing south toward the back of the sprawling complex of buildings in front of us, "and try to imagine open fields and farmland as far as you can see." It was obvious he couldn't begin to visualize my early adolescent farmland years. Initial sadness from missing the open lands I once roamed with my dog Butch quickly gave way to fond memories, as I closed my eyes—briefly recalling the hayfields and nearby Compton Creek and Dominguez Hills in the background.

Jeff and I jumped back into the car and headed deeper into West Compton, to the middle school I'd attended. "It really looks bad," Jeff blurted out, as we drove slowly past Walton, asking "How old is the school?" Graffiti covered some outside walls, and at least one of the many damaged classrooms' windows was boarded with plywood. The school was about fifty years old, but the signs of years of neglect showed from the poverty that had gripped Compton and its school district for over a quarter century.

We continued visiting more westside neighborhoods, especially near Centennial High School located in the city's far northwest corner. This area, bordering Watts and unincorporated parts of South Central LA, had been the residential beachhead for African Americans in the late 1940s and early 50s. And it was where the first Black-owned businesses started.

The most beloved of these businesses for three generations of African Americans was Naka's Broiler, located across the street from Centennial High. Nathaniel and Katherine Banks, Texas natives, opened their little restaurant in 1956. The couple divorced several years later, but "Mama Naka," as customers adoringly called her, became a revered community fixture for sixty years.

"There seems to be way fewer Mexican folks here," Jeff noted in northwest Compton. In fact, Black residents on the streets and driving along Central Avenue were still the majority in this corner of Compton.

We continued our drive and headed back to the old barrio to meet Father Stan Bosch, a local Catholic priest and social justice activist with a reputation for practicing what he preached. Father Stan wanted to meet at Sacred Heart Church, one of two Compton churches he served. We parked in front of the chapel that'd been there since I was a kid. After the larger, new church was built at the end of the block, the chapel became a community center for parishioners. Every home that'd once occupied the eastern side of N. Culver Street, including ours and our grandmother's house next door, were long gone. A row of small administrative offices lined the back of the parking lot between the old and new chapel.

Father Stan greeted us warmly at his office. A White man in his early forties with sandy-brown colored hair and a close-cropped white beard, he looked more like an aging surfer boy than a clergyman. The old, Irish priest I remembered from the 1950s had worn traditional long black robes. Father Stan sported khaki pants and a collarless short-sleeve black shirt.

After quick introductions, I think I stunned him when I looked around and peered through the office windows, announcing, "I'm sitting in the same space where I was born fifty-two years ago," referring to my home that had once stood in the same spot.

"Welcome home, Al," said Father Stan.

It felt strange yet comfortable. And we left that meeting with an agreement to return soon for much longer discussions about Compton and the father's work with Latino/a parishioners. That July day in 2000 was the first of what became many summers to follow, in which I learned more about the city's status and people. But for Jeff, the trip seeded what would turn into a nearly decade-long commitment to Compton and its youth.

TWENTY

Our Town, Our Kids

Timing is everything. Added inspiration for reacquainting myself with my hometown came unexpectedly in the summer of 2002. A documentary film came out about teachers and students at Dominguez High School, my alma mater. I had to go see *OT: Our Town—A Famous American Play in an Infamous American Town* right away.

I was skeptical, due to the "Infamous" in Scott Hamilton Kennedy's subtitle. "I bet this film is about gangs at my old high school," I told Susan as we planned to see it in San Francisco. She suggested I give it a chance.

Thoughts of high school days came back on the thirty-mile trip north to the city. I hadn't been on the Dominguez High campus since freshman year at UCLA in 1967, when I'd returned to the relatively new high school to watch former basketball teammates play. Trepidation mixed with eagerness to see what the campus looked like in the film, given Compton schools' challenges in recent decades.

San Francisco's Roxie, a century-old independent movie theater near the Mission District, was almost empty that Saturday afternoon. And my low expectations for the documentary seemed to be met in the opening scenes:

254

a graffiti-marked Compton landscape appeared, with the music of N.W.A.'s "Straight Outta Compton" and George Benson's "The Ghetto" playing in the background. Next came the worn-looking buildings of Dominguez High with a police squad car cruising the campus.

But within two minutes, I was mesmerized by the sensitive, poignant story about two teachers who used tough love and captured the hearts of a group of teenagers at Dominguez High while they struggled together to mount the first student play at the school in decades. The film laid bare the experiences of Catherine Borek, Karen Greene, and their students as they grappled with huge challenges in a poor high school, in a district that had only recently regained control from the state.

With no funding, props, or lights, the group turned Thornton Wilder's classic 1938 play, *Our Town*, into a Compton-style drama. There is no theater on campus, and a stage wasn't even available, until right before the play's performance in the school's cafeteria building.

At its core, the documentary covers how Black and Brown students overcame self-doubt, fear, and many personal and familial difficulties to successfully stage a play at Dominguez. Along the uncertain and bumpy path to pulling off the play in front of a packed audience of family and friends, Borek and Greene also encountered doubt and apprehension. But they triumphed.

Tears streamed down my cheeks after the final act of the play ended, as I saw the student cast members hug and kiss one another, family members, and their proud teachers. The standing ovation from the audience and students' smiles told it all: the feelings of accomplishment, joy, and pride in knowing how hard work and dedication had paid off.

The film, shot primarily in the cafeteria, touched me at so many levels. That same cafeteria was where I'd attended school dances—though during a vastly different time. And it's where I'd organized a meeting to help ease racial tensions as the student body president.

I'm sure most viewers saw the film as a lesson in perseverance and faith. For me, it mainly reinforced the need to understand Compton and its people more deeply, to search beyond the tropes and stereotypes about a place defined only as dangerous, criminal, and violent.

The African American and Latino/a youth in the play and their dedicated teachers represented an unexamined, inspirational slice of life in Compton that the media had largely ignored. This was the other side of Compton that I saw the more time I spent there.

The minute I returned home after viewing *OT: Our Town*, I reached out to Borek and Greene to arrange to meet them. I met with Borek initially during my next visit to Compton, in fall 2002. Catherine Borek, a twenty-one-year-old White woman and recent graduate of Portland's Reed College, had moved to the LA area to begin her first teaching job. "The first time we drove through Compton," she said with a smile on her face, "it was scary [because] I had, of course, the gangsta-rap image in my mind, drive-by shootings and all of 'The Boyz n the Hood' images." Accompanied by a friend as they meandered through city streets, she wondered "Are they noticing my skin color?"

Borek had been accepted into the Teach for America (TFA) program. Founded in 1990, TFA places young college graduates in under-resourced rural and urban schools as non-credentialed teachers. After an intensive summer training session in one of several locations nationally, these mostly liberal-minded, social justice-oriented wanna-be teachers are placed by TFA in schools with high teacher turnover.

Of her four California choices at the time, Catherine said, "I wanted Compton the whole time," adding with a giggle, "except for the fact they paid the least." She began there in 1996 as an English teacher at Centennial High but was soon transferred to Dominguez High after the district's count of students at each school shifted placements.

Catherine's eyes sparkled in recalling the transfer to Dominguez, which had less staff, as being "one of the biggest blessings" for allowing her to work through beginning teachers' mistakes. "I was focusing less on the kids, except in their reaction to me: Would they react badly to the White teacher? Would they accept me? Would they react badly to a young teacher?"

Unlike Centennial on the city's northwest side, the demographics of the student body on the far east side were flipped: Dominguez High had about 40 percent African American and 60 percent Latino students. In fact, Catherine's seventh period class, which was a favorite, was mostly Latinos/as. "They were the class that when the bell rang," ending the school day, "if they were in the middle of reading a poem . . . , they would stay." By the end of the academic year, Catherine had committed to staying at Dominguez "so I could see that seventh period class graduate in 2000."

Back in high school, Catherine had loved taking drama classes. She persuaded the school administration to allow her to teach a drama class, and the idea was born to stage a production. She plastered posters on campus hallways and interested about forty students in trying out.

From the start, putting on the play was no cakewalk. Few students could commit to regular after school rehearsals, Catherine said, recounting that many "had a job, had to babysit, had something going on." She soon appreciated, from working with the student cast members, the harsh realities many of them faced in Compton in the 1990s.

For instance, Ebony volunteered for the lead narrator role in the three-act play. An extremely bright, articulate student, she shared in the documentary that her birth mom had been a prostitute. Ebony was adopted by a single, divorced mother who'd moved her children to Compton when Ebony was in fifth grade.

Arguably the documentary's star, Ebony declares at the beginning, "Compton—home of gangsta rap and gangsters. That's all people know about Compton, that's all people think of Compton."

She went on to become a student at UC Berkeley, where I met her at her dormitory in October 2003. We talked about life in Compton and at Dominguez High and her experiences in the play. "I can't say enough about those teachers. I think they [Ms. Borek and Ms. Greene] are the reason that so many of us now, this generation of students that are coming out of Dominguez . . . are pushing and are trying to succeed." Ebony credits these and other teachers for helping to turn around the Dominguez culture by planting seeds of opportunity and success.

She also benefited from parental support and advocacy. "I think I've been college bound since I was in kindergarten, probably prior to that," she said, noting that her mom taught her how to read at age three. That doesn't mean her young life was challenge free. Although she always excelled in school, Ebony shared that Compton schools weren't ideal preparation for the super-competitive college environment she was in now. Despite not being able to assist with this educational transition, Ebony's mother was helping by telling her, "Do it on your own."

I certainly could identify with her mama's message, and Ebony's conundrum. Like my own parents, those of Ebony and other Compton students who'd had little formal classroom instruction could still understand and promote education as the key to a better life.

Karen Greene, the other teacher and collaborator on the play, knew the challenges of Compton's kids from having grown up there. Karen's schooling experience was different from the majority of her peers, though, because she was in the GATE (Gifted and Talented Education) program beginning in first grade and attended a high school outside Compton. Yet she knew kids in her neighborhood who experienced the threat of gangs, a home without two parents, teen pregnancy, and more.

Karen also brought substantial knowledge and training in the arts to Dominguez. The UC Berkeley graduate went on to receive a fellowship to work for the Social Outreach Theater in Washington, DC, before working in Los Angeles and Denver for a while. "I wanted to find ways of bringing the arts back to Compton," she said, after she began teaching at Dominguez High in 1999.

I entered these extraordinary teachers' world for a bit when Ms. Borek invited me to speak to one of her English classes in fall 2004. Walking through the hallways of Dominguez High was painful, due to the shabby-looking classroom buildings and walls spot-painted to cover up graffiti. But I was super excited to meet Catherine's students. After sharing a little about Compton's history, I asked students about their hopes and dreams. "How many of you want some day to own a nice home, live in a nice neighborhood, and drive a nice car?" All hands quickly shot up. I continued with, "To have these things in America today you need a college education. How many of you want to go to college?" Only a few students didn't raise their hands. "Do your parents want you to go to college?" brought similar responses.

Then I shared my own story of parents who were poor, had limited education, and yet had a desire for their kids to attend college. I told the students all this so they could understand that the unlikely journey through higher education was possible, adding that, "When I was a student a long time ago at Dominguez, there were a few teachers like Ms. Borek who supported my dream to go to college. And though college was difficult for me way back when, I followed my dreams and the dreams of my parents."

I could tell my message had sunk in when Ms. Borek's students began asking questions about college life. One question, though, made me laugh. "When you were at Dominguez long ago," a boy asked with a curious look on his face, "did you have to walk through the LA River to get to school?" The school borders the river. My response generated lots of giggles. "No, I'm old, but I ain't that old. There were bridges across the river when I was your age."

As I left Catherine's class and walked to the parking lot, I thought about how the odds were stacked against these kids and their parents, who faced a difficult, sometimes insurmountable hill to keep them safe and in school, much less help prepare them for college. "How do they manage? How do they keep hope alive?" Driving away from the campus that afternoon, one thought stuck in my head: the students I met sure were lucky to have Ms. Borek as a teacher.

In the years following my return to Compton, I also learned about community-based and faith-based organizations and leaders working tire-lessly to help and protect Compton's young people. I met not only other committed teachers, but parents who pushed hard for a better educational system. I also reconnected with one of my former Stanford students, Luz Herrera, who had recently set up a one-person legal practice in Compton. Together we began to lay plans to connect residents and programs in the city dedicated to helping kids.

Born in Tijuana and raised in East Los Angeles, Luz had been a Chicana student leader at the Farm and had enrolled in at least one of my courses. She emailed me in 2002 to say she'd established a private practice in a small office in my hometown to serve the growing Latino population.

Inspiration was something Luz understood. She'd had no idea about lawyering until she had an opportunity as a high school student to meet an attorney who worked for the Mexican American Legal Defense and Edu-cation Fund. Then she found out in college how lawyers had used litigation strategies to cement civil rights victories in the 1960s and 70s. "Learning about this history helped me envision a role for myself in the legal profession. I wanted to be a lawyer who used her legal training to open doors for others."

I could have stamped "future social justice lawyer" on Luz's forehead by the time she graduated from Stanford and was headed to Harvard Law

School in 1996. She turned down more lucrative offers afterward to set up a solo law practice in Compton. "For me it is simple," Luz recalled, "I went to law school because I wanted to represent people like the ones who sell homemade tamales door-to-door and the street vendors. They are the working poor. They are entrepreneurial immigrants. They are those individuals who struggle to make full rental and mortgage payments on time. Establishing my own practice allowed me the opportunity to fuel the fire that burned in my belly."

Luz was instrumental in gathering like-minded folks in the city to meet with us and discuss issues facing Compton youth. The widening circle of people I met through the informal group we formed, Compton Community Partners, exposed me to more people and programs making a difference locally.

The Partners sometimes met at El Nido Family Center, an independent nonprofit working throughout LA that had been founded in the 1920s by the National Council of Jewish Women. At one of these meetings, I met Mark Deese, a remarkable Compton parent and community activist. Unlike many other parents who fled during the 1980s and 90s, Mark hadn't given up on Compton and its schools.

He'd grown up in LA and visited his grandparents' home in Compton almost every weekend. They had helped found the Little Zion Baptist Church when African Americans were just becoming the majority on the westside. Mark, in turn, had moved with his wife and small children to Compton around 1985 because of its affordability. "It had been on the downswing at that particular time," he recalled in 2003.

He had also developed friendships with several classmates at California State University, Northridge, who'd grown up in Compton. "I wanted to be a part of [this] Afrocentric community," he stated emphatically. "When we came in, we were literally embraced by the block club [members], which were predominantly Black . . . and they were the most infectious, most influential, most active advocates for building a better community that I've seen anywhere in any community."

Mark's school involvement was hereditary. His mom, a super-active PTA member, visited the local school so often that he "actually thought mom was like a part owner in the schools." Besides PTA membership, Mark participated in a decades-long, dogged effort advocating to improve Compton schools because, he said, "I thought we could change it in a timely fashion. All my kids excelled in elementary and middle school, but it's when they got to high school . . . the credibility in education began to drop among schools . . . and it just fell through, like the Grand Canyon."

With hopes of tapping into his activism on behalf of Compton's kids, I invited him in 2009 to the annual celebration of a Bay Area nonprofit organization that I wanted to export to Compton: the Mural Music and Arts Project, founded by Sonya Clark Herrera, with roots in East Palo Alto, a city that resembles Compton.

I flew Mark to the Bay Area and hosted him at the event, where students discussed the importance of the organization in their lives and how it inspired them to succeed, while sharing their artwork and pride about it. Mark was clearly touched and psyched about steering an offshoot in Compton. But when I reached out after getting the ball rolling, to confirm his partnership with me, I learned, sadly, that he'd become too ill from diabetes to take on the task. He died four years later from complications of his illness.

Few parents become as engaged as a Mark Deese or a Bernice "Mama" Woods, taking their advocacy for improving education to school board meetings and city hall chambers. But I knew from reading newspaper articles and such that there were hundreds of Compton parents who clamored for better schools and safety. These Black and Latino parents condemned campus violence, advocated for better police protection, more school resources, and improved facilities.

Other advocates did so despite not being parents. That held true for Father Stan Bosch, whom Jeff and I had met in 2000 and whose work among parishioners in Compton's two Catholic parishes was inspirational. Stan was intent on going beyond simply providing religious services to his flock, about 90 percent of whom were Latinos/as. He had worked for eleven years with former gang members in Santa Ana in Orange County and in East Los Angeles. These localities are among the most ethnically homogeneous Latino communities in California.

Father Stan arrived in Compton in 1997 and quickly began working to give voice to his parishioners' concerns about public safety and policing. In summer 2000, gang violence had spiked again, especially between Latino and Black gangs. "It felt like there was a dark cloud over this place," the priest recalled of his first few months, and "the demands have been so radical and extreme—life and death—that's it's difficult to leave this place emotionally after a long day."

A proposal to disband the Compton Police Department, promoted by the city's controversial and mercurial Black mayor, Omar Bradley, was the big political issue for Compton residents in 2000. But for Father Stan, this was a moral and ethical issue too, and it deeply affected his parishioners. These Latinos/as believed in having some law enforcement presence to help keep violence in check, yet they had no representation in city government at the time.

"The police situation is really a lightning rod and an opportunity for us to stir our people," the priest told an *LA Times* reporter, regarding the voice of Latinos who made up about 70 percent of Compton's population. Father Stan mobilized parents to march every week to city hall to express concerns before the mayor and city council. Mayor Bradley, in his hyperbolic response, condemned the priest for inciting what he called a "dangerous situation" that could lead to "a race war."

Father Stan escorted me from his office in Our Lady of Victory Church that June 2000 day on his way to a meeting with African American ministers to discuss an ecclesiastical effort to help calm tensions between Black and Latino gang members. I clearly remember his words as we parted. "You know, professor," he said while cupping his hands in the manner of prayer, "it's all about the young people and their parents. If we can provide a better future for them, Compton will be a better place."

His final comments bring to mind a proverb I heard long ago—and hold dear. It goes something like this: "When you help change the life of a child for the better, you will change the family for the better. And when you help change a family, you help change a community for the better."

Among those who practice this proverb daily are public middle school classroom teachers I call the "Vanguard 3." The three at Compton's Vanguard Learning Center (VLC, formerly Vanguard Middle School) were among a community of people committed to local youth and to helping improve the lives of African American and Latino/a students. And the three are more than simply teachers to so many students.

Mr. Inge, Mr. Lane, and Mr. C all believe in what is called the "whole child approach." As soon as they began their teaching careers at Vanguard, they quickly realized that acknowledging and embracing what students brought with them to the classroom—both good and bad—was necessary to create a positive learning environment.

Mr. Lane shared the bedrock philosophy of their work as follows: "The students don't care how much you know [as a teacher]; they want to know how much you care." These guys really cared, and they helped change the lives of thousands of young people in Compton over the years, all for the better.

I deeply admired the work of the Vanguard 3, one of whom I knew quite well. Mr. C is my son Jeff. He had partnered with Matt Lane, whom I'd met in summer 2001, when the two were members of the same "Teach Compton" cohort of soon-to-be-teachers. Like Teach for America, this program brings to the Compton Unified School District new college graduates willing to jump immediately into classrooms after a summer training session. I don't think I would've had the guts to do this at age twenty-two.

In Jeff's case, he'd had experience working with middle school students in west Philly for three years as a UPenn student. What he hadn't prepared for were the large class sizes at VLC, or being asked to teach a seventh-period journalism class. "What am I supposed to do with this many students during the last period of the school day, on a subject I have no idea how to teach?" he'd asked the principal. "Just get them working on something," he said Mrs. Holmes replied. Student numbers weren't the only challenge, based on the scene Jeff shared of stepping into the journalism class the first day: "There were forty-two eighth graders in that class, in a classroom with one dusty old computer with a floppy disk and no other resources." No wonder he described the first few weeks at the VLC as being "a time of excitement mixed with fear."

Despite his father being a college professor and his mother a teacher, Matt Lane, a young White man from Portland, Oregon, also felt challenged early on. He'd attended the University of Southern California in Los Angeles and majored in sociology and African American studies. The plan was to pursue a social justice–related career in law or something else to benefit marginalized communities. Then during senior year at USC, Matt saw an ad one day in the student newspaper for Teach Compton and jumped at the opportunity.

Regis Inge was the veteran teacher of the trio. A native of nearby Gardena, he came from a long line of family members who attended Tuskegee University, many of whom became public school teachers or administrators in Alabama. His mother was a kindergarten teacher, too. Seeing how hard she'd worked, such as spending nights preparing arts and crafts projects and other things for her students, had dissuaded him from the teaching path. But as a social work major at Tuskegee, a friend had asked him to help tutor a local student one early Saturday. "I didn't know how to start tutoring this little girl until Phil told me to do some basic math with her," Regis retold the story. "'Okay, What is 2+2?' I asked the little girl, and she hesitated for a moment and then said 'B.' Okay, let's start over. 'What is 1+1?' and she said 'A.'"

Taken aback by how unprepared this young African American first grader was for school, he was hooked. "I needed to help this child," he realized, though his mom gave him mixed encouragement because of the difficulties one faces when trying to make a difference as a teacher.

Regis Inge landed his first teaching job at the VLC at age twenty-five. Back then in 1995, the school had about 60 percent Black and 40 percent Latino/a students. And he remembered feeling as underprepared as Jeff would later feel, that first day in his classroom. In fact, Regis ran through all his prepared lesson plans for the whole day by 10:30 that morning. Luckily, during a morning break, he found a senior teacher who loaned him some lesson plans.

It didn't take Regis long to understand the "whole child" concept and to be aware of "all that [students] bring to the classroom." To help them, he said, involved patience that included listening to students' stories. Some came from stable working-class families, but others, he recalled, were "foster care kids, poor children with single mothers, some with no father role models, and others exposed to gangs." Regis's teacher playbook is inspirational: "I learned how to build trust, understand their situations, help them with their self-esteem and confidence, and not judge them. I try to get them to the next level with a 'you can do it' philosophy and a goal to figure out their gifts."

Mr. Inge supported the first-year fellow teachers right away, he said, recognizing that they had "great potential to be important figures in students' lives because there were so few men teachers and positive male role models for VLC kids." They in turn learned from Regis's tips of "being persistent and giving your students love—sometimes tough love—and encouragement." Mr. C and Mr. Lane also took to heart his advice to have fun with the students—that "work and play go together"—was as important as leading with the heart and by example.

Given Inge's take, it's not surprising that, when a reporter asked him if Kendrick Lamar (a famous recording artist from Compton who attended Vanguard) was his greatest student success story, he didn't give a pat answer. "At least in fame and fortune," Mr. Inge replied to the journalist, "but all former students who reach their potential and use their gifts to find a good job and a stable life, this is how I measure success." His response broadly epitomizes what the Vanguard 3 practiced daily at VLC, while collectively logging forty years at this Compton middle school. The Vanguard 3 shared a mission to help students beat the odds by being committed teachers, mentors, and male role models.

The rewards of teaching in a Compton public school were enough that Matt Lane, who'd planned to stay two or three years before switching career paths, taught at the VLC for thirteen years (before his wife's job took them to Oakland). "It was the hardest thing I ever endured," Matt recalled about his first year at VLC. In part, he noted, "the system [in Compton schools] was incredibly broken." Yet he added, "I learned so much and had to challenge myself to be comfortable as a White male and to understand my White privilege as I came to face-to-face with many kids who didn't know White people."

Besides emulating Regis Inge's approach based on love, respect, compassion, and empathy, Matt took his advice to participate in after-school activities, when teachers and students can interact in a different light. In particular, he teamed up with Mr. C to jump headfirst into coaching school sports teams.

Having served as a "dad coach" for three children's soccer, baseball, and basketball teams, I find it hard to imagine how these young teachers juggled teaching and coaching at the same time. Despite the adjustments, Mr. Lane and Mr. C began to build strong relationships with the students in their first-year classrooms and on the field.

In fact, I learned the sports aspect was a highlight of their years working with Compton kids. "Teaching a sport," Matt said, was like having a "classroom on the field." For Mr. C, it was also a respite from teaching huge numbers of students during the day. The bonds of camaraderie they earned with students also "opened spaces," as Jeff referred to it, for students to share the good and bad stuff of their lives.

Among the frequently heard "bad stuff" was what Mr. Lane likened to student behavior that resulted from a "PTSD [post-traumatic stress disorder] because of neighborhood gang violence and unstable home life." The Vanguard 3 also cited troubling issues of abuse that some students experienced in the foster care system, and tensions between some Latino/a and Black students. In addition, undocumented students inevitably brought anxieties with them to school about being apprehended by "La Migra" (ICE, Immigration and Customs Enforcement). Students also had limited life experiences outside their Compton neighborhoods on which to build healthier perspectives. "We all wanted students to believe in themselves," Mr. Inge told me, "and we wanted to expose them to new things."

On the flipside, I heard about student resiliency, about students' eagerness to learn once they'd tasted academic achievement, and the bonds of friendship between diverse kids, building self-esteem and more. These factors fueled teachers like the Vanguard 3 to stay committed.

I had a front-row seat to see the good things VLC students brought to the table when Mr. C teamed up with his brother Greg to create a program to reward students for their achievements, on and off the field. By that time, Greg had completed his mechanical engineering degree from Stanford (in 2005) and started an unanticipated eight-year-long NFL career. High school academic success and athletic talent meant he was admitted to Harvard and invited to the Cambridge campus to observe a spring football practice. But the practice began at 6:30 in the morning—on a frozen field, with temperatures in the thirties. Stanford had also admitted him, and head football coach Tyrone Willingham soon asked him to join Stanford's program as a walk-on punter. He jumped at the opportunity, although his chances of ever playing as a walk-on were low.

In his freshman year, Greg convinced Willingham and his staff to try him at the wide receiver position he loved the most. That opportunity was life changing. By junior year, Greg was not only seeing substantial playing time, but he had a scholarship.

His experiences at Stanford, academically and athletically, had taught him a critical life lesson that he now imparts to high school student athletes through his nonprofit in San Diego, The Athlete Academy. "You must work hard to create opportunities," he always says with conviction, "and you definitely have to be prepared when that opportunity knocks on your door."

After graduation from Stanford, opportunity knocked again when James Lofton, a Stanford alum and NFL Hall-of-Fame wide receiver who coached with the San Diego Chargers, gave Greg a tryout. That offer came after NFL team scouts had visited the Stanford campus to assess potential league hopefuls. Greg took the chance and participated in the Chargers rookie mini-camp and then its six-week training camp. Greg went on to earn a two-year stint as a wide receiver with the San Diego Chargers followed by six years with the Miami Dolphins, Minnesota Vikings, and New Orleans Saints.

Knowing how sports figures can influence youth, Greg initially teamed up with his brother to establish Charging Forward for Academic Success, a program for VLC student athletes. The program fostered academic success and created opportunities for participants to attend events outside Compton. Greg provided the funding, and Jeff, the logistics, with help from Matt Lane.

I vividly remember the first of these events held during a football game on a beautiful, bright sunny day in San Diego. The Charger's stadium was full and noisy. But no group was louder than the VLC students, who were bursting with pride and energy while showing off their new "CF" T-shirts. Though they were seated in a section of the stadium high above us, Susan, Lauren, and I could hear them shouting, "Charging Forward, CPT" (CPT for Compton) and "Cama—rillo! Cama—rillo! Cama—rillo!" every time Greg was out on the field.

"Look at their faces, man," I shared with Jeff, as we marveled after the game at their ear-to-ear smiles, especially after Greg exited the locker room to greet them and sign programs. Most of the students had never been to

San Diego before, which is only about 100 miles from Compton. As hungry teens, they jumped at Jeff's offer to cover any food orders. "Hot dogs, popcorn, hamburgers, you name it, they ate it," he said. "I just hope they don't throw up in the van on the way back to the CPT."

Susan, Lauren, and I attended another very special Charging Forward event a few years later. Greg had arranged for the event to be at the ESPN Zone in the LA Live entertainment facility in downtown Los Angeles. It would celebrate the first Charging Forward graduates to head to college. I was seated next to Jeff at the podium when, with tears welling in his eyes and pride in his voice, he called each young man to his side, introduced them, and shared their challenges and triumphs. Greg later presented each with a laptop computer, as a gift of love and congratulations for their admission to four-year universities.

Charging Forward's largest—and final—event was in 2010. Called "Camp Camarillo," it attracted nearly a hundred participants from Compton's three high schools. Several former Charger teammates of Greg's, including standout out defensive end Luis Castillo, and one of his Miami Dolphins teammates, former Heisman Trophy–winner Ricky Williams, helped him run skill-building sessions for the student athletes. Richard Sherman, a Dominguez High School alumnus and recent graduate of Stanford (who became an NFL All-Pro defensive back), also joined the group.

Susan and I had arrived at LAX airport early that day to pick up Lauren to attend the Camp Camarillo event with us; she had recently graduated from UCLA. On the drive from Westwood to Compton, Lauren asked us to stop in Watts so she could drop off a gift for Diamond, a student she'd tutored through a UCLA-related program for several years (as she was also pursuing an educator's path).

As I sat in Centennial High's football bleachers on that warm July day in Compton, with Susan and Lauren at my side, a wave of nostalgia gripped me. While watching the young men in Camp Camarillo, I hoped more opportunities would be made available to them, as college had opened up worlds for me that I couldn't have imagined at their age. Programs like Charging Forward were, ultimately, about more than sports and rubbing elbows with star athletes. They were about creating opportunities for disadvantaged kids to excel. Or, in Lauren's relationship with Diamond, about building bonds of friendship and caring that shored up a teen who lived in the challenging environment of the projects near Centennial High.

I had routinely visited my hometown over the last decade. But this day in Compton, with my entire family present, felt different. Having used my skills as a historian to trace the city's evolution, I now fully understood how and why these kids from Compton faced such enormous challenges, most of which were not of their own making. But this event went beyond gathering data to foster long-term changes; it was about direct impacts to help build youth a stronger foundation for life—just as my foundational college years had done for me. I had come full circle back to my roots that July day.

I thought about the city's many hard-working parents, trying mightily to make ends meet to provide for their children. And about all the heroes and champions in the city I'd had the opportunity to meet and know.

As Camp Camarillo ended, the former VLC kids huddled around Jeff and Greg, trading hugs and high fives everywhere. My heart was filled with happiness, pride, and hope for Compton's future.

TWENTY-ONE

Generations of Changemakers

After a decades-long legislative effort, the governor of California signed Assembly Bill 101 into law in October 2021. The AB 101 legislation meant that, beginning in the 2025 academic year, every state high school will include ethnic studies in its curriculum, with a semester-long version being required for graduation. California is the first state in the nation to mandate this requirement that has been the end result of work by so many people, including me.

I am beyond excited about this new curriculum's potential to help California's young adults understand matters of race, ethnic background, class status, gender identity, and more, which are fundamental to understanding American society. As a historian with a few miles on my odometer, I also deeply believe they are key to keeping democracy alive, while lamenting the fact that today's efforts to push the needle of social justice further along is as difficult now as when I was younger. I also firmly believe educating our young people through a lens of ethnic studies about social and racial justice will help advance a more equitable society. This stems partly from seeing, over the past decade, how the ethnic studies curriculum I've helped implement in two Bay Area high schools has changed the trajectory of some students' lives and that of their families—just as taking the first ethnic studies course offered by UCLA did for me over fifty years ago. That course served as a transformative steppingstone to helping me understand and appreciate more fully my community of origin, my family's history, and my own early life experiences.

Now, hundreds of thousands of high schoolers across the Golden State, and perhaps millions in the years ahead, will have the opportunity to be inspired by these courses and what they learn. This hope provided motivation as I worked with California Assemblyperson José Medina to support passage of AB 101.

I was absolutely committed to the spirit and substance of the proposed legislation that, in April 2019, Medina and I testified about before the Assembly Committee on Education in California's Capitol Building. But the experiences that day meant much more, as I reflected on the two-hour, solitary drive home from Sacramento on a beautiful spring afternoon.

The mission to promote ethnic studies is part of a much larger project to advance social change and racial justice through education. I thought about how my life's journey is tied to this project and to the connections that bind me to so many like-minded people within my generation as well as to those who came before—and younger people today.

My work with Assemblyperson Medina is emblematic. He'd enlisted my help many months before we'd met in person in his office the day of our presentations to the Assembly Committee. We held much in common, such as coming of age in California in the second half of the twentieth century. A former teacher, José's passion for ethnic studies had begun at the University of California, Riverside, in a Chicano studies course taught by dear friend, colleague, and mentor Carlos E. Cortés, the founding director of Chicano studies there.

Intergenerational connections were also on my mind after that statehouse visit, for good reason. As Medina and I'd walked the corridors of the ornate State Capitol Building on the way to the committee hearing room, we crossed paths with Assemblyperson Lorena S. González. "Hello Professor," Lorena said as the two of us approached an elevator, "I hope you remember me." "Of course, I do," I immediately replied, while giving her a hug. Lorena not only co-sponsored AB 101 but was my advisee at Stanford some twenty years earlier. She went on to earn her law degree from UCLA. And before her election to the State Assembly in 2013, she'd worked as a community activist and supporter of workers' rights, including being the CEO and Secretary-Treasurer of San Diego and Imperial Counties Labor Council, AFL-CIO.

González and Medina were among the Latino/a politicians committed to advancing social change and racial justice issues for Californians. And they were the embodiment of that change. When I graduated from UCLA in 1970, for example, you could easily count Latino/a state lawmakers on one hand. Today the California Latino Legislative Caucus has thirty-eight members as a powerful voice in the state legislature.

I saw Lorena again, in May 2019, for a very special occasion at the State Capitol. As chairperson of the California Latino Legislative Caucus, she was master of ceremonies for the annual Latino Spirit Awards celebration in which I was honored alongside others who'd made contributions in health, education, technology, journalism/media, the arts, and other areas. I was one of two recipients of the Latino Spirit Award in Achievement in Academia. Guess who was the other? Professor Carlos E. Cortés.

Each Spirit Award recipient was escorted down the aisle of the state legislature by three members of the caucus. When we halted at the front of the room, I could see my family members smiling in the gallery above us. It was also wonderful being hosted by Lorena, taking photos with caucus members, and introducing her to my family. The ceremony got me thinking about other former students with influential positions. One of my earliest students, Maria Echaveste (Stanford class of 1976), became the highest-ranking Latina in a presidential administration when she was appointed deputy chief of staff during President Clinton's second term. She'd enrolled in the first Chicano history lecture course I taught in 1975. Two years later, Xavier Becerra (Stanford class of 1980) took the same course. The former twelve-term member of the U.S. House of Representatives, and former California attorney general, Xavier currently is U.S. Secretary of Health and Human Services in the Biden administration. It was a very special, inter-generational moment when I last saw him and Carolina Reyes, his spouse, at the Stanford University degree ceremony for the Program in Comparative Studies in Race and Ethnicity (CSRE). Carolina had also been one of my

In the post–World War II decades, as suburban development replaced agricultural lands there, people of color were allowed to purchase homes and/or rent property in East Palo Alto. Like in Compton, White folks began to leave in droves during the 1960s. By the 1980s, East Palo Alto was mostly Black, and like Compton, was becoming a majority Latino city over the next twenty years.

When Jeff began working at EPAA in 2010, Latinos were two-thirds of all residents, Blacks were 16 percent, and Asian/Pacific Islanders, 7 percent. During this demographic transition, the city also suffered from growing poverty and rising crime rates. The crack cocaine epidemic and gang violence also destabilized the new city as it grappled with problems that included a school district starved for resources.

East Palo Alto Academy, as a charter school with a direct university relationship, emphasized curricular innovation, project-based learning, and college readiness. Including a Chicano history segment in Ms. Castillon's history courses dovetailed with this innovation. Besides assisting Irene with course content, I developed a workshop through Stanford's History Department and Program in Comparative Studies in Race and Ethnicity for undergraduate students to mentor EPAA juniors on their history project research and presentations. Susan, recently retired from her school counseling position, coordinated this Stanford mentoring program.

I vividly recall attending three student exhibitions at the school as a "community" panel member. It was a huge deal for them to develop a PowerPoint presentation and explain their projects before three adults and Ms. Castillon. Each presentation surpassed expectations. One stood out in particular. Lucia, an undocumented child of immigrants from Mexico, covered the history of the Chicano movement of the 1960s with passion and knowledge, while connecting the dots between that and her own family's journey. We all sat there mesmerized, wiping tears from our eyes, in witness of her confidence, grasp of knowledge, and ease with which she addressed topics. "Wow!" I said in the comments segment after Lucia's presentation, "I couldn't have expected any better presentation from one of my Stanford undergraduate students." She smiled as her cheeks blushed red.

Before we left that afternoon, I asked Lucia about future plans. "I want to go to college and become a teacher like Ms. Castillon," she said. In fact,

Lucia attended Loyola Marymount University in Los Angeles, earning a degree in Chicano/Latino studies and secondary education. Susan and I attended her 2018 commencement ceremony, before she went on to achieve an MA degree and teacher credential from Stanford's Teacher Education Program the following year. Lucia Gonzáles Cabrera is now a fourth-year history teacher at East Palo Alto Academy—"just like Ms. Castillon!"

Castillon, in 2013, was hired by Jeff when he became founding director of the new Luis Valdez Leadership Academy in San José. Irene joined as a history teacher and academic dean of the new charter high school. It is named after the legendary Chicano activist, playwright, film director, and screenwriter and serves a predominantly Latino student body in East San José.

Irene and I continued our collaborative work with two other history teachers at the school to implement Mexican American history as a ninth-grade requirement in LVLA's social studies curriculum. A year-long course was soon available, with an impact that was more robust from being a full-blown course of study.

To further this high school effort, I developed a two-quarter long, service-learning based course at Stanford. Called "Teaching Mexican American History in High School," it involved undergraduates traveling weekly to the LVLA campus to assist the history teachers and to mentor their students. This course was based on a deep treasure trove of knowledge produced by two generations of historians, and it foreshadowed the ethnic studies course requirement legislation I was helping promote.

When the first group of LVLA students were completing their high school years, Castillon left a voicemail about the course's impact. "Profe, you have to see what so many of our seniors have written in their college essays about learning Chicano history," she stated. "It's heartwarming, even beyond my expectations." I asked Irene to share with me a few of the students' statements. Reading these statements reinforced why I'd supported taking Mexican American history to high school history classrooms in the first place.

Carla (not her real name) confided that, "During middle school, I am sad to say that I was ashamed of where I was from and rejected my ethnic identity." But, she added, after "I started high school, I began to find self-love again because I was able to take a Mexican American history class that taught me about my history and portrayed my history as empowering." For Chris, the course brought history alive: "It felt good being able to relate to something, for once, in history." For Maria, the course not only helped build skills essential to learning, but it fostered a civic consciousness. "This class . . . taught me to think critically about the past and current events as they relate to social justice and tolerance."

I was not surprised by such claims, given my experience with taking a Chicano history course as a UCLA junior. What took me aback were the statements about the course's inspirational influence on future plans. "This class has taught me the importance of pursuing higher education in order to challenge the status quo," Maria stated emphatically, and "I want to attend college to learn how to empower my community and to advocate for the rights of people who have been impacted by systemic racism and oppression." "I would like to be a Mexican American teacher that shows young Chicanos, such as myself," Chris wrote, "the great heroes that we had and the great protests that our ancestors accomplished for us." "Because education has changed my life," Chris added, "one career that I want to pursue is teaching . . . because I know that I will be a great influence for students who have been affected by poverty, gangs, and violence in their communities." And Carla shared, "I plan on exploring majors in ethnic studies and theater and performing arts to achieve my long-term goal of being a culturally empowered teacher."

And so, what I helped put in motion during five years of working with LVLA has been like ripples in a pond, extending pride in community into goals about reaching out to make future communities strong. Engaging with Mexican American history gave students a platform to better understand their lives and to develop healthier perspectives on their families, communities, and society. The course also helped instill skills and confidence in students as they enter higher education and envision impactful careers.

Considering that Latinos are 56 percent of all K–12 students in California, and that those who are poor often attend under-resourced schools, what I witnessed with the ethnic studies–related course implementation at LVLA was nothing short of transformative. In 2018, when the first cohort of participating seniors graduated, over 80 percent were admitted to four-year universities, and 50 percent enrolled. By comparison, about 27 percent of

California's Latino students enrolled into colleges and universities (and only 12 percent nationally). To be sure, the Mexican American history curriculum was only part of what facilitated educational success and college readiness for LVLA students, but it appeared to be a powerful part. I observed the same types of impacts with many East Palo Alto Academy students.

These results reinforce my deeply held belief that social, political, and economic change—as well as racial justice—are achievable. Social justice warriors of all stripes from generations past believed this as well, inspiring them to work tirelessly to break down walls of exclusion and open portals of opportunity to a quality education and other foundational elements for social change.

The progress made, then and now, is cause for celebration. But there is no room for patting oneself on the back. As a historian, I've studied periods of progressive social and political change in American history and the reactions against them from people, groups, and institutions hell-bent on preserving the status quo. As a people, we are in the middle of one of those periods again. Powerful forces have arrayed to strategically turn back the hands of time to an era when White supremacy, in all its destructive ways, reigned unchecked. Undermining the voting rights of citizens of color is one strategy used, despite that this is tantamount to undermining democracy itself. This undemocratic approach has gained great momentum in "red states" in recent decades, aided and abetted by U.S. Supreme Court rulings that have chipped away at constitutional guardrails established by the Voting Rights Act. The result is that not since the Civil War has the foundation of our democracy been under such enormous stress.

A majority of the U.S. Supreme Court also recently supported making it illegal to consider an applicant's race or ethnicity in college admissions. This is part of college affirmative action policies, established in the 1960s, routinely being in the crosshairs of conservative politicians and organizations. From the late 1970s through the 2010s, the Supreme Court primarily ruled in favor of cases that steadily chipped away at the foundations of these policies. An exception I was involved in occurred with the University of Michigan (*Gratz v. Bollinger*, 2000), in which the Court ruled that race and ethnic status *can* be used as one of many factors considered for higher education admissions. Yet a 2023 ruling by the Supreme Court made it so colleges and universities, including private institutions, can now no longer use race/ethnicity to build diverse student bodies.

An argument used against affirmative action policies is that institutions practice "colorblind" admissions. At its root, this argument is willfully *blind* to the enduring racial inequities in American society. Besides, making college admissions fair and race neutral isn't the goal of the backlash. Outlawing affirmative action–related policies is about pealing back rights and opportunities that conservative Whites believe were taken from them by "big government" in favor of "racial minorities."

Terminating these policies has gone hand in hand with a right-wing political agenda to dismantle other socially progressive policies. The U.S. Supreme Court's ruling in 2022 to overturn *Roe v. Wade* and the ban of gender-affirming care in many red states are other examples of battles in the so-called culture wars.

To support this war, misinformation has been spread that has stoked fear in the hearts of millions of people that their way of life is threatened. Extremist politicians use this strategy to mobilize Republican Party loyalists and to promote recovery of an America they claim has been lost. This strategy has also inspired White supremacists to take off their gloves, march in public, and engage in hate crimes of various sorts with impunity.

It is not surprising that, in many GOP-controlled states, race and ethnic studies curricula in K–12 schools and at universities have also been targeted. More than twenty-five states have considered and/or established educational policies restricting teaching the history of racial inequality in public schools. The focus, under the cover of removing content that "may cause guilt" among some students, has been banning books and erasing histories about racial discrimination and oppression in our national past (for instance, avoiding discussion of slavery, and Jim and Jaime Crow). But the real goal is to keep people ignorant. It is part of an effort to continue to sow hate, fear, anxiety, and a "we versus them" mentality in messaging that divides rather than unites.

I shudder to think how young people of color and their parents in red states will manage to keep hope alive during this struggle for the soul of our nation. I am angry whenever I think about the impact on the children of immigrant parents when they hear right-wing politicians bashing and demeaning them. And I am alarmed when I read about policy-related assaults on programs of diversity, inclusion, and equity on some university campuses.

However, when I feel sickened by all that is happening to erode the multiracial democracy generations of American fought to create, I have an antidote. I need only remind myself of all the good people fighting the fight to preserve gains made and to expand the beachhead of a more equitable, inclusive society.

I think about all the fair-minded, socially progressive folks I know who are committed to doing this work every day—especially for young people. I've met many of them in Compton: teachers like Catherine Borek at Dominguez High School, and equally dedicated community activists like Abigail López-Byrd. A native of Compton, she co-founded a nonprofit called Color Compton with her husband Marque Byrd. This organization is devoted to building relationships among the city's youth of color while they create art and explore their identity and community history; this is exactly the type of program I'd once hoped to establish in the city of my youth.

When lamenting the efforts of a growing number of legislatures in red states to dismantle diversity, equity, and inclusion-related programs on their college campuses, I am heartened to see how the many young faculty I helped hire, as special assistant to the provost, during my last decade at Stanford are expanding the institutional footprint for the study of race and ethnicity for the next generation. I also step away from despair by thinking about my familia of former students. Some work in the public sector and with nonprofits that are supporting ordinary people. Others became K–12 teachers and college professors across California and the nation and are teaching less whitewashed versions of U.S. history and ethnic studies to future generations.

In my immediate familia, I am inspired by my own children—Jeff, Greg, and Lauren—all educators. After leaving Compton, Jeff spent ten years leading charter high schools in East Palo Alto, East San José, and East Oakland prior to becoming a leader of Stanford's Teacher Education Program (STEP). He now helps train a richly diverse cohort of future secondary school teachers.

Greg also pursued an educational career after retiring from the NFL. He earned an MA in educational leadership at San Diego State University

(SDSU). He then served as an academic coordinator in the athletic department at the University of San Diego and in a similar position at SDSU. Most recently, he founded The Athlete Academy.

Lauren, who beautifully exemplifies all the values we hoped our children would internalize, earned her BA from UCLA and MA degree from Stanford. She became a Spanish teacher, first at a San José public high school and now at Mountain View High School. She also leads the Ambassadors Program, a leadership organization that promotes inclusion by providing support for immigrant students, multilingual learners, freshmen, and transfer students as well as for low-income students and their families. She also crosses paths with Jeff in her role as a STEP lecturer who shares her classroom experiences in designing equitable groupwork for diverse students. At both high schools, she has garnered Teacher of the Year awards. Most recently, I am proud to say, she was named one of the five California State Teachers of the Year for 2023. With over 300,000 public school teachers in California, how extraordinary that Catherine Borek is one of the other recipients of this honor!

I think, as well, about Susan and my grandchildren. When our children, their spouses (Sharon, Josephine, and Matt), and our grandkids gather for family festivities, the ethnic and racial diversity of the group brings joy to my heart. A U.S. postal stamp could be made of our grandkids to represent the multiethnic, multicultural, and multiracial heritage of California's children: they are African American, Tongan/Guamanian, Japanese, Irish/British/German, Hungarian, Mexican, as well as Jewish, Catholic, and Protestant.

It was for their sake, and that of all of California's children, that I had testified before the California Assembly Education Committee in 2019. It means so much to me that our seven grandkids will have opportunities to learn about the previously overlooked history of people of color. If, by chance, a high school teacher one day asks our grandchildren to read this book written by their "Papa" as part of their ethnic studies curriculum, I hope my stories will give special meaning to their lives and be an inspiration to many others.

ACKNOWLEDGMENTS

The recollections of family and friends are everywhere in this memoir, and I am so thankful for their help. I am grateful to so many of my Walton Junior High School and Dominguez High School classmates who graciously shared their stories about families and neighborhoods in Compton. Recounting my days at UCLA with old buddies was fun. Reconnecting with all of these friends was truly special.

I also want to give a big shout-out to some friends and colleagues who read and commented on all or parts of the manuscript. Thanks go to Maggie Andersen for her enthusiastic embrace of my project and to Sharon Markenson for using her English teacher skills to edit some of my early chapters. The suggestions of Laura E. Gómez were enormously important for helping me rethink parts of my story, and the thoughtful comments provided by Gustavo Arellano and Geraldo Cadava were right on target. Barbra Rodriguez's professional skills and insights as a development editor were hugely valuable. The support and encouragement of Kate Wahl, editor of Stanford University Press, throughout the process were always offered with consummate professionalism and grace.

I am deeply indebted to the dozens of Compton folks who shared their oral histories with my students and me. They provided an abundance of personal stories about their experiences in the city. The cooperation of Greg Williams, director of the Gerth Archives and Special Collections at California State University, Dominguez Hills, is greatly appreciated, especially his support to include my Compton-related documents and Camarillo family archive in CSUDH's library.

It was extra special to recall family events and memories with my dear big brother Art "Harpo" and sister Annie—they were touchstones for helping me resurrect stories about the barrio and our familia. My parents and my López uncles helped me ground the stories even further back in time.

Familia means everything to me. Our children—Jeff, Greg, and Lauren—and our grandchildren were the inspiration for me to write this book. No one provided more love, heart, and soul to this memoir project than my life partner and spouse, Susan. After all these years, she is still my best friend and "No. 1" editor.